World Religions

Nihil Obstat: Rev. William M. Becker, STD
             Censor Librorum
             13 November 1997

Imprimatur: †Most Rev. John G. Vlazny, DD
             Administrator of the Diocese of Winona
             13 November 1997

Genuine recycled paper with 10% post-consumer waste. Printed with soy-based ink.

The publishing team included Michael Wilt, development editor; Barbara Allaire, John Ferrie, and Stephan Nagel, consulting editors; Rebecca Fairbank, copy editor; Gary J. Boisvert, production editor, page designer, and typesetter; Maurine R. Twait, art director; Penny Koehler and Genevieve Nagel, photo researchers; Tom Lowes, cover photographer and map artist; and Patricia Deminna, indexer.

The acknowledgments continue on page 268.

Printed in the United States of America

Printing: 9 8 7 6 5

Year: 2006 05 04 03 02

ISBN 0-88489-486-X

Saint Mary's Press
Christian Brothers Publications
Winona, Minnesota

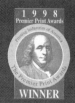

World Religions won the 1998 Best of Category in textbooks for the Premier Print Award from the Printing Industries of America. Chosen from thousands of entries, the Premier Print Award goes to those firms who demonstrate a unique ability to create visual masterpieces.

World Religions

A Voyage of Discovery

Jeffrey Brodd

with a foreword by Gregory Sobolewski

Contents

The Roman Catholic Church and Non-Christian Religions

by Gregory L. Sobolewski

My Lutheran grandfather was trouble for my father when my father first started dating my mother. My grandfather seldom went to church, but he complained to my Catholic dad in a heavy accent about "those damn Cadlics." Dad felt a lot better when he discovered that his future father-in-law was talking about automobiles rather than religion.

Until that discovery, my dad feared my grandfather because my dad loved his fiancée deeply, and he didn't want religion to get in the way. He also never talked with my mom's father about their religious differences, and so he presumed the worst. This example of a misunderstanding from one particular family serves as an analogy for situations often encountered in the human family at large. We sometimes fear that which we do not understand; we sometimes ignore it; we sometimes even attack it.

When our misunderstandings are about things like automobiles, little is at stake. But when matters of faith are at issue, the stakes can be high. Matters of faith are serious for those whose faith matters. Christians learn from the Bible that "all things work together for good for those who love God, who are called according to his purpose" (Romans 8:28). Thus Christians believe that love of God casts out

fear, ignorance, and hostility, and transforms our life. In a word, Christians *hope*. Christians hope that differences can first be tolerated, then understood, and finally celebrated. The inspiration offered by the Bible's promise of things working together for good, along with Christian discussions of faith, are causes of hope for good relations among the world's many religions.

Together with all Christians, Roman Catholics view the truth about persons and their relationships with God, with one another, and with the world, through the lens provided by the words and deeds of Jesus of Nazareth. Jesus made the outstanding claim that his very presence brought the Kingdom of God. Not a place or an institution, the Kingdom of God comes from one's knowing God through Jesus.

Jesus stated that "'I am the way, and the truth, and the life. No one comes to the Father except through me'" (John 14:6). Jesus could see that his hearers recognized the presence of the Kingdom of God through the choices they made in their lives. He prompted them to see God more clearly and then to act accordingly, with love. Knowing that change of this kind is difficult to achieve, Jesus stated further that "'I will ask the Father, and he will give you another Advocate, to be with you forever. This is the Spirit of truth, whom the world cannot receive, because it neither sees him nor knows him'" (John 14:16–17). Christians believe that this Holy Spirit is the actual presence of God in our life today—even as we read this page.

Through Jesus of Nazareth, the family of God (Father, Son, Holy Spirit) became the family for all persons. As God's Son, Jesus invited human beings to know God fully. In God's holy spirit, the family prospers with inspired acts of love. The love within those who believe in Christ heals their wounds, promotes their dreams, and guides their relationships with God, other persons, and the planet. The presence of this love is not a matter of preference for Christians, like automobiles, video games, or nail polishes. It is a matter of truth for the Christian family because Jesus of Nazareth is experienced through the ages as the only complete revelation of God's familial love for all persons.

Together with all Christians, Roman Catholics do not negotiate God's love among life's spiritual options. Rather, Catholics accept that Jesus of Nazareth conclusively extended God's irreversible and full love out of the family of God and into the family of humanity. Thus Christians can really live life hopefully, restraining fear and not being paralyzed by it. Christians are at home with God, even as we are amazed by the unsurpassable mansion that Jesus called the Kingdom of God.

Catholics believe that the Kingdom of God preached by Jesus is most fully present in the Roman Catholic church, which is obligated to bring the good news of God's family of love to all persons. Within the Catholic church, the biblical promises of hope are fully preserved even as they are understood and applied freshly for people in every age. Mother Teresa of Calcutta (1910 to 1997) is a remarkable example of how the love of God hopes without fear. She cared unconditionally for society's discarded persons—outcast because of poverty, disease, age, or uselessness.

Roman Catholic leaders attempt to clarify how the Kingdom of God can be seen today, and how it might become more effective. Regarding non-Christian religions, Catholic leaders have never been more welcoming than they have been in the last thirty-five years. At the Second Vatican Council (1962 to 1965), the Catholic magisterium (the teaching authority of Roman Catholic popes, cardinals, and bishops) stated:

The catholic church rejects nothing of those things which are true and holy in these religions. It regards with respect those ways of acting and living and those precepts and teachings which, though often at variance with what it holds and expounds, frequently reflect a ray of that truth which enlightens everyone. (*Declaration on the Relation of the Church to Non-Christian Religions*, number 2)

This insight is remarkable! The family of God includes not only persons who are baptized in Jesus Christ but also those who entered into other relationships with God. Non-Christians can, and do, speak truthfully of God. Church teaching encourages Catholics to recognize that the non-Christian religions of the world strive for the common good of the human family.

In the New Testament, we read that God "desires everyone to be saved and to come to the knowledge of the truth," and that the one mediator between God and humanity is Jesus Christ (1 Timothy 2:4–5). Given the Catholic church's respect for non-Christian religions, it should come as no surprise that the church teaches that salvation through Christ is available to all. To return to our family analogy, we would not deny the necessities of life to a member of our family simply because she or he lived in a different place or had a different lifestyle. So it is with God's desire that all be saved:

There are those who without any fault do not know anything about Christ or his church, yet who search for God with a sincere heart and, under the influence of grace, try to put into effect the will of God as known to them through the dictate of conscience: these too can obtain eternal salvation. (*Dogmatic Constitution on the Church*, number 16)

The church itself is a necessary sign of God's saving actions in Jesus Christ. The church is Christ's body on Earth, testifying to and advancing his saving actions for all people, Christians and non-Christians alike.

Having affirmed what is true and holy in non-Christian religions, as well as the availability of salvation to all, one might ask: Has Roman Catholicism traded away the truth of Jesus? Has it trampled on the memories of the Catholic missionaries who for centuries brought faith in Jesus to lands far and wide? The Gospel according to Matthew ends with the resurrected Jesus saying these words:

"All authority in heaven and on earth has been given to me. Go therefore and make disciples of all nations, baptizing them in the name of the Father and of the Son and of the Holy Spirit, and teaching them to obey everything that I have commanded you. And remember, I am with you always, to the end of the age." (28:18–20)

With these words, Jesus presented his followers, for all time, with what is known as a missionary mandate. God loves all people and desires that all be saved. The church is obligated to be missionary, to "go and make disciples," because it believes and participates in God's all-encompassing plan for salvation. This mandate goes hand in hand with the respect the church holds for non-Christian religions. For example, some years ago Pope John Paul II spent a day praying for peace with members of many religions. It was his Christian "faith conviction," the pope said, that made him turn to the representatives of the world's religions "in deep love and respect" ("The Challenge and the Possibility of Peace," number 2). Christian faith conviction, with its missionary mandate, promotes genuine understanding among the world's many faiths.

My grandfather and his new son-in-law, my father, may have had different tastes in automobiles, politics, and sports, but they were united in loving the woman who was daughter to one and wife to the other. Their friendship was based not in particular details of cars and sports, but in the welfare of the one woman they each loved differently. In a similar way, the church encourages Catholics to advance the common truths of God recognized by all religions, even as Catholics observe their own particular and unsurpassable truth known by faith in Jesus Christ, and even as the various religions practice faith in their own unique ways.

Roman Catholics continuously offer God's familial love to all humanity when they present the love of God as taught and demonstrated by Jesus Christ. Today Catholics are required to increase their respect for truth found in non-Christian religions. On the day that Pope John Paul II prayed for peace with leaders from many religions, he recognized the common ground among the religions. In the following excerpt from Pope John Paul's address to the gathering, he highlights the importance of this common ground, for it is at the heart of creating a peaceful world:

With the world religions we share a common respect for and obedience to conscience, which teaches all of us to seek the truth, to love and serve all individuals and peoples, and therefore to make peace among individuals and among nations.

Yes, we all hold conscience and obedience to the voice of conscience to be an essential element in the road toward a better and peaceful world. Could it be otherwise, since all men and women in this world have a common origin and a common destiny?

If there are many and important differences among us, there is also a common ground whence to operate together in the solution of this dramatic challenge of our age: true peace or catastrophic war. ("Challenge and Possibility of Peace," number 2)

Jeffrey Brodd's exposition of our world's religions in this book is a fascinating exploration of thousands of years of humans' spiritual hunger and satisfaction. The leaders of the Roman Catholic church encourage Catholics to honor Jesus Christ as they develop esteem for non-Christian religions. Like new in-laws, Catholics rely on the biblical promise of hope that "all things work together for good for those who love God, who are called according to his purpose" (Romans 8:28).

PART 1
Points of Departure

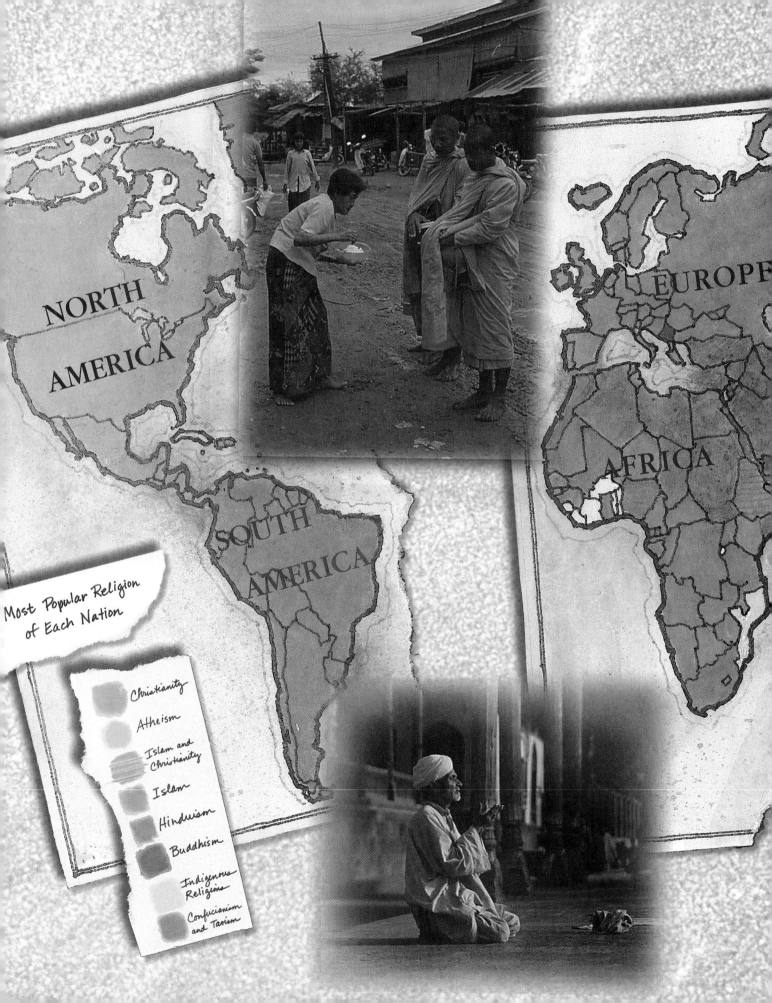

NORTH AMERICA

SOUTH AMERICA

EUROPE

AFRICA

Most Popular Religion of Each Nation

- Christianity
- Atheism
- Islam and Christianity
- Islam
- Hinduism
- Buddhism
- Indigenous Religions
- Confucianism and Taoism

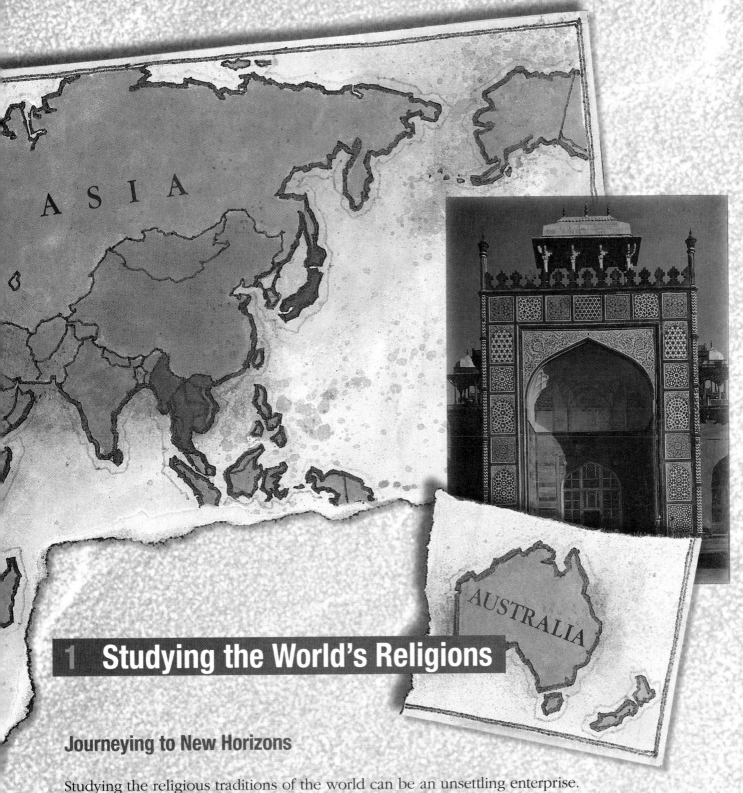

1 Studying the World's Religions

Journeying to New Horizons

Studying the religious traditions of the world can be an unsettling enterprise. Religions answer life's most profound and important questions. But there are many religions, each offering its own answers. How can this be? We all share a common humanity, so can more than one true answer to each of life's questions be found? If ultimate reality, or God, is truly ultimate, can more than one God exist? And if there is only one ultimate reality, crowning the summit of our spiritual selves, can there be multiple paths to the summit?

This Chinese painting from the ninth century depicts the Buddha and the Four Passing Sights. These sights raised religious questions that led to the founding of Buddhism.

The Nature of a Religious Tradition

Let us begin our voyage by mapping out the territory. As we explore this great variety of religions, what can we expect to find? In general, what is the nature of a religious tradition?

All religions tend to answer the same fundamental questions. Most religions also have a number of basic elements in common, such as doctrines, sacred stories, and rituals. Together these elements form a tradition. To better understand the nature of religious traditions, we can begin by looking at these two sets of features—religious questions and basic elements.

Religious Questions

The rest of this book describes the answers that various religions give to life's basic questions. All people, by virtue of being human, face certain fundamental questions. These questions are universal, because humans are spiritual beings. Along with being physical, rational, and emotional, we have the capacity for self-reflection; we have a conscience; we can ponder our own nature. In a word, we are *spiritual*.

Not everyone chooses to answer fundamental religious questions by adhering to a religious tradition. Some people understand themselves to be "spiritual," but do not consider themselves "religious," or adherents of a specific religion. Religions, however, hold certain advantages for those grappling with religious questions. They offer answers that have been tested by time, in some cases by thousands of years. Religions are also fortified by the richness of tradition and by the shared experience of community.

Regardless of how one chooses to answer them, religious questions are inevitable. Let us consider the primary ones.

What Is the Human Condition?

The initial religious question asks about the basic nature of the human condition. Are we

Raising such questions can be unsettling because it requires that we look beyond the safe haven of our own set of answers, and consider the answers of others. It is like embarking on a voyage, journeying far from the familiar surroundings of home, and encountering strange and challenging places and ideas. But like all voyages, the study of religions reveals new horizons. Most important, it enriches our understanding of the many ways of being human. Our journey, though it may prove unsettling at times, will be marked by discovery.

1
The terms *spiritual* and *religious* often mean different things to different people. What does each term mean to you?

by nature good, or are we evil? Are we somewhere in between, originally good but now flawed in some way?

Suffering is an important aspect of the human condition. All religions recognize that we suffer. The question is, Why do we suffer? If we are by nature good and in no need of greater perfection, then of course suffering is not our fault. But if we are evil, or somehow flawed, perhaps we deserve to suffer. A religion typically offers a means of overcoming suffering in order to attain salvation.

What Is Salvation?

Religions, in general, are deeply concerned with **salvation.** This is a complex issue. Depending on the religion, salvation can relate to this life or to the afterlife, and it often relates to both. It is therefore helpful to consider two aspects of salvation.

Salvation in this life can be described as **transcendence,** or overcoming the limitations of the human condition. We can respond to these challenges of being human in many ways. Some people may simply try to ignore the challenges by allowing a certain numbness of the spirit. Others may become workaholics in an attempt to block out life's problems. Some hide behind a veil of drugs or alcohol. Unlike these responses, however, religious transcendence brings us face-to-face with the human condition. It enables us to live fully in the human condition, with all its joys and sorrows, while maintaining an underlying state of tranquillity and joy. In many traditions such joy is said to be indescribable; it simply must be experienced in order to be known.

Some religions emphasize the experience of transcendence in this life, and teach a form of salvation in the here and now. For other religions, salvation is not finally attained until the afterlife. This leads to the question of human destiny.

What Is Our Destiny?

As spiritual beings, one of the things we ponder is our destiny. Where are we going, ultimately? Most (though not all) of the religions provide answers to this question, and these answers are closely linked to the issue of salvation.

According to some religions, human beings face two possible destinies, one of which is salvation, and the other, a form of condemnation. The question of destiny is far more complex for religions that teach that human beings live more than one lifetime. In this case the immediate destiny after this life is generally not the ultimate, final destiny, but just another step toward the final destiny.

In Christianity the cross is often used as a symbol of salvation. This mosaic is from a church in Ravenna, Italy.

What Is Right, What Is Wrong?

Along with questions of salvation and destiny, religions must answer the question that is at the heart of **ethics:** How are we to act while living in the world?

Religions tend to focus a great deal of attention on the ethical question, resulting in significant teachings on what is right and what is wrong. Obeying these ethical or moral teachings is usually a crucial part of the quest for salvation.

What Is the Nature of the World?

Along with answering questions about human beings, religions also answer questions about the world. Where did the world come from? Is it real, or is it just some kind of cosmic illusion? Is the world sacred, perhaps even living? Or is it merely matter? Is the world a help or a hindrance to the religious quests of humans?

Such questions belong to the general category of **cosmology**—the understanding of the nature of the universe. The answers to cosmological questions tend to determine how much interest a religion has in the natural world. Some religions express such interest through support of scientific inquiry and theories regarding the natural world, while others tend to be suspicious of science.

What Is Ultimate Reality, and How Is It Revealed?

Finally, there is the religious question of ultimate reality, or (especially for Western traditions) God. Theistic religions are those that hold a belief in God, or in multiple gods. These religions teach a certain theology, or doctrine regarding the divine. The theologies of the world's religions include a range of basic perspectives: **monotheism** (belief in only one God), **polytheism** (belief in many gods), and **pantheism** (belief that God is in all), to name but a few.

Nontheistic religions do not hold a belief in a personal god or gods. In some cases such religions teach that all reality is essentially one thing, and that human beings are part of the ultimate reality.

Most religions also teach that the ultimate reality, whatever form it takes, is somehow revealed to humans. This is called **revelation,** and it usually takes place through sacred stories or myths, or through various types of religious experience. These are among the basic elements of religions described in the next section.

Basic Elements of Religions

Now that we have mapped out some of the primary questions to which religions respond, let us explore some of the common motifs through which they offer their answers. Some of these basic elements of religions are quite familiar and will need little explanation at this point. Others are less familiar; it will be helpful to understand them before embarking on our study of the religions themselves.

Religious Experience

Religions begin with the religious experiences of individuals. Some of these beginnings are famous and easy to identify. When the Buddha experienced enlightenment un-

The religious experience of Moses is depicted in *Moses Before the Burning Bush,* by the Italian painter Raphael (1483–1520).

2

The degree to which religion and science are compatible varies greatly depending on the particular religion. Drawing from your own knowledge and experience, describe how you see the relationship between religion and science.

der the *bodhi* tree, Buddhism was born. When Muhammad began to experience revelations from Allah, Islam began. Other beginnings are not so easily identified. Religious experience, moreover, can be part of anyone's religious life; obviously it does not always result in a new religion.

What is commonly known as **faith** belongs to the category of religious experience. But this form of faith differs from **belief.** One *believes* in some creed or doctrine, whereas one simply *has* faith. When asked by an interviewer if he believed in God, the great psychologist Carl G. Jung responded: "I *know.* I don't need to believe. I know" (*C. G. Jung Speaking,* page 428). Jung knew, undoubtedly, because he experienced God through faith.

As we journey through the world's major religions, we will encounter numerous types of religious experience, some of them quite astounding. Generally speaking, within the theistic religions God is experienced as a holy presence who is other (that is, as a being distinct from the individual). This experience of the holy other is often characterized by two separate emotions: fear and fascination. A well-known example of this type of experience is the revelation of God to Moses on Mount Sinai, through the burning bush. Moses was fearful of God, yet drawn in fascination toward the divine presence.

In nontheistic religions, religious experience usually takes the form of **mysticism.** A basic type of mysticism involves the individual becoming one with the divine through inward contemplation. We will explore this type of mysticism beginning with chapter 3, on Hinduism. In our study of primal religions, we will see another form of religious experience known as the vision quest.

Religious Beliefs and Teachings

For many people, the most obvious and basic element of religion is belief. Adherents of a religion believe in something, namely, the creeds, doctrines, or teachings of their religion. Christians believe, for example, in the Apostles' Creed and in the doctrine of the Trinity.

Belief in creeds and doctrines is more prevalent in Christianity than it is in most other religions. Such teachings cover the full range of life issues. Ethical teachings are an important category, as are teachings on salvation and on the nature of the world.

Doctrines, creeds, and other teachings generally stem from religious experience, taking form as the mind attempts to make sense of the content of revelation. These teachings are often recorded in sacred texts, or scriptures.

Sacred Stories, or Myths

The concept of **myth** may not be so familiar to us, because we no longer live in a predominantly mythic world. We now tend to base our perspectives on science and history, acquiring knowledge through empirical observation and rational thinking. Myths are both nonhistorical and nonrational. But this is not to say that they necessarily conflict with history and science, nor that they are false or *irrational.* On the contrary, myths are, by definition, sources of sacred truth. Myths are also powerful, for they give meaning to life.

Myths take the form of sacred stories that are passed along from one generation to the next. Many times they are conveyed orally, though some religions record their myths in scripture. Myths are often set in primordial time, a period in the distant past somehow set apart from the ordinary time of the present. They commonly tell of the origins of humans and the world. Myths set forth fundamental knowledge regarding the nature of things and the proper way to live.

The story of Creation, contained in the opening chapters of the Book of Genesis, is a perfect example of such a sacred story, or myth. It provides knowledge about a number of basic issues: the world was created by God; human beings were created in the image of God, and we are by nature good; we are meant to have "dominion" over the other creatures; and so forth. These mythic ideas depend neither on science nor on history, but they remain sacred truths for Jews, Christians, and Muslims alike.

3
Like the terms *religious* and *spiritual, faith* tends to mean different things to different people. What does faith mean to you?

4
Myth is not as strong an element in the modern, scientific world as it was in earlier ages. Still, as the example of the Genesis account of Creation suggests, some of our basic perspectives about life are derived from mythic sources. What other mythic truths are prevalent in our society—truths based on neither science nor history, but that give life meaning and direction?

Ritual and Worship

Worship is an important basic element of religions, taking a variety of forms and occupying much of an individual's religious life. Most of these forms of worship involve some formal practice, or **ritual.** Like belief, ritual is very familiar to most of us. In many cases a ritual re-enacts a myth. For example, one of Christianity's primary rituals is the Eucharist, or Holy Communion. It is a re-enactment of the sacred story of the Last Supper that Jesus shared with his disciples, as recorded in the Gospels of the New Testament.

Religious Communities

All religions involve communities, and for most people the communal aspect of religion is a significant and attractive feature. A sense of community, of belonging to a group such as a tribe or a parish or a congregation, is usually empowering for individuals. The shared experience of community also fortifies religions themselves, and often results in some form of organization, usually including a hierarchy of leadership.

Sacred Entities, Art, and Architecture

5
Identify at least two examples of sacred entities, art, or architecture in your community. Compare the two examples in terms of how they express religious ideas and provoke emotions.

The sacred architecture of cathedrals, temples, and other structures of worship, and the art within them, are among humanity's more beautiful cultural achievements. Other sacred entities, whether natural (such as mountains and rivers) or of human construction (such as cities), also are highly significant for some religions. In India, for example, Hindus consider almost every major river sacred.

A Student's Approach to the World's Religions

Now that we have mapped out some of the prominent features of religions, let us consider in greater depth the challenges and rewards of this voyage on which we are about to embark.

First we can recall the issues that might make our journey unsettling on occasion. It would seem that by definition, ultimate reality must be the same for all humans. Certainly the monotheistic religions consider God to be the God of all. If this is the case, how can there be more than one true religion? Are the religions saying essentially the same thing, even though they are using different words filtered through different historical and cultural frameworks? Are they in basic agreement about the truth? If so, does the matter of choosing a religion simply come down to personal preference?

These are difficult questions, and it is unrealistic to hope that they will all be answered satisfactorily by the end of our voyage. Besides, religion itself is grounded in a mystery that we cannot necessarily expect to penetrate. We can, however, make considerable progress toward understanding these challenges by being clear about *how* we approach the study of the world's religions.

Two Approaches to the Study of Religions

The challenges of studying the religions of others are rather minimal for those who are not religious themselves. Most people, however, are religious and must see the religions of others from within their own tradition. This can be especially difficult from the point of view of religious traditions that rigidly maintain their own version of the truth while rejecting the versions of others. But many religions are highly tolerant of the perspectives of others.

In the face of these challenges, the study of world religions is enriched when approached in two ways. The first is the comparative approach. Friedrich Max Müller, one of the founders of the study of comparative religions, pointed out that to know just one religion is to know none. As we move from chapter to chapter, the basic elements of religions, along with the common questions they strive to answer, will become clearer. Studying many religions will enable us to know each one, including our own, more precisely.

Second, it is imperative that we approach the study of religions with **empathy,** which is the capacity for seeing things from another's perspective. An often-quoted Native American proverb advises, "Never judge other people until you have walked a mile in their moccasins." The need to cultivate empathy is one of the most challenging—and rewarding—aspects of the study of religions.

Destinations and Discoveries

Before we embark on our voyage, let's briefly chart our course and set forth some specific objectives. This chapter is followed by a look at primal religions, focusing on the Aborigines of Australia, the Yoruba of Africa, and the Plains Indians of North America. We then explore the religions originating in South Asia, the region including India, Sri Lanka, Pakistan, Nepal, Bhutan, and Bangladesh. This section covers Hinduism, Buddhism, Jainism, and Sikhism.

We move next to the religions originating in East Asia, especially China and Japan. These religions are Confucianism, Taoism, Zen Buddhism, and Shinto.

Finally, we study religions originating in the Middle East and the areas surrounding the north coast of the Mediterranean Sea. We examine first Zoroastrianism and the religions of ancient Greece and Rome, and then turn our sights to Judaism, Christianity, and Islam.

As for our objectives, we can specify three, though surely our discoveries will extend beyond them. For one thing, we can strive to become knowledgeable about the answers each of the religions offers to the religious questions outlined earlier in this chapter. All the religions are treasure troves of wisdom, and everyone can benefit from exploring them. Secondly, we can become better acquainted with the basic elements of the world's major religions through our study of abundant examples of each element. Finally, and this objective relates to much of what has been said in this chapter, we can expect to emerge from this course with a greatly enhanced understanding of the people who adhere to these religions.

Raise anchor! Let the voyage begin.

6
It is important to cultivate empathy, the capacity for seeing things from another's perspective, when studying the religions of others. Try applying the Native American proverb on empathy by "walking a mile in the moccasins" of a family member or close friend. What do you think life looks like from that person's perspective?

Glossary

belief. Conviction of the truth of religious assertions such as a tradition's creeds, doctrines, or teachings.

cosmology. The understanding of the nature of the universe.

empathy. The capacity for seeing things from another's perspective, and an important methodological approach for studying religions.

ethics. A basic element of religions that deals with how we are to act while living in the world.

faith. Experience of the divine or holy presence; faith is characterized by its spontaneity and its self-evident truth for the individual.

monotheism. The belief in only one divine being.

mysticism. A category of types of religious experience characterized by communion or union with the divine through inward contemplation.

myth. A story that is passed along orally (and in some cases is recorded in scripture) that tends to answer questions of origins and serves as a source of sacred truth.

pantheism. The belief that the divine reality exists in everything.

polytheism. The belief in many gods.

revelation. The transmission of the divine will or knowledge to human beings, typically through myths or some form of religious experience.

ritual. Formal worship practice, often based on the re-enactment of a myth.

salvation. The general deliverance from the shortcomings of the human condition; for some religions, salvation is gained through a form of transcendence in this life, and for other religions, it comes through attaining a good destiny in the afterlife.

transcendence. Salvation in this life, which enables us to live fully in the human condition, with all its joys and sorrows, while maintaining an underlying state of joy and tranquillity.

GREAT SANDY DESERT

GREAT DIVIDING RANGE

AUSTRALIA

GIBSON DESERT

GREAT VICTORIA DESERT

Perth

Sydney

Melbourne

TASMANIA

SAHARA DESERT

Nile

AFRICA

Niger   Oyo Ife

YORUBALAND

Lake Victoria

KALAHARI DESERT

Atlantic Ocean

DRAKENSBERG MOUNTAINS

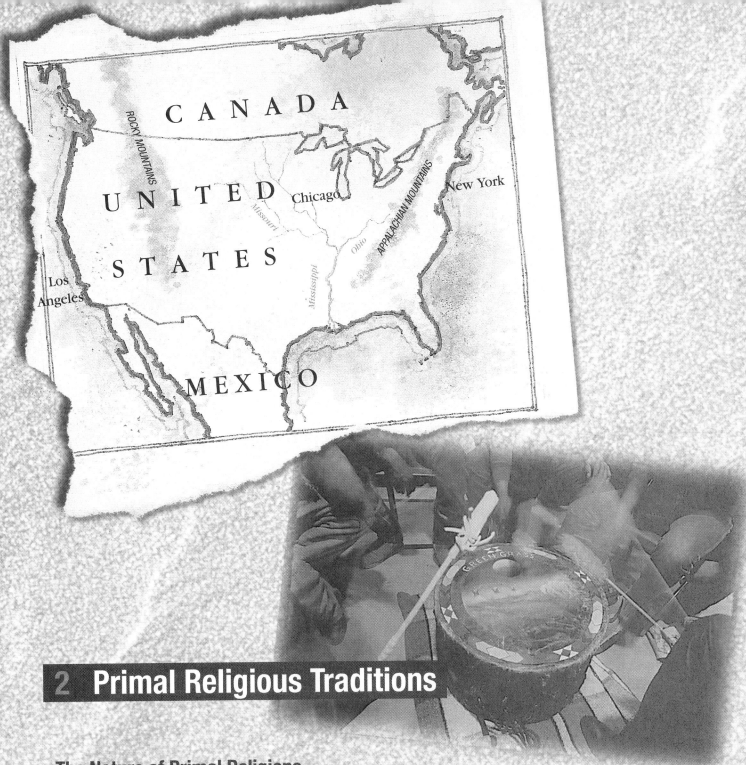

2 Primal Religious Traditions

The Nature of Primal Religions

Since prehistoric times, small groups of people throughout the world have practiced their own unique forms of religion. Some of these religions continue to be practiced, especially among the native inhabitants of Australia, Africa, and the Americas. We refer to these religions as "primal" because they tended to come first, relative to the other religious traditions we will study in the remaining chapters of this book.

Beginning our study with these first religions is a good idea for several reasons. For one thing, primal religions provide special insight into two of the basic elements of religions touched on in chapter 1: myth and ritual. Primal peoples have tended to preserve a mythic orientation toward life. Their myths, and the rituals that re-enact them, remain essential sources of knowledge and power for all aspects of their lives.

Another reason for studying primal religions first is that all religions stem, more or less directly, from primal beginnings. For example, the ancestor of Judaism, the religion of the ancient Israelites, was in its early stages a primal religion, exhibiting features similar to those discussed in this chapter. It is the same for other religions, such as Hinduism in India or Shinto in Japan. They are rooted in the primal traditions of early peoples.

Along with having orginated first, primal religions are generally the traditions of nonliterate people, which means that they do not depend on scriptures or written teachings, as do most other religions. What they lack in written texts, however, they often make up for in oral material—myths or stories that are passed down from generation to generation.

Primal religions tend to be the traditions of tribal peoples, organized in small groups who dwell in villages as opposed to large cities. There are exceptions, however, such as the city-dwelling Yoruba of Africa. In this and other ways, primal traditions are diverse. It is therefore crucial that we avoid making sweeping generalizations.

In light of this vast diversity, this chapter does not attempt to describe all primal religions. Instead it focuses on three rather specific examples: the Aborigines of Australia, the Yoruba of Africa, and the Plains Indians of North America. Once we have considered each of these traditions in turn, we can reflect on some general themes that tend to be common to primal religions.

The Australian Aborigines

The Aborigines, the native people of Australia, were largely unaffected by outsiders until the arrival of Europeans some two hundred years ago. The Aborigines maintained traditions extending many thousands of years into the past. In some areas, notably in the northern and central regions of Australia, these traditions remain largely intact today.

Australia is a continent of great diversity. Its climate and terrain range from lush forested mountains to harsh deserts, and these differences have produced a variety of social groups that speak about forty separate languages and have differing customs. Australia's primal religious life is diverse as well, but it has enough common elements that we can speak of one Aboriginal religion while acknowledging its varying manifestations.

The Dreaming: The Eternal Time of the Ancestors

The foundation of Aboriginal religion is the concept of the Dreaming. According to Aboriginal belief, the world was originally formless. Then at a certain point in the mythic past, supernatural beings called **Ancestors** emerged and roamed about Earth. The Ancestors gave shape to the landscape and created the various forms of life, including the first human beings. They specified the territory each human tribe was to occupy, and determined each tribe's languages, social rules, and customs. When the Ancestors had finished and departed from Earth, they left behind symbols of their presence, in the form of natural landmarks, rock paintings, and so on.

This mythic period of the Ancestors is called **the Dreaming.** In a very real sense, this period lives on, for the Aborigines believe that the spiritual essence of the Ancestors remains in the various symbols they left behind. The sites at which these symbols are found are thought to be charged with sacred power. Only certain individuals are allowed to approach them, and they must approach the

sites in a special way. Rather than taking the shortest route to the sites, they follow the paths that were originally taken by the Ancestors in the Dreaming. This ritual re-enacts the mythic events of the Dreaming, and through it the Aborigines re-create their world as it existed in the beginning. This gives them access to the endless sources of sacred power of these sites. The Aborigines inhabit a mythic geography—a world in which every notable landmark, whether it be a rock outcropping, a watering hole, or a cave, is believed to have great religious significance.

The spiritual essence of the Ancestors is also believed to reside within each individual. An unborn child becomes animated by a particular Ancestor when the mother or another relative makes some form of contact with a sacred site. Usually this involves a ritual that draws the Ancestor's spiritual essence into the unborn child.

Through this connection each Aborigine is a living representation of an Ancestor. This relationship is symbolized by a **totem**—the natural form in which the Ancestor appeared in the Dreaming. The totem may be an animal, such as a kangaroo or snake, or a rock formation or other feature of the landscape. The

1

Chapter 1 stressed the importance of feeling empathy—the capacity for seeing something from another's perspective—when studying world religions. Striving to understand the Aboriginal concept of a mythic geography offers a good opportunity for practicing empathy. Think of a favorite outdoor area, such as a place in the wilderness, a beach, a park, or your backyard. Imagine that every notable landmark has great religious significance and that your every move within the area is undertaken as if it were a religious ritual. Now describe the area and your experience of being there.

Far right: An initiation dance. *Center:* Aborigine men paint initiates' bodies in preparation for initiation ceremonies. *Right:* An Australian Aborigine in ritual attire.

2

Every society has rituals that re-enact origins, just as the Aborigines do. Some contemporary rituals are religious in nature, while others involve patriotism and other aspects of society. Think of as many such rituals as you can, and list each one, briefly explaining how it is a re-enactment of an original event.

individual or group will always be identified in certain ways with his or her totemic Ancestor. The system of belief and ritual based on totems is called totemism. Totemism is a motif that is common to many primal traditions.

The Ancestors of the Dreaming also continually nourish the natural world. They are sources of life of all kinds. In order for this power to flow forth into the world, the human beings associated with each particular Ancestor must perform proper rituals.

The supernatural, the human world, and the world of nature are thus considered to be delicately interrelated. Aboriginal religious life seeks to maintain harmonious relationships among these three aspects of reality.

Animating the Power of the Dreaming: Aboriginal Religious Life

Religion, for the Aborigines, is the entire process of recreating the mythic past of the Dreaming in order to tap into its sacred power. This is done primarily through ritual, the re-enactment of myth. It also involves maintaining the structure of society as it was originally established by the Ancestors. This, in turn, requires the performance of certain rituals, such as those of initiation. Let us consider more closely each of these aspects of Aboriginal religion.

For Aborigines, ritual is essential if life is to have meaning. It is only through ritual that the sacred power of the Dreaming can be accessed and experienced. Furthermore, Aborigines believe that the rituals themselves were taught to the first humans by the Ancestors in the Dreaming.

Behind every ritual lies a myth that tells of certain actions of the Ancestors during the Dreaming. For example, myths that describe the creation of the kangaroo, a chief food source of the Aborigines, spell out precisely how and where the act of creation took place. Rituals that re-enact these myths are performed at the corresponding sacred sites in order to replenish the local population of kangaroos.

Taboo:
The Basis of Aboriginal Social Structure

Aboriginal society is carefully structured. Certain people are forbidden to participate in certain rituals. The basis of this structure is

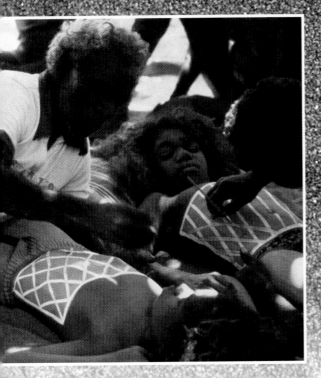

the concept of **taboo,** which dictates that certain things and activities, due to their sacred nature, are set aside for specific members of the group and are forbidden to others. Violation of this principle has been known to be punishable by death.

The sites and rituals associated with certain Ancestors are for men only. Others, such as those connected with childbirth, are for women only. Restrictions are also based on maturity and on an individual's amount of religious training. Usually the older members of the tribe are in charge of important rituals.

For young people, religious maturity and training are achieved in part through the elaborate initiation rituals practiced throughout Aboriginal Australia.

Initiation: Symbolic Death, Spiritual Rebirth

Even before birth each Aborigine possesses the spiritual essence of her or his totemic Ancestor. Initiation rituals serve to awaken young people to this spiritual identity, and at the same time redefine their social identity within the tribe. The rituals bring about the symbolic death of childhood, which prepares the way for the spiritual rebirth that is a nec-

essary step toward adulthood. Meanwhile, throughout the course of these rituals, myths of the Dreaming are taught to the young people. In this manner they learn the essential truths about their world and how they are to act within it.

Both boys and girls undergo initiation, though usually the rites are especially elaborate for boys. As an example, we will consider the male initiation rites practiced in the nineteenth century by the Dieri tribe of south-central Australia.

The initiation rituals of the Dieri took place around a boy's ninth birthday (though the age could vary) and lasted for months. In the first ritual, intended as a symbolic death, the initiate's two lower middle teeth were knocked out and buried in the ground.

Other rituals followed, including circumcision (removal of the foreskin of the penis), which for many Aboriginal tribes is the symbolic death par excellence. According to one myth, two Ancestors had shown the Dieri in the Dreaming how to circumcise with a stone knife.

The main initiation ritual was called the Wilyaru. The intiate stood with his eyes closed

3
To what extent does our society apply restrictions similar to those of the Aboriginal concept of taboo?

as men took turns cutting their forearms and letting their blood fall on the youth, until he became caked with dried blood. This blood served to connect the boy symbolically with his relatives. Next, wounds were inflicted on the boy's neck and back, intended to leave scars, yet another symbol of death. At this point the boy was given a bull-roarer, a sacred instrument consisting of a piece of wood attached to a long string made from human hair. The bull-roarer recreated the sound of the deities, and because of its great power, was taboo for women.

These initiation rituals were followed by a period of months during which the boy was alone in the wilderness, until his wounds healed and the blood wore off his skin. When he returned to his tribe, he was greeted with much rejoicing and celebration. His rites of initiation completed, the boy had become a man.

It might be difficult for an outside observer to understand the reasons for these various rituals. But this simply illustrates the great power of myth. Aboriginal myth creates a reality that is unique to the Aborigines, a world of their own in which such initiation rituals not only make sense but are essential if life is to have meaning. The power of myth, and the performance of ritual to re-enact myth, are basic features of all primal traditions.

An African Tradition: The Religion of the Yoruba

Africa, the second largest continent in terms of land mass, is home to some four hundred million people and several hundred different religions. Our study will be confined to just one of them: the religion of the Yoruba. While hardly representative of all African religions, the Yoruba tradition is similar enough to some others to serve as a good example. Yoruba society, today consisting of about sev-

4
Rituals of initiation are another aspect of primal traditions that occur in contemporary society, though generally not as elaborately. What sorts of experiences have you undergone that have served as rituals of initiation, marking your passage from childhood to adulthood?

en million people, has endured for over one thousand years. Theirs is an ancient religion that has produced some of the greatest artwork on the African continent.

The Yoruba and Their Universe

The Yoruba live in the western regions of central Africa, in the modern nations of Nigeria, Benin, and Togo. Yoruba does not designate a unified nation, but rather a group with a common language and culture. Throughout their history the Yoruba have favored living in cities. Some of these cities, such as Ife, Oyo, and Ijebu, have been quite large. The cities have tended to maintain independence from one another. Ife, however, has always been the center of Yoruba religion, because it was there, the Yoruba believe, that the god Orisa-nla first began to create the world.

The Yoruba regard the cosmos as being divided into two separate worlds: Heaven and Earth. Heaven is the invisible home of the gods and the ancestors. Earth is the visible world of normal experience, and home to human beings, who are descended from the gods. Earth is also populated by a perverted form of human beings, the witches and sorcerers, who can cause disastrous harm if not controlled.

The purpose of the Yoruba religion is to maintain the balance between the human beings of Earth and the gods and ancestors of Heaven, while guarding against the evil deeds of sorcerers and witches.

Gods and Ancestors: The Inhabitants of Heaven

It is relatively common for primal traditions to hold a belief in both a supreme god and a host of less powerful deities. The supreme god of the Yoruba is Olorun, and the many deities the Yoruba worship are known as **orisa.**

Olorun, the High God

The Yoruba believe that Olorun is the primary, original source of power in the universe. All other life forms ultimately owe their existence to him. But Olorun is distant and remote, and not involved in human affairs. He is therefore hardly worshiped at all, except in prayer. No shrines or rituals are assigned to him, and no sacrifices are made on his behalf. Instead, many other gods, the *orisa,* function as mediators between Olorun and human beings.

Orisa

The *orisa* are lesser deities, compared to the supremacy of Olorun. But in the religious life of the Yoruba, the *orisa* are truly significant. All are sources of sacred power and can help or harm human beings, depending on how well the rituals designed to appease them are carried out.

Hundreds of *orisa* exist. Some are worshiped by all Yoruba, others by only one family group. One of the more significant *orisa* is Orisa-nla, whom most Yoruba believe created Earth. Ogun, the god of iron and of war, has a special status. Originally he was a human being, the first king of the city of Ife. After he died he became a god, and now he inhabits the border area between the ancestors and the rest of the *orisa.* The most complex of the *orisa* is Esu, who contains both good and evil properties. Precisely because of this, Esu mediates between Heaven and Earth. Worship of Esu is included when worshiping any other *orisa,* and he has a place in every shrine.

Esu's dual nature as both good and evil, and his corresponding role as mediator between Heaven and Earth, make him a **trickster figure,** a sort of mischievous supernatural being. Tricksters are significant in many primal traditions throughout the world.

5
The Yoruba *orisa* are a type of divinity unfamiliar to most of us. What aspects of the *orisa* do you find most interesting?

Far left: The amulets on this Yoruba mask illustrate the impact of Islam in Africa. As primal traditions develop throughout history, they incorporate elements of other religions.
Left: Esu, the most complex of the Yoruba *orisa,* is depicted in this sculpture.

The Ancestors of the Living

Along with the deities, the heavenly world is inhabited by the ancestors, deceased humans who have acquired supernatural status. Similar to the *orisa,* the ancestors possess sacred power that can help or harm the living. Therefore, they too are worshiped through rituals at special shrines.

There are two types of ancestors. Family ancestors, whose worshipers include only their own families, gained their supernatural status through having earned a good reputation and having lived to an old age. The second type are the deified ancestors, who were once very important human figures known throughout Yoruba society, and who are now worshiped by large numbers of people.

Connecting Heaven and Earth: Ritual Practitioners

We have noted that the purpose of Yoruba religion is for humans to maintain balance between themselves and the heavenly gods and ancestors. Now that we have become acquainted with some of these heavenly beings, it is time to consider the ritual means of connecting them to the earthly, human world.

Several different types of ritual practitioners can be found among the Yoruba. They perform the vital function of mediating between Heaven and Earth. For whatever religious need a worshiper is attempting to fulfill, there is a specialist who can facilitate communication with the appropriate deity or ancestor.

The head of the family, for example, is responsible for worshiping the family ancestors, which is done in the home at the family shrine. The king, or chief, of each city is in charge of its annual festivals, along with performing a host of other religious functions. The many Yoruba priests oversee the various rituals carried out at the shrines of each *orisa.*

Among the priests who engage in specialized services are **diviners.** Diviners practice the art of **divination,** through which one's future can be learned. To become a diviner requires years of training, and the role is usually

6

Worship of deceased ancestors occurs in many religious traditions. Do we "worship" ancestors in our society?

passed from parent to child. Divination is an extremely important aspect of Yoruba religion because knowledge of one's future is considered essential in order to determine how to proceed with life. The procedure itself involves an intricate system of hundreds of wisdom stories, which the diviner knows by memory. Particular stories are determined to be relevant for each individual. From the stories, the individual's future can be interpreted.

Another ritual specialist is in charge of mediating between the ancestors and the living. Wearing an elaborate ceremonial mask and costume, the ritual specialist becomes a living representation of an ancestor by dancing at festivals. When an important person dies, this ritual specialist imitates that person and conveys comforting messages from the deceased to the living.

The prevalence of these ritual practitioners clearly illustrates the importance of mediating, and thereby of maintaining balance, between the worlds of Heaven and Earth. Most primal religions share the understanding that the boundaries between the human and the supernatural realms are very thin, and can be easily crossed over.

Religion of the North American Plains Indians

Humans first came to North America some forty to sixty thousand years ago. They migrated from Asia by crossing over the Bering Strait (situated between Russia and Alaska), which at that time was dry land. They gradually spread out and eventually inhabited large regions of both North and South America.

These first inhabitants of America, or Native Americans, formed many diverse cultural groups, each with its own religion. As an example, we will consider the religion of the peoples of the North American Plains. Basic aspects of religion were shared in common by these peoples despite their diversity—there are more than thirty tribes and seven distinct languages among the peoples of the Plains.

The Plains are vast, stretching from the Canadian provinces of Alberta, Saskatchewan, and Manitoba southward to the Gulf of Mexico, bordered on the west by the Rocky Mountains, and on the east by the Mississippi River. The culture that we now associate with this area formed relatively recently, after the arrival of horses from Europe in the seventeenth century. Domestic horses enabled the Plains Indians to become great hunters of buffalo and other game. Numerous tribes migrated into the Plains region, exchanging ideas with one another. This exchange was aided by the use of a common sign language understood by all the tribes. The religion of the Plains is therefore somewhat representative of Native American religion in general. Today this religion serves as the model of pan-Indian religion, a recent and popular movement uniting many tribes from across North America. As a result, Plains religion continues to be of vital interest to native peoples throughout the continent.

Our investigation highlights a few of the religious features common to the Plains peoples, beginning with the basic beliefs of one of the largest and most influential tribes, the Lakota.

Basic Beliefs of the Lakota

The Lakota, also known as the Western Sioux (although *Sioux* is pejorative, from an enemy tribe's term for "snakes"), inhabited western Montana and Wyoming, the eastern regions of the Dakotas, and parts of Nebraska. They are an especially important tribe for a number of reasons. They are remembered for

A Young Man's Vision Quest

John Fire Lame Deer (1903–76) was born on the Rosebud Reservation in South Dakota. In his lifetime he was a rancher, a rodeo cowboy, and a reservation police officer, but he is best known as a Sioux, or Lakota, holy man. In this excerpt from his autobiography, Lame Deer describes his experience of a vision quest.

I was all alone on the hilltop. I sat there in the vision pit, a hole dug into the hill, my arms hugging my knees as I watched old man Chest, the medicine man who had brought me there, disappear far down in the valley. He was just a moving black dot among the pines, and soon he was gone altogether. (P. 11)

Night was coming on. I was still lightheaded and dizzy from my first sweat bath in which I had purified myself before going up the hill. I had never been in a sweat lodge before. I had sat in the little beehive-shaped hut made of bent willow branches and covered with blankets to keep the heat in. Old Chest and three other medicine men had been in the lodge with me. I had my back against the wall, edging as far away as I could from the red-hot stones glowing in the center. As Chest poured water over the rocks, hissing white steam enveloped me and filled my lungs. I thought the heat would kill me, burn the eyelids off my face! But right in the middle of all this swirling steam I heard Chest singing. So it couldn't be all that bad. I did not cry out "All my relatives!"—which would have made him open the flap of the sweat lodge to let in some cool air—and I was proud of this. I heard him praying for me: "Oh, holy rocks, we receive your white breath, the steam. It is the breath of life. Let this young boy inhale it. Make him strong."

The sweat bath had prepared me for my vision-seeking. Even now, an hour later, my skin still tingled. But it seemed to have made my brains empty. Maybe that was good, plenty of room for new insights. . . .

Sounds came to me through the darkness: the cries of the wind, the whisper of the trees, the voices of nature, animal sounds, the hooting of an owl. Suddenly I felt an overwhelming presence. Down there with me in my cramped hole was a big bird. The pit was only as wide as myself, and I was a skinny boy, but that huge bird was flying around me as if he had the whole sky to himself. I could hear his cries, sometimes near and sometimes far, far away. I felt feathers or a wing touching my back and head. This feeling was so overwhelming that it was just too much for me. I trembled and my bones turned to ice. . . .

Slowly I perceived that a voice was trying to tell me something. It was a bird cry, but I tell you, I began to understand some of it. That happens sometimes. I know a lady who had a butterfly sitting on her shoulder. That butterfly told her things. This made her become a great medicine woman.

I heard a human voice too, strange and high-pitched, a voice which could not come from an ordinary, living being. All at once I was way up there with the birds. The hill with the vision pit was way above everything. I could look down even on the stars, and the moon was close to my left side. It seemed as though the earth and the stars were moving below me. A voice said, "You are sacrificing yourself here to be a medicine man. In time you will be one. You will teach other medicine men. We are the fowl people, the winged ones, the eagles and the owls. We are a nation and you shall be our brother. You will never kill or harm any one of us. You are going to understand us whenever you come to seek a vision here on this hill. You will learn about herbs and roots, and you will heal people. You will ask them for nothing in return. A man's life is short. Make yours a worthy one."

I felt that these voices were good, and slowly my fear left me. I had lost all sense of time. I did not know whether it was day or night. I was asleep, yet wide awake. Then I saw a shape before me. It rose from the darkness and the swirling fog which penetrated my earth hole. I saw that this was my great-grandfather, Tahca Ushte, Lame Deer, old man chief of the Minneconjou. I could see the blood dripping from my great-grandfather's chest where a white soldier had shot him. I understood that my great-grandfather wished me to take his name. This made me glad beyond words.

We Sioux believe that there is something within us that controls us, something like a second person almost. We call it nagi, what other people might call soul, spirit or essence. One can't see it, feel it or taste it, but that time on the hill—and only that once—I knew it was there inside of me. Then I felt the power surge through me like a flood. I cannot describe it, but it filled all of me. Now I knew for sure that I would become a *wicasa wakan*, a medicine man. Again I wept, this time with happiness.

I didn't know how long I had been up there on that hill—one minute or a lifetime. I felt a hand on my shoulder gently shaking me. It was old man Chest, who had come for me. He told me that I had been in the vision pit four days and four nights and that it was time to come down. He would give me something to eat and water to drink and then I was to tell him everything that had happened to me during my hanblechia. He would interpret my visions for me. He told me that the vision pit had changed me in a way that I would not be able to understand at that time. He told me also that I was no longer a boy, that I was a man now. I was Lame Deer. (Lame Deer and Erdoes, *Lame Deer, Seeker of Visions*, pages 14–16)

having led a confederacy of tribes in the defeat of Custer and his troops in the Battle of Little Bighorn in 1876. In 1890, as the wars against the whites came to an end, more than two hundred Lakota were massacred at Wounded Knee, South Dakota. Today about one hundred thousand Lakota live on reservations in Manitoba, Montana, and North and South Dakota.

The Lakota name for the supreme reality is **Wakantanka,** sometimes translated as "Great Spirit," or the "Great Mysterious," but literally meaning "most sacred." Wakantanka actually refers to sixteen separate deities. The number sixteen is derived from the number four (multiplied times itself), which is the most sacred number in Plains religion. It refers to the four directions (north, south, east, and west), which are especially relevant to peoples living in the wide open regions of the Plains.

The creation of the world and the arrival of the first human beings are explained in detailed myths that celebrate the activities of the various supernatural beings involved. One of the more significant beings is Inktomi (meaning "spider"), the Lakota trickster figure. As the mediator between the supernatural and human worlds, Inktomi taught the first humans their ways and customs. Inktomi also serves another important function. Numerous stories tell about Inktomi's mistakes and errors of judgment, and offer an important moral lesson for children: Do not behave as Inktomi did!

Basic to any religion are beliefs regarding death and the afterlife, or human destiny. The Lakota believe that four souls depart from a person at death, one of which journeys along the "spirit path" of the Milky Way. The soul meets an old woman who judges it and either allows it to continue on to the otherworld of the ancestors, or sends it back to Earth as a ghost. Meanwhile parts of the other souls enter fetuses and are reborn in new bodies.

The beliefs of other Plains tribes are similar in many ways to those of the Lakota. We will now explore two rituals that are common to all Plains Indians.

7
Imagine yourself living in the open wilderness of the North American Plains. Why do you suppose the Lakota understood their supreme reality as being closely related to the four directions?

The Vision Quest

The **vision quest** is common to many primal traditions throughout the world. It is a primary means for an individual to gain access to spiritual power in order to assure greater success in activities such as hunting, warfare, or curing the ill.

The vision quest is done under the supervision of the medicine man, who issues specific instructions prior to the quest, and later interprets the content of the vision. Before setting out on the quest itself, the participant undergoes a ritual of purification in the sweat lodge.

The sweat lodge is used on numerous occasions, and is a common element among Plains Indians and Native American traditions in general. It is a hut made of saplings and covered with animal skins, making it dark and airtight. The structure of the lodge is representative of the universe. Heated stones are placed in the center, and water is sprinkled over them by the medicine man. The intense heat causes the participant to sweat profusely, leading to both physical and spiritual purification.

Once purified in this fashion, the person goes off alone to a place far from the camp, usually to a hilltop. There, he or she (women participate in vision quests, though not as frequently as men) endures the elements for a set number of days, without food or water. Depending on the medicine man's instructions, the person might perform certain rituals, carefully structured around a central spot.

Eventually the vision comes, usually near the end of the stay. It arrives in the form of an animal or some other object or force of nature. A message is often communicated along with the vision. When the individual returns to camp, the vision and the message are interpreted by the medicine man. The lessons derived from the vision quest are an important influence for the rest of the person's life.

On some occasions the participant acquires a guardian spirit, which can be in the form of an animal, an inanimate object, or a ghost. The guardian spirit continues to protect and to instruct the person, especially at times of great need.

Along with the ritual of the vision quest, the actual moment of receiving the vision, or guardian spirit, is a form of religious experience, one of the basic elements of religions discussed in chapter 1. This type of religious experience is common to many primal traditions of the world.

The Sun Dance

Whereas the vision quest focuses on the individual, the **Sun Dance,** another ritual common to all tribes of the Plains, is undertaken for the benefit of all. It occurs at the beginning of summer and is, in part, a celebration of the new year. In the past it also functioned as a preparation for the great annual buffalo hunt.

A sacred leader, usually the medicine man, presides over the Sun Dance. A variation of this occurs among the Blackfeet, who inhabit Alberta, Saskatchewan, and Montana. They choose as their leader a woman of outstanding moral character. Leading the Sun Dance is both a great honor and a grave responsibility.

Left: A Native American man during a vision quest, 1908
Above, right: A Native American man emerges from an underground sweat lodge, 1937.

For all tribes the major task in preparing for the Sun Dance is the construction of the lodge. A cottonwood tree is carefully selected, felled, and ritually carried to a chosen spot, where it is set upright. This tree becomes what scholars call the ***axis mundi,*** the axis or center of the universe—itself an important and common theme for primal traditions. As the connecting link between Earth and the heavens, the tree is also representative of the supreme being. The lodge is constructed around the tree in a manner that is representative of the universe with its four directions.

The performance of the Sun Dance features long periods of dancing while facing in the direction of the sun, which is revered for its life-giving powers. Music and drumbeats accompany the dancing. Some of the dancers skewer the flesh of their chests, and attach themselves to the tree with leather thongs. They then pull back from the tree as they continue dancing, until eventually their flesh tears. Because they believe that their bodies are the only things they truly own, the dancers regard bodily mutilation as the only suitable sacrifice to offer to the supreme being.

Owing to this practice of bodily mutilation, the U.S. government once outlawed the Sun Dance. Now it is again legal, and it is popular among tribes of the North American Plains.

Common Themes, Diverse Traditions

While being careful to point out the vast diversity of primal religions, we have also noted some specific elements that are common to many of them: totemism, taboo, the trickster figure, the vision quest, the *axis mundi.*

Upon reflection it is also clear that our three examples of primal religions share certain general themes. For these religions the boundaries between the supernatural and the human worlds are very thin, and easily crossed. Among the Australian Aborigines, for example, the sacred power of an Ancestor of the Dreaming is believed to enter the individual at the time of conception. The Yoruba commonly turn to divination to acquire knowledge of their destinies from the *orisa.* Meanwhile, communication between the ancestors and the living is thought to be regularly maintained.

A closely related theme involves the all-encompassing nature of religion in primal societies. The secular and the sacred are not separate. Rather, the universe is full of religious significance, and humans are constant participants in drawing on its sacred and life-giving powers. This is vividly illustrated by the fact that Native American languages have

8
The Indians of the Northern Plains traditionally lived off the land, depending on hunting and fishing to feed themselves. What elements of the vision quest and Sun Dance rituals can you identify that are related to this lifestyle?

9

In general, primal religions understand the boundaries between the human and the supernatural realms to be very thin, and easily crossed.

Drawing from the religious traditions of the Aborigines, the Yoruba, and the Indians of the Northern Plains, identify as many examples as you can that illustrate this understanding.

no words for *religion;* it pervades life, so there is no need to set it apart.

Another fact common to the primal religions, one we have not yet emphasized, is that they are all engaged in change. Too often, students of religion have regarded these traditions as static, unchanging monoliths. In fact, primal religions have constantly been changing. American Indians, for example, were once Asians, and the religions of the Plains peoples changed markedly when horses arrived from Europe in the seventeenth century. Australian Aborigines are very well equipped to accommodate modern changes. Once a new tradition has been ac-cepted, they agree that the Ancestors themselves had established it long ago in the period of the Dreaming. The innovation becomes part of their eternal reality.

One of the powerful consequences of this ongoing change is the remarkable adaptability of primal peoples. Though it is common to hear the assertion that these cultures will inevitably be lost from the face of the Earth, the primal religious traditions are not necessarily doomed. On the contrary, the level of participation among native peoples in their own traditional ways seems to be growing. These traditions now bear the imprint of modernity, but their ancient foundations live on.

Glossary

Ancestors. For the Australian Aboriginal religion, Ancestors are supernatural beings (or deities) who emerged and roamed the Earth during the time of the Dreaming, giving shape to the landscape and creating various forms of life. When the word *ancestors* is lowercased, it refers to the deceased, who can assist the living while requiring religious devotion (as among the Yoruba, for example).

axis mundi (Latin: "axis of the universe"). Common to many religions, an entity such as a mountain, tree, or pole that is believed to connect the heavens and Earth, and is sometimes regarded as the center of the world; for example, the cottonwood tree of the Plains Indians' Sun Dance.

divination. The use of various techniques, such as throwing bones or shells and then interpreting the pattern in which they fall, for gaining knowledge about an individual's future or the cause of a personal problem; important among many religions worldwide, including that of the Yoruba.

diviners. Ritual practitioners who specialize in the art of divination; very important among the Yoruba.

Dreaming, the. The mythic time of Australian Aboriginal religion when the Ancestors inhabited the Earth.

orisa (aw-ree-sah'; Yoruba: "head source"). The hundreds of various Yoruba deities who are the main objects of ritual attention, including Orisa-nla, the creator god; Ogun, the god of iron and of war; and Esu, the trickster figure.

Sun Dance. Ritual of the Lakota and other tribes of the North American Plains that celebrates the new year and prepares the tribe for the annual buffalo hunt, performed in the late spring or early summer in a specially constructed lodge.

taboo (sometimes spelled tabu). A system of social ordering which dictates that specific objects and activities, due to their sacred nature, are set aside for specific groups and are strictly forbidden to others; common to many primal peoples, including the Australian Aborigines.

totem. A natural entity, such as an animal or a feature of the landscape, that symbolically represents an individual or group and that has special significance for the religious life of that individual or group; a common motif among Australian Aborigines and other primal peoples.

trickster figure. A type of supernatural being who tends to disrupt the normal course of life, found among many primal peoples; for example, Esu among the Yoruba and Inktomi among the Lakota.

vision quest. A means of seeking spiritual power through an encounter with a guardian spirit or other medium, usually in the form of an animal or other natural entity, following a period of fasting and other forms of self-denial; common to many primal peoples, including the Lakota and other tribes of the North American Plains.

Wakantanka (wah-khan-tankh'-ah; Lakota: "most sacred"). Lakota name for the supreme reality, often referring collectively to sixteen separate deities.

PART 2
South Asia

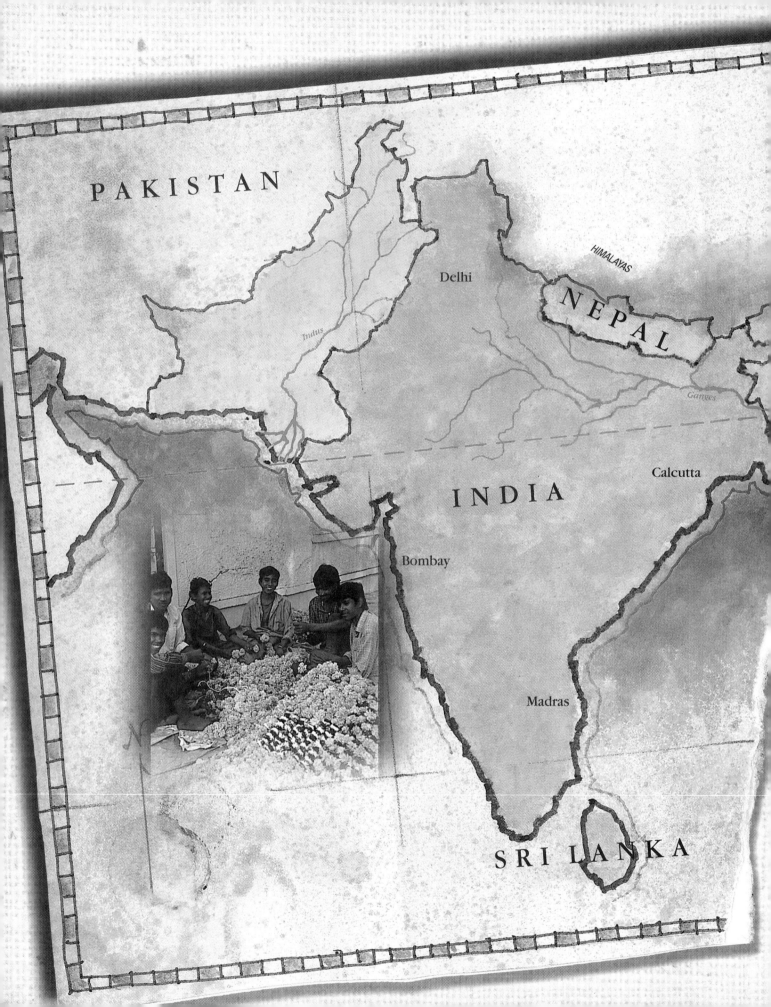

PAKISTAN

Delhi

HIMALAYAS

NEPAL

Indus

Ganges

INDIA

Calcutta

Bombay

Madras

SRI LANKA

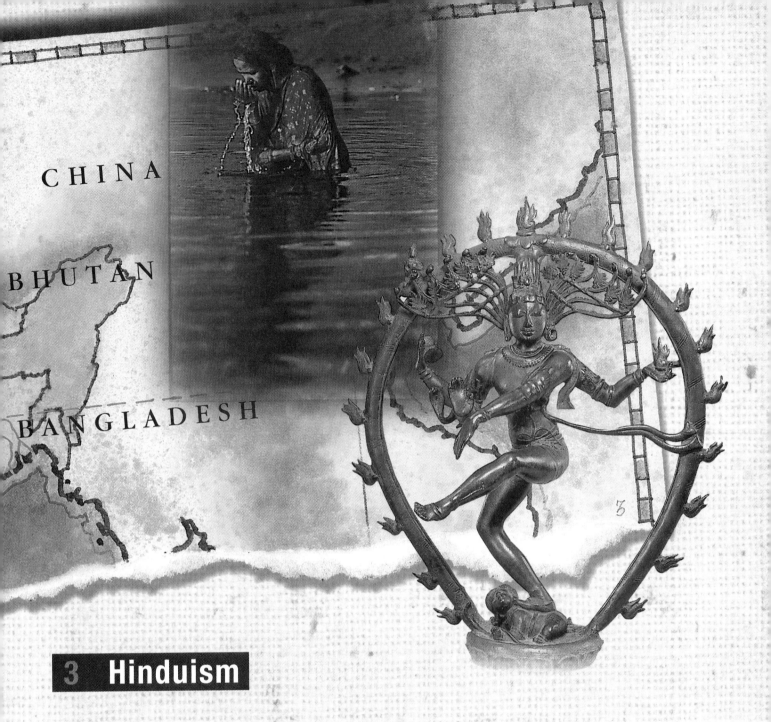

CHINA

BHUTAN

BANGLADESH

3 Hinduism

There is only one God, but endless are his aspects and endless are his names. Call him by any name and worship him in any aspect that pleases you, you are sure to see him. (Shri Ramakrishna, quoted in Prabhavananda, *The Spiritual Heritage of India*, page 353)

Many Rivers to One Ocean

The great holy man Shri Ramakrishna (1836 to 1886) speaks for the majority of his fellow Hindus when he emphasizes the harmony and tolerance that are so characteristic of his religion. A harmony of many different beliefs and practices all aiming for the common goal of salvation, like many rivers converging into one ocean, Hinduism also tends to be highly tolerant of other religions. True to the ideals of Hinduism, Shri Ramakrishna lived what he taught. Mastering from early boyhood a variety of Hindu paths of worship, he later became a Muslim and then a Christian, all the while, from his own perspective, becoming more and more profoundly a Hindu.

Throughout the ages, harmony amid diversity, and tolerance toward other faiths have characterized Hinduism. The **Rig Veda,** Hinduism's earliest sacred text at nearly four thousand years old, declares: "God is one but men call him by many names" (quoted in *Source Book in Indian Philosophy,* page xxvii). The great twentieth-century Hindu, Mahatma Gandhi, echoes the ancient wisdom of the Rig Veda: "Even as a tree has a single trunk, but many branches and leaves, so is there one true and perfect Religion, but it becomes many as it passes through the human medium" (*Moral and Political Writings of Mahatma Gandhi,* volume 1, pages 542–543). Like Ramakrishna, Gandhi revered Christianity and placed the Sermon on the Mount from the Gospel of Matthew alongside Hinduism's Bhagavad-Gita as his favorite religious texts.

In this chapter we will consider the main aspects of the vast diversity of beliefs and practices that together form Hinduism. We will chart many rivers, but it is important not to forget that all flow eventually into one ocean.

Human Destiny: From Worldly Realms to the Divine Beyond

To learn about Hinduism depends first of all on understanding a perspective of reality—the universe, human beings, and the divine—that is fundamentally different from common Western perspectives. Because Hinduism emphasizes above all else the concerns of human beings, we shall chart the Hindu perspective on reality by considering human destiny. It is best to begin this story at its conclusion, for the final destiny of salvation returns the individual back to the original source.

Mahatma Gandhi considered the Bhagavad-Gita and the Sermon on the Mount his favorite religious texts.

Salvation: Returning to the Sacred Source

For all Hindus, salvation is the ultimate goal, the ocean into which all the rivers of Hinduism eventually flow. For most it is a distant goal, not to be attained in this lifetime. Hindus believe in reincarnation (which is described in detail later in this chapter) and thus anticipate a long series of lifetimes, so they can afford to be very patient regarding the goal of salvation. Hinduism is not in a hurry.

The Hindu term for salvation is **moksha,** which means "liberation" or "release." It is a release from this ordinary, finite, limited realm of existence into the infinite ocean of the divine. *Moksha* is an experience characterized by infinite being, infinite awareness, and infinite bliss. The details of this experience defy description, for it is a realm completely beyond this world. Never again to be reincarnated, the Hindu who has attained *moksha* is united forever with the divine, having returned to the sacred source.

The Divine: One Ocean, Many Names

Hinduism's perspective on the nature of the divine differs profoundly from that of Western religions such as Christianity. Rather than believing in one personal God who created all things and exists independently of them, most Hindus believe that all reality—God, the universe, human beings, and all else—is essentially one thing. At the same time, Hindus worship many gods and goddesses.

Monism: All Is Brahman

Though there are exceptions, Hindus generally believe in **monism,** the doctrine that all reality is ultimately one. All rivers, all lakes, even all droplets of rain can correctly be regarded as sharing a common essence, originating from the ocean and eventually returning to it. In the same way, monists believe that all forms of reality—gods and goddesses, plants and animals, the material universe, and humans—share a common essence. Hindus call this essence **Brahman.**

Infinite and eternal, Brahman is the ground of existence and the source of the universe. It is discoverable only through profound contemplation, and its true nature is not revealed on the surface of things. Brahman is impersonal, without characteristics that can be seen, heard, or even intelligibly thought about in the mind. The **Upanishads,** the ancient philosophical texts that form the basis of Hindu doctrines, teach that Brahman can only be described as *neti, neti . . . :* "not this, not this. . . ." Whatever the senses can perceive, whatever the mind can ponder, these are not Brahman, for Brahman is beyond the reach of human perception and thought. Just as atomic particles are invisible and yet are the basic building blocks of matter, so does Brahman reside beneath all surfaces, forming the essence of all things.

Ultimate reality, called Brahman when referring to the essence of all things, can be described in another way as well. The Upanishads teach that ultimate reality can be understood through inward contemplation of the self. The ultimate reality within is named **Atman,** the eternal self.

The fundamental discovery of the Upanishads is that Brahman, ultimate reality understood through contemplation of the universe, and Atman, ultimate reality understood through contemplation of the inner self, are in fact one and the same. Brahman is Atman; all reality is one.

One of the most famous passages in the Upanishads consists of a dialog between a father and a son. Svetaketu asks his father:

"Please, sir, tell me more about this Self."

"Be it so. Put this salt in water, and come to me tomorrow morning."

Svetaketu did as he was bidden. The next morning his father asked him to bring the salt which he had put in the water. But he could not, for it had dissolved. Then said Uddalaka:

"Sip the water, and tell me how it tastes."

"It is salty, sir."

"In the same way," continued Uddalaka, "though you do not see Brahman in this body, he is indeed here. That which is the

subtle essence—in that have all things their existence. That is the truth. That is the Self. And that, Svetaketu, THAT ART THOU." (*Upanishads*, page 70)

"That art thou" (*tat tvam asi* in Sanskrit) is one of the most frequently cited passages in all of Hindu literature. Brahman is Atman. This is monism. All reality—the universe, oneself, and everyone else—shares one essence. And that one is Brahman. Or that one is Atman. The terms are interchangeable.

Polytheism: 330 Million Gods

The divine is thought ultimately to be one essence. And yet Hindus subscribe to polytheism, believing in many gods and goddesses (traditionally, 330 million!). We can best understand this apparent contradiction by continuing to think of the ocean. Though we speak of different oceans that fill separate areas of the earth's surface, there is in reality only one body of water. One person could be surfing in the Pacific while thousands of miles away her cousin is sailing on the Atlantic, each enjoying apparently different oceans. But ultimately they form one body of water.

Hinduism generally regards the 330 million deities as extensions of one ultimate reality, many names for one ocean. We will consider the more important gods and goddesses in some detail later in this chapter. For now it is helpful to understand how they function. Because the divine reality of Brahman or Atman is beyond the reach of the senses and of thought, humans need accessible points of contact with the divine. Hinduism's many deities provide this, each with its own personal characteristics. Hindus can freely worship whichever gods and goddesses they like. Given the vast number of deities, at least one will surely provide an effective point of contact with the divine.

Many Worlds, Many Lifetimes: Hindu Cosmology

All religious traditions set forth a cosmology—an explanation regarding the nature of the universe. Hindu cosmology presents a radical alternative to the great Western religions and modern science.

Before describing *what* the Hindu universe is, it is appropriate first to consider *why* the universe is. For if everything is ultimately and originally one thing, all unified in the divine Brahman, why does there appear to be anything else? What happened in the first place that caused the human need to seek salvation? Such questions are of obvious interest, and yet they have no easy answers. Hinduism tends to regard such issues as great mysteries. Just as Brahman itself is ultimately a mystery, beyond the reach of logical explanation, so, too, its creative energy flows forth mysteriously. This universe—this ordinary, finite, limited realm of existence—somehow has come to be. Humans call it home, at least for now. The important thing for Hindus is to deal with the universe as it is, to seek the salvation that eventually will bring freedom from the world's bonds.

Cycles of Creation

The West has generally stressed the linear progression of time, from a distant beginning (such as the six days of Creation recounted in the Book of Genesis, or the big bang theory of modern astrophysics) to an eventual end of creation as we know it. Hinduism, on the contrary, charts time and creation in ongoing cycles.

The cyclical cosmology of Hinduism declares that the universe undergoes long periods of creation and destruction, a rhythmic pattern that repeats itself endlessly. The end of the present period is drawing near—although millions of years remain. As the end of

1

Imagine that you are Svetaketu's father. Describe another analogy that might answer his question about the self.

2

What are some ways you are aware of that people make contact with the divine? Briefly explain two or three possibilities.

A small selection from the pantheon of Hindu gods:
Center: Vishnu and his consort, Lakshmi
Clockwise from top left: Krishna as a boy; Vishnu; Agni, god of fire; Ganesha, pictured in a stage production of the *Mahabharata*

the cycle approaches, the destructive forces already at work will gradually gain the upper hand, eventually bringing all of creation to a deep stillness and long pause. Then the entire universe will be re-created: the galaxies will be remade; souls will arise again and come to inhabit the various life forms; Hinduism itself will evolve all over again.

Reincarnation

Amid the cyclical pattern of the universe, each individual is also created and re-created repeatedly, until finally attaining release from this realm through *moksha*. According to the doctrine of **samsara,** or "wheel of rebirth," the soul is reincarnated from one life form to another. Accounts vary as to precisely what is reincarnated. At the very least, it is the individual's self, or atman, the divine spark within that is destined eventually to be reunited with its source. Most aspects of the personality are generally not thought to be transmitted into the next life form. For instance, individuals usually cannot remember past lives.

Reincarnation occurs on a vast number of levels of existence, including the various life forms of this earth and other similar worlds, gods and goddesses in the many Hindu heavens, and demons in its many hells. Like all realms of *samsara,* even those of the gods do not last forever—they are not Brahman. A soul might enjoy heavenly pleasures for ten thousand years, but then the wheel of rebirth is destined to continue, and a soul will continue being reincarnated until *moksha* is achieved.

Reincarnation puts an interesting twist on the problem of mortality. On one hand, to die without attaining liberation must be considered a defeat, because the soul is then destined to remain on the wheel of rebirth. On the other hand, the prospect of reincarnation denies death at least some of its sting. Death is not final for Hindus—in fact, it is likely to be experienced again!

In the **Bhagavad-Gita,** Hinduism's most popular sacred text, the god Krishna teaches Arjuna, a great warrior, about many important religious issues, including reincarnation. The process of death and reincarnation is analogous to getting undressed at night and putting on a different set of clothes in the morning. As Krishna explains to Arjuna, the eternal self puts on new bodies in a similar fashion:

Never have I not existed,
nor you, nor these kings;
and never in the future
shall we cease to exist.

Just as the embodied self
enters childhood, youth, and old age,
so does it enter another body;
this does not confound a steadfast man.

· · · · · · · · · · · · · · · ·

As a man discards
worn-out clothes
to put on new
and different ones,
so the embodied self
discards
its worn-out bodies
to take on other new ones.

(Bhagavad-Gita, 2:12,13,22)

Law and Order: Divine Principles in the World

Two important principles, *karma* and *dharma,* serve to connect the divine with this world. These principles form the crucial link between the realm of *samsara* and the divine source. By providing a basis for a moral life in this world, *karma* and *dharma* thus serve to permeate the earthly life with spiritual significance.

Karma

Karma functions hand in hand with *samsara. Karma* literally means "action" or "deeds." As the principle that determines the nature of each reincarnation, *karma* is best understood as the moral law of cause and effect. Every action produces a justified effect based on its moral worthiness. *Karma* thus

Krishna, right, counsels Arjuna, in a stage production of the *Mahabharata*.

determines all the particular circumstances and situations of one's life. Just like a law of physics (for example, motion: for every action there is an opposite and equal reaction), *karma* is a law of nature, and it functions independently of any deity or of a formal day of judgment. Individuals are automatically held to be morally responsible for their actions; as the old saying goes, "As you sow, so shall you reap."

Karma permeates the realm of *samsara*, such that an individual's *karmic* record stays with the soul from reincarnation to reincarnation. *Karma* thus determines the life form into which the soul is born, whether it be a deity or other supernatural being, a human, or an animal. Of the various life forms, only humans have the will to affect the status of their *karma*. Therefore, being human is both a privilege and a demanding responsibility.

Karma secures a high degree of justice, in theory at least. For unlike followers of Western religions, Hindus have an easy answer to the question, Why do bad things happen to good people? Because, based on the evil deeds of past lives, they deserve it! The criminal can never escape justice, and the saint will never be denied a just reward. Due to this foolproof feature, the law of *karma* has been called the most logical system of divine justice the world has ever known.

Dharma

With the law of *karma* in effect, people are held responsible for their actions. However, some standard is needed by which individuals can judge the rightness or wrongness of their actions. This standard is **dharma,** or ethical duty based on the divine order of reality.

Dharma is of central significance. The term itself is Hinduism's closest equivalent to our term *religion*. More than just a specific list of rights and wrongs, *dharma* is the complete rule of life. For every activity there is a way of acting that conforms to *dharma*. Hindus

4
In the right-hand column of a sheet of paper, write the main actions you have taken during the last twenty-four hours. Then, in the left-hand column, write what caused you to take each action. Is it possible for an action to lack a cause? Why or why not?

look to four different sources when seeking guidance about *dharma* in particular situations. These sources, in order from highest to lowest level of authority, are (1) divine revelation, as expressed in the sacred scriptures; (2) sacred tradition, as passed on from generation to generation; (3) the practices and example of those who are considered the wisest members of society; and (4) conscience.

Whenever Hindus strive to fulfill desires, *dharma* provides limits to their pursuits. *Dharma* also shifts the focus from satisfying private cravings to caring for others. In its ultimate effect of nourishing unconditional concern for the world, *dharma* has much in common with the primary Christian ethical principle of unconditional love.

The Hindu perspective on human destiny has, as we have seen, a significant effect on the lives of individuals. Individuals, however, are part of the larger social order. In the next section we will examine Hindu society and the ways it influences an individual's identity.

Hindu Society: Mapping the Individual's Identity

Despite their sometimes dizzying complexity, the many aspects of Hinduism are for the most part in harmony. Basic principles are interconnected. *Karma,* the moral law of cause and effect, is based in *dharma,* ethical duty. *Dharma,* in turn, is connected to another aspect of Hinduism, its social order. A person's particular *dharma* is determined by gender, caste, and stage of life. Amid this social order, Hindus are free to choose from among four legitimate goals. Together these circumstances map an individual's identity.

The *dharma* of women, for example, has traditionally emphasized obedience toward men—first the father, then the husband, and finally the sons. The duties of caste and stage of life, which figure prominently in constituting the *dharma* of men, are less relevant for women. Women's primary role of providing for the welfare of the family, though, has always been of central importance in Hinduism.

Doing One's Job: The Caste System

Throughout its history Hinduism has divided society into four distinct classes, or **castes**—**brahmin** priests; **kshatriya** warriors and administrators; **vaishya** producers, such as farmers, merchants, and artisans; and **shudra** servants and laborers. The original term used for these divisions means "color," which is apparently related to the fact that the original inhabitants of India were much darker than the fair-skinned Aryans who invaded and conquered most of India during the centuries of Hinduism's beginnings. The Aryans considered it important to prevent the two racial groups from intermingling, so they distinguished their own classes—the *brahmin, kshatriya,* and *vaishya*—from that of the native peoples, the *shudra.*

The original four classes were divided and subdivided until over three thousand distinct categories emerged. These categories correspond primarily to differing occupations, especially with respect to men. For women the primary significance of caste pertains to whom they can marry; traditional *dharma* provides specific rules regarding marriage with respect to caste. An additional category consists of the "outcastes," those who are considered to be outside of society altogether. This group includes the "Untouchables," who only recently have begun to enjoy some legal rights, thanks to the work of Mahatma Gandhi. He renamed the outcastes *Harijan,* "God's children."

In general the caste system is rigidly based on heredity. One is simply born to a lifelong caste identity, as determined by *karma,* which directs the soul into whatever situation it deserves. The Upanishads explain:

Accordingly, those who are of pleasant conduct here—the prospect is, indeed, that they will enter a pleasant womb, either the womb of a *[brahmin],* or the womb of a *kshatriya,* or the womb of a *[vaishya].* But those who are of stinking conduct here—the prospect is, indeed, that they will enter a stinking womb, either the womb of a dog, or the womb of a swine, or the womb of an outcast[e]. (Chandogya Upanishad 5.10.7)

In this way *karma* can be seen to justify the caste system itself. One does not just happen to be born an outcaste; it is deserved, based on the "stinking conduct" of a previous life. Likewise for the *brahmins* who, due to

5

Hindu society is rigidly separated by caste identity. Is Western society separated in any ways that are similar to the caste system?

their meritorious *karma* in previous lives, deserve their privileged position. They have lived in conformity to their *dharma,* and are now closer to salvation because of it.

Karma determines caste identity, and caste, in turn, determines the specific *dharma* governing a person's actions. For example, the ethical duties of a *brahmin* differ from those of a *kshatriya.* A most striking example of how caste identity determines *dharma* is contained in the Bhagavad-Gita. Arjuna, a great warrior (thus of the *kshatriya* caste), is poised to enter a crucial battle. But as he considers the gruesome tasks that lie before him, including the killing of kinsmen and old friends, he hesitates, wondering if he should avoid battle. But the god Krishna, disguised as Arjuna's charioteer, reminds Arjuna of his *dharma:*

Look to your own duty;
do not tremble before it;
nothing is better for a warrior
than a battle of sacred duty.

The doors of heaven open
for warriors who rejoice
to have a battle like this
thrust on them by chance.

If you fail to wage this war
of sacred duty,
you will abandon your own duty
and fame only to gain evil.

(Bhagavad-Gita, 2:31–33)

6
Describe each of the Hindu stages of life, comparing each stage to a similar stage in Western society.

Acting One's Age: Four Stages of Life

Age is also a determining factor in an individual's *dharma*. Hindu society distinguishes four stages of life, each with its own set of specific duties. The stages are especially relevant for males.

Upon undergoing an initiation ritual at about the time of puberty, the Hindu boy enters the first stage, that of the student. Characterized by intensive study of the Vedas (vay'duhz) and other sacred literature, this stage lasts until marriage. The second is the householder stage, in which the worldly tasks of pursuing a career and raising a family are central. Women are involved in this stage along with their husbands.

The birth of the first grandchild marks the beginning of the third stage, called the forest-dweller stage. A man may choose to ask his wife to accompany him through this stage, which allows retreat from worldly bonds (sometimes literally by dwelling in the forest) in order to engage fully in the spiritual quest. The fourth stage is that of the **sannyasin**, or wandering **ascetic**. This stage is for those forest dwellers who have developed a readiness to return to society, but in a manner such that they remain detached from the normal attractions and distractions of social life. Engaged with the world but not attached to it, the *sannyasin* is described in the Bhagavad-Gita as "one who neither hates nor desires" (5:3). For women who have accompanied their hus-

A Hindu marriage ceremony marks the start of the householder stage of life.

bands into the forest, it is natural that they, too, might advance to the fourth stage. If so, husband and wife live detached from each other, having transcended the ordinary ways of this world, including those of marriage.

Seeking One's Desire: Four Goals of Life

Liberation from *samsara,* in the Hindu view, is the only perfect form of salvation. *Moksha* is the ultimate goal of life. But what if we enjoy this world, welcome the challenges of this life, and relish its fruits? What if we have no real desire to leave this world, so much so that reincarnation itself is looked upon positively, as yet another opportunity to seek the many pleasures of existence?

Sensual Pleasure

Hinduism embraces such pleasure seeking, even as it teaches the ultimate goal of liberation. Pleasure, or **kama**, is a legitimate aim of life. No religion denies that humans desire pleasure. Religions differ drastically, however, in their judgments as to the goodness or rightness of fulfilling this desire. Hinduism tends to surpass most religions in its outright celebration of the pursuit of pleasure. *Kama,* which refers mainly to the pleasures of sensual love, is to be embraced by whosoever desires it, provided that the lovers remain within the limits of *dharma.* So legitimate is the pursuit of *kama* that some of Hinduism's sacred literature is devoted to the enhancement of sensual love.

Material Success

Despite its complete legitimacy, the appetite for *kama* is believed to have a limit. Eventually the fulfillment found in love will no longer satisfy completely. A yearning arises for something else. For most people this yearning is for **artha**, material success and the social power and prestige that accompany it. Just as North American secular society tends to embrace the pursuit of money, Hinduism celebrates the goal of *artha.* But *artha,* too, eventually proves unfulfilling. In due time people experience a yearning to strive

for something beyond pursuits that provide only for personal and material needs.

Harmony with *Dharma*

This yearning leads to the third goal, which is called **dharma**. As the third goal of life, *dharma* maintains its meaning as the general principle of ethical duty. But when *dharma* is embraced as the primary goal of life, it is no longer merely a duty, begrudgingly performed. It is now that which is most desired. The profound joy of living in harmony with *dharma* is known firsthand. No one needs to tell the Hindu who pursues this goal that "it is more blessed to give than to receive." The blessings of *dharma* give fuel to its fire. Yet even perfect harmony with *dharma* is a limited joy, destined eventually to lead to even deeper yearnings. After all, the world for which the ethical person is concerned—even if the concern is unconditional—is still the world of this realm, afflicted with the unending pains of *samsara.*

The Bliss of *Moksha*

All Hindus are destined to seek the fourth goal of life: the infinite being, awareness, and bliss of *moksha,* the great ocean into which all rivers eventually flow. And the paths to *moksha* that are available to Hindus are as numerous and diverse as the rivers of India. In the next section we will consider the three major paths to salvation.

7
Reflect on a goal you have had and have achieved. Was the satisfaction of achieving the goal permanent? Did it cause you to desire to achieve new goals? From the experience, what did you learn about desire?

Three Paths to Salvation

Hinduism embraces three great paths to *moksha*. People have different talents and strengths, and each of the three paths draws primarily on one of the following human tendencies: to be active, to gain knowledge, and to experience emotional attachment. The paths are not mutually exclusive; in practice, Hindus often follow more than one. All three are revered as effective means of moving closer to the ultimate goal of liberation.

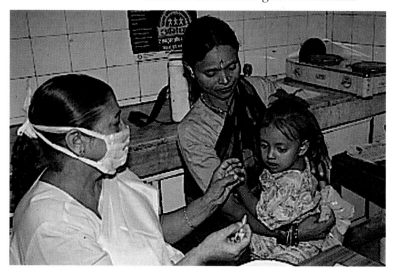

For the Active: The Path of Works

For the majority of people, those engaged in the day-to-day tasks of earning a living and raising a family, those for whom physical activities come most naturally, the favored means of seeking liberation is the **Path of Works.** Simple to understand and to practice, this path has everything to do with living in accordance with *dharma*.

As we have seen, *dharma* in its most general meaning is ethical duty, and includes observance of many traditional aspects of Hinduism: household rituals, public ceremonies, and social requirements, such as conforming to dietary laws and marriage restrictions. *Dharma* also involves an ongoing concern for the world, as exemplified in the most influential modern advocate of the Path of Works, Mahatma Gandhi. For Gandhi, re-

ligion itself is none other than concern for the world expressed through social service:

I am being led to my religion through Truth and Non-violence, i.e., love in the broadest sense. I often describe my religion as religion of Truth. Of late, instead of saying God is Truth I have been saying Truth is God, in order more fully to define my religion. . . .

The bearing of this religion on social life is, or has to be, seen in one's daily social contact. To be true to such religion one has to lose oneself in continuous and continuing service of all life. Realization of Truth is impossible without a complete merging of oneself in and identification with this limitless ocean of life. Hence, for me, there is no escape from social service; there is no happiness on earth beyond or apart from it. (*Moral and Political Writings of Mahatma Gandhi,* volume 1, page 461)

In all its aspects, the Path of Works is marked by an attitude of unselfishness. When doing the actions, one must avoid selfishly claiming credit for having accomplished something. This is challenging, for humans tend to be inclined toward selfishness. As Krishna remarks in the Bhagavad-Gita, "Deluded by individuality, the self thinks, 'I am the actor'" (3:27). If every accomplishment requires a pat on the back, the bondage of individuality is strengthened, and the self is further removed from the universal ocean of Atman, its true source and essence. The Path of Works succeeds when one does the opposite, performing the right action without needing to claim the credit.

In a similar way, selfish attachment to the results of action must be avoided. Krishna instructs Arjuna:

Be intent on action,
not on the fruits of action;
avoid attraction to the fruits
and attachment to inaction!

(Bhagavad-Gita 2:47)

Do the right thing only because it is right. Be a good student, not because it will earn a good grade, but because being a good student is right in itself. Mahatma Gandhi was a doer of great deeds, but he did not act in order to be rewarded by the fruits of his labors, whether in the form of praise by others or even a sense of self-satisfaction. He simply did what he perceived to be the right thing to do.

For the Philosophical: The Path of Knowledge

The shortest but steepest ascent to liberation follows the **Path of Knowledge.** This path is intended for those with talent for philosophical reflection. It requires the follower to devote a great deal of time to learning and meditation. These demands render the path of knowledge most practical for members of the *brahmin* caste.

Whereas the Path of Works emphasizes the doing of right actions over wrong ones, the Path of Knowledge emphasizes the attainment of knowledge over ignorance—knowledge of the true nature of reality. But this is an enormous challenge, for this is knowledge of a very special sort, amounting to profound insight that is far beyond merely knowing about the subject matter. To attain this knowledge is to live it, to be that which is known, to experience the true nature of reality. With this experience, reached through profound contemplation of the innermost self, comes a full awareness of truth, a certitude that has the power to transform the knower, thus leading to liberation.

Various Approaches of the Schools

Different teachings within the Path of Knowledge offer varying specifics regarding the true nature of reality. The most important are those of three schools of Hindu philosophy: Vedanta, Yoga, and Sankhya. In the midst of their diversity, the three approaches are in harmony regarding the same basic task: the attainment of knowledge over the ignorance that binds the self to *samsara.*

Vedanta. The school of **Vedanta** is most faithful to the predominant monism of Hinduism. Even within Vedanta, though, the characteristic diversity of the religion is apparent. We will focus our attention on the most prominent form of Vedanta, that espoused by the great medieval philosopher Shankara (788 to 820). The majority of Hindus who traverse the Path of Knowledge embrace this philosophy.

Shankara's understanding of reality amounts to the basic monism predominant in Hinduism: All reality is essentially one—Brahman, the indescribable, impersonal ultimate. The world and all finite beings within it are the stuff of *maya*, cosmic illusion. In a state of ignorance, people are tricked into thinking of their individual self as being ultimately real, just as the world of a dream seems real to the dreamer.

This persistent sense of individuality prevents one from experiencing the truth. As a droplet of ocean spray appears for a moment

8

"Do the right thing only because it is right." Must right actions be rewarded, or should they be their own reward?

9

What do you think might be some differences between the knowledge sought by a Hindu on the Path of Knowledge and the knowledge sought by a student working on a college degree?

M.C. Escher's lithograph, *Waterfall*, demonstrates the Hindu concept of *maya*, or cosmic illusion. For the person viewing Escher's work, as for the individual trapped in *maya*, the world is not as it seems.

to have an existence separate from the ocean, so do individuals imagine themselves to exist independently of Brahman. But in an instant the droplet is absorbed back into the ocean, indistinguishable from its infinite source. So too it is the destiny of the individual eventually to be absorbed back into the infinite source. For despite the illusion of separateness, in truth all are one. The atman, the self that is deep within, is really the eternal Atman, the infinite self. And Atman is Brahman.

When this truth is experienced, the Path of Knowledge has been followed to its end: liberation of the self from *samsara* into the ocean of Brahman. But as the Upanishads warn, it is an arduous path, demanding that a unique kind of knowledge be applied to a difficult lesson:

Subtler than the subtlest is this Self, and beyond all logic. Taught by a teacher who knows the Self and Brahman as one, a man leaves vain theory behind and attains to truth. (Upanishads, page 17)

Yoga. Emphasizing physical and psychological practices, **Yoga** understands well the connection between the self and the other parts of our human makeup—the body and its sensations, the mind and its thinking, and the subconscious. The objective of the yogi, or practitioner of Yoga, is to free the eternal self from bondage by stripping away the many levels of personhood in which it is wrapped.

The most famous version of this teaching sets forth eight steps:

1. Moral preparation through abstaining from five acts: harming living things, lying, stealing, acting unchastely, and being greedy
2. Moral preparation through observing five virtues: cleanliness, calmness, self-control, studiousness, and prayerfulness
3. Sitting in a posture that promotes comfort while discouraging drowsiness. Eighty-four postures are described; the most popular is the lotus position, with feet crossed and resting on the thighs, hands crossed in the lap, and eyes focused on the tip of the nose.
4. Breathing properly so that the entire body is brought into a simple rhythmic pattern
5. "Closing the doors of perception": withdrawing the senses from any contact with objects
6. Concentrating on one thing so that the mind empties itself of all other thoughts
7. Meditating, an ever deepening state of concentration moving toward the final step
8. Going into **samadhi**, a trance-like state in which self-consciousness is lost, and the mind is absorbed into the ultimate reality

In *samadhi* the knower becomes that which is known; the Path of Knowledge has been traversed to its goal. Although in practice the yogi normally comes back out of the trance, its transforming power leads to final liberation.

Sankhya. Contrary to Hinduism's predominant monism, **Sankhya** asserts that reality is composed of two distinct categories: matter, and an infinite number of eternal selves. Somehow, for reasons beyond explanation, selves get entwined with matter, thereby becoming bound to the world of *samsara*. Such is the origin and the predicament of human beings. As in the practice of Yoga, the task of the follower of the Sankhya approach is to free the eternal self from the bondage of the personality. The basic teachings of the Sankhya school are important for Jainism and Buddhism, and thus will be considered in more detail in those chapters.

For the Emotional: The Path of Devotion

Based in loving reverence for one's chosen god or goddess, the **Path of Devotion** is most suitable for those to whom emotional attachment comes naturally. In contrast to the inward journey of the Path of Knowledge, this path directs spiritual energy outward, in worship of the deity. Such worship is beneficial because the gods and goddesses look with favor upon their devotees, and answer their prayers. Most important, the Path of Devotion moves its adherents closer to salvation. Worship requires a focusing of attention on the divine, and away from the finite self. Through worship, the Path of Devotion helps to reduce the individuality that binds the self to *samsara*.

Gods and Goddesses

The issue of Hinduism's vast number of gods and goddesses, together with its predominant monism, were addressed earlier in this chapter. However, more remains to be said about the deities themselves. Some have been a part of Hinduism from the beginning, while others are being newly acknowledged.

The vast variety of gods and goddesses points to an important fact about the Path of

For Hindu ascetics, knowledge and devotion are the paths to salvation most likely to be followed.

The Quest for Truth

Shubhabrata Dutta, known as Shuvo to his friends, is a young Hindu man studying at a U.S. university. He offers the following thoughts on the role of Hinduism in his life:

As far as I can remember, the first time I really thought about Hinduism was in sixth grade, through some sayings of Shri Ramakrishna. Before that, although I attended all the religious festivals (there are lots of them!), I never really questioned or understood my faith. The saying of Ramakrishna that left a deep impression on me was, "If you put zeroes after a one, it makes a great number, but if you erase the one, the zeroes by themselves are not of any worth. Likewise, if we remove God from the creation, the creation, by itself, does not make any sense."

I was struck by the depth and the intelligence of the analogy. I thought that only a great scholar could have come up with this kind of simple but deep uttering. So I asked my father, himself a devotee of Shri Ramakrishna, about the scholarly career of Shri Ramakrishna, and found out to my surprise that Ramakrishna could not even sign his name properly. That was a real shock! But much later I came to realize that the unscholarly way of Shri Ramakrishna may very well answer the questions philosophers have been asking for the last three thousand years. In light of Ramakrishna's life, I understood Hinduism with all its complications; I realized that it is not that complex after all if we can just "live the life." And above all, being a "true" Hindu is no different than being a "true" Muslim or a "true" Christian. Religions are not God but many "ways" to God. One who quarrels about the ways but forgets about the destination is nothing but a fool.

Being a Hindu is very simple, actually, at least from my point of view. Being a Hindu is no more than being an *honest* human being. I have written the word *honest* in italics to show that it is *the* most important thing in being a Hindu. There are no universally held dogmas (except perhaps the prohibition against eating beef), no unanimous theological or philosophical doctrines, and no single ethical practice. From both inside and outside, Hinduism looks like a total mess, an enormous forest of ideas and practices of very dissimilar (and sometimes totally opposite) nature. What then can I believe? What path shall I choose? What is the right way? A Hindu will say, "Through self-examination you will find the answers. All you need is a burning desire to know the truth, and the rest will follow automatically." I believe in this, and to my great joy, the greatest spiritual personalities of India also believed in it and showed it in their lives.

As a Hindu, I grew up with certain concepts that may seem funny to other people. One of them was the omnipresence of Life. I was taught the saying from the Upanishads, *"Sarvam khalidam Brahman,"* "Everything is permeated by Brahman," and also that all the deities are associated with particular things. So I pick up a penny from the street and touch it to my forehead because money represents the goddess Lakshmi, or I scrupulously avoid touching any paper with my feet because I fear that Saraswati, the goddess of learning, might get angry with me. Such practices are necessary sometimes and unnecessary at other times. Why? Because, as Swami Vivekananda said, "A man does not proceed from falsehood to truth, but he moves from lower truth to higher truth." As a Hindu I believe that a certain ritual or a particular belief is necessary until I reach a point where it no longer helps me toward my *moksha,* my liberation. *Moksha* is beyond both evil and good. Anything that helps me to attain my *moksha* is *relatively* good, anything that turns me away from it is *relatively* bad. In the famous words of Shri Ramakrishna, "First you pluck out the thorn of ignorance using the thorn of Knowledge. But then you throw both of them away." What remains then? Indescribable bliss.

As a Hindu, I have the rarest fortune to hear the perennial song of hope from the Upanishads: "Listen, O children of Immortal bliss, I have known Him who is as bright as sun and lives beyond the ocean of Death. He who knows Him becomes immortal." I cannot imagine why Hindus have been accused of negativism or pessimism. If I really know that there is a world infinitely greater, infinitely truer, and infinitely more blissful than this one, why shouldn't I hurry to go to that world? Certainly we cannot blame the student who gives up watching *Star Trek* in order to study enough to get an A on an exam.

As a matter of fact, Hindus have taken Jesus' advice literally: "'Strive first for the kingdom of God and his righteousness, and all these things will be given to you as well'" (Matthew 6:33). Social structure, economic progress, and advancement of art and entertainment are all good, but then this question always comes up: "For what? What is this all for?" And for me there is only one answer: It is for God, for the ultimate good of humanity.

To me, being a Hindu means to be on a quest for Truth. "Religion is realization," Swami Vivekananda so succinctly put it. Religion is not so much about *knowing;* it is about *being.* I can read many books but still be spiritually blind; another may become illumined without reading a single book.

I have been associated with Ramakrishna Mission for over twelve years, and in those years I have been blessed to meet some very saintly people. I have seen, in their lives, that being religious does not make a person morose or pessimistic. Rather it makes one blissful. One such man, while walking with me along the Ganges on a beautiful summer evening, told me, "Shuvo, it is like walking toward Light; each step brings newer hope, newer bliss, it is so light that I feel I can fly, that I can take out my heart and throw it into the sky and it will burst into a thousand pieces and then I will become free, forever."

Devotion: a typical Hindu is devoted to more than one deity, depending on the specific needs of the day. Still, it is common to choose a personal deity as the object of special devotion. We will single out for consideration some of Hinduism's most popular deities: Vishnu, Shiva, Kali, and the *avatars* Krishna and Rama.

Among the 330 million gods is an important triad: Brahma, the Creator; Vishnu, the Preserver; and Shiva, the Destroyer. Brahma, though still highly thought of, is rarely worshiped anymore. Today, as for centuries, Vishnu and Shiva are worshiped by millions. As his role as the Preserver would suggest, Vishnu, with his four arms and his various symbols of power and goodness, is regarded by his devotees as their supreme protector and example of moral perfection. It is notable that Shiva, a god known for destruction, should be so popular. In fact, this fits logically within the Hindu cyclical cosmology, for the destruction brought about by Shiva makes way for new creation.

The cycle of destruction and creation is similarly a primary theme of the popular goddess Kali, herself a wife of Shiva. Black in color and wearing a necklace of skulls, she is a bloodthirsty goddess who is a violent destroyer of her enemies. Toward her devotees, though, she shows steadfast care and affection, providing for their needs. The great Ramakrishna was one of her millions of devotees.

Avatars

An **avatar** is an incarnation, or living embodiment, of a deity, generally of Vishnu, who is sent to earth to accomplish a divine purpose. The relationship of the *avatar* to the deity from which he comes is illuminated in the Bhagavad-Gita. Here Krishna, an *avatar* of Vishnu, actually speaks as Vishnu when he addresses Arjuna:

Though myself unborn, undying,
the lord of creatures, I fashion nature,
which is mine, and I come into being
through my own magic.

Whenever sacred duty decays
and chaos prevails,
then, I create
myself, Arjuna.

To protect men of virtue
and destroy men who do evil,
to set the standard of sacred duty,
I appear in age after age.

(4:6–8)

Krishna has a prominent role in the epic poem the *Mahabharata* (mah-hah-bah'rah-tah) of which the Bhagavad-Gita is but a small section, but also is very popular in another role. Krishna is the somewhat mischievous and always amorous cowherd, often accompanied by adoring bands of female cowherds. Beautifully depicted in Hindu art, these scenes symbolize the loving adoration of souls (the cowherds) for God (Krishna). Krishna is also frequently depicted with his favorite consort, Radha. The intensity of their feelings is clearly expressed, and they function as a symbol of perfect love.

Rama is another popular *avatar.* He is the hero of the *Ramayana,* an epic poem from ancient times that continues to have enormous influence among Hindus. Like Krishna, Rama is an incarnation of Vishnu. Through the centuries, he has come to be so highly regarded that many Hindus revere him as the supreme deity.

The Bhagavad-Gita

As we have seen, the Bhagavad-Gita contains ideas that are relevant to many aspects of Hinduism. Still, it is most closely associated with the Path of Devotion. The content of the Bhagavad-Gita acknowledges the fruitfulness of both the Path of Works and the Path of Knowledge, but tends to favor the Path of Devotion. This central passage, in which Krishna again addresses Arjuna, is especially revealing as to the universal appeal of this path to salvation:

Whatever you do—what you take,
what you offer, what you give,
what penances you perform—
do as an offering to me, Arjuna!

You will be freed from the bonds of action,
from the fruit of fortune and misfortune;
armed with the discipline of renunciation,
your self liberated, you will join me.

I am impartial to all creatures,
and no one is hateful or dear to me;
but men devoted to me are in me,
and I am within them.

(9:27–29)

Aspects of Daily Devotion

If we were to ask a follower of the Path of Devotion to describe Hinduism, we would most likely learn first and foremost of the various acts of worship practiced from day to day. Along with a host of individual practices, such as prayer and visits to temples and shrines, Hindu worship includes numerous household and community rituals, pilgrimages to holy places, and veneration of the ever present and much adored sacred cows.

Household and village rituals. Typically, Hindu households maintain shrines to chosen deities, containing some form of image or symbol. Along with the tending of a sacred fire and ritual bathing, domestic worship includes daily devotional rites before the shrine. Though the use of clay figurines and other material representations of deities may appear to be a form of idolatry, or idol worship, in fact it is not. For the image itself is not worshiped, but rather the god or goddess it is representing. In this manner the households of India are homes to millions of "masks" of deities.

On regular occasions the village joins together in worship. Often this occurs at the local temple, where ceremonies are conducted by a priest. Villages also celebrate annual festivals in honor of certain gods; sometimes these can last for days. For example, a festival in honor of Saraswati, the goddess of wisdom and patroness of education and the arts (and hence a popular goddess at schools), can involve days of celebration before a life-size image that has been specially crafted for the festival. On the final day, the image is given a funeral and disposed of—amid the

The cow represents life for Hindus. Mahatma Gandhi said that the cow is "the mother to millions of Indian mankind. Protection of the cow means protection of the whole dumb creation of God."

cheers of smiling devotees! The cycle of creation and destruction applies to the worship of the deities as well.

Holy places. Pilgrimages to holy sites, some very long and arduous, are another common form of devotion. Sometimes the destination is a temple or other site of a great festival. It can also be a natural entity, such as a river. Most rivers are regarded as sacred. The most famous river of them all—and the one deemed most sacred—is the Ganges. Thought to fall from its heavenly source of Vishnu's feet onto Shiva's head and out from his hair, the water of the Ganges is sacred enough to purify all sins. Pilgrims seek its banks to partake in ritual baths, and the ashes of the dead are swallowed by its life-giving water.

Cow veneration. Mahatma Gandhi referred to the protection of cows as the "central fact of Hinduism," and "one of the most wonderful phenomena in human evolution." For him, and for millions of fellow Hindus, the cow represents life. It provides for Hindus in a multitude of ways and yet suffers along with them. Therefore Hindus venerate cows, worshiping them like deities, and on regular occasions decorating them with garlands and anointing their heads with oil. In the past, the killing of a cow was sometimes a capital offense.

Gandhi's words on the encompassing significance of cow veneration provide a fitting conclusion to this section:

The cow to me means the entire sub-human world. Man through the cow is enjoined to realise his identity with all that lives. . . . The cow is a poem of pity. One reads pity in the gentle animal. She is the mother to millions of Indian mankind. Protection of the cow means protection of the whole dumb creation of God. (Gandhi, *Young India,* page 804)

10
Discuss the differences between your own experience of worship and the worship of a Hindu on the Path of Devotion.

Hinduism in the Modern World

All traditional religions face challenges posed by the modern world. Scientific and secular views can erode the authority of perspectives based in ancient myths. The plurality of other religious traditions constantly becomes more familiar, offering new alternatives. And new movements, some in response to these very threats, arise within a tradition, thus challenging the old ways.

In the case of Hinduism, the modern world seems to pose an especially acute challenge. India, home to a vast majority of the world's Hindus, is also the world's largest democracy, and sets itself apart from religion, as a secular state. For its many citizens who tend to equate Hinduism with India, and for whom the ancient religious principles of *dharma* provide basic patterns of existence, the interplay of the secular state with traditional religion is frequently unsettled and contentious.

In this section we will consider several of the issues and figures of modern Hinduism, in an attempt to make sense of the contemporary situation.

Those Whom Hindus Revere: Religious Leaders

India is alive with significant religious figures, holy people in various roles who tend to provide continual spiritual nourishment for a tradition in the grip of change. *Brahmins* tending to ancient rituals; gurus, or enlightened teachers, teaching the truths of the Upanishads to the young; *sannyasins* bearing the serenity of spiritual transcendence even as they walk amid their fellow villagers: all give nourishment to Hinduism, connecting it with its illustrious past and directing it toward its future.

The role of women is continually changing in Indian society.
Above: Gandhi stands among workers in England.
Right: Women in modern Bombay

Mahatma Gandhi

The one figure who has loomed larger than any other holy person of recent times, and in most every way a symbol of Hinduism as the past meets the future, is Mohandas K. Gandhi (1869–1948), reverently called Mahatma, meaning "great souled." His steadfast efforts to stand up to oppression through nonviolence and civil disobedience forever changed the nature of India, and of Hinduism. And yet his assassination by a Hindu extremist in 1948, just months after his long goal of Indian independence from British rule had been accomplished, is darkly symbolic of the modern challenges that Hinduism faces, now as much as then.

Although for most Indians today the lifetime of Gandhi is part of the distant past, as a religious figure he lives on. His insights continue to fuel Hinduism's tendency to accept all wisdom as lighting the way to the divine. In villages all across India, statues of Gandhi, under the protective guard of Vishnu's multiheaded cobra, remind Hindus of his revered presence.

The Sacred Amid the Secular: Contemporary Issues

A seemingly countless number of pressing issues are emerging as traditional Hinduism and secular India continue their journey together into the twenty-first century. We shall consider three of them.

The Caste System

The complex social distinctions based on the caste system, especially those of the outcastes, have come under careful scrutiny during the twentieth century. Significant changes have occurred, some quite recently.

In a major development, one for which Gandhi struggled for years, the Indian government in 1948 ruled that discrimination against outcastes was officially forbidden. Governmental programs since that time, similar to affirmative action programs in the United States, have sought to further promote the economic and social rights of these people. Among some upper-caste Indians, such programs are meeting harsh resistance. In general, attitudes based in something so deeply traditional as the caste system tend to change slowly. Such is the case as India struggles with this issue.

Women in Hindu Society

Traditional Hindu society has always been strongly patriarchal—under the domination of men. Typically, women's *dharma* has required them to be obedient to men. But, as is the case with Hinduism in general, opinions on the topic of women's roles in Hinduism differ. Depending on the locale, especially on whether it is a city or a village, the degree to which Hindus follow such traditional teachings varies considerably. For many urban Indians, the norms are clearly changing.

One of the most striking examples of the controversial treatment of women in Hinduism—and of the vast changes that have occurred in some cases—is the practice of **sati**, the burning of a widowed wife. The following passage from a Hindu text called the Padmapurana sets forth some of the traditional teachings, both on *sati* and on the general obedience expected of a wife:

A wife must eat only after her husband has had his fill. If the latter fasts, she shall fast, too; if he touch not food, she also shall not touch it; if he be in affliction, she shall be so, too; if he be cheerful, she shall share his joy. She must on the death of her husband allow herself to be burnt alive on the same funeral pyre; then everybody will praise her virtue. (Quoted in Noss, *A History of the World's Religions,* page 118)

Although the authority of such texts has been questioned throughout the history of Hinduism, *sati* became a common practice in Hindu life. Since 1829 *sati* has been officially forbidden. Occasionally it still occurs, though this is very rare. In some ways traditional

The secular state of India and the traditional religion of Hinduism tend to disagree over some important issues. How does religion relate to the secular state in your country?

Hinduism has been able to conform to modern norms. However, other aspects of the traditional place of women are changing much more slowly.

Hindus and Muslims

Islam and Hinduism have experienced a long history of contact, beginning in the eighth century. The contact has not always been peaceful. This is not surprising when one considers that these two religions are vastly different from each other. Still, for centuries, Hindus and Muslims (adherents of Islam) have lived side by side in South Asia. For the most part, they have influenced each other's religious traditions very little (the substantive Muslim influence on the artistic and scientific life of India is a different matter).

In recent decades, relations between Hindus and Muslims have remained uneasy, at times erupting into violence. Due to pressure from within the Muslim community, in 1947 India was partitioned to form the divided nation of Pakistan (the eastern part of which is now Bangladesh), thus providing a Muslim homeland. This turned into a bloody ordeal in which many followers of both religions were killed. The assassination of Gandhi occurred in its aftermath. More recently another bloody outbreak of violence erupted in the ancient city of Arodhya, where a Muslim mosque stood on the site traditionally regarded as the birthplace of the *avatar* Rama. In 1992, after months of tense standoffs, some three hundred thousand Hindus stormed the mosque and tore it to the ground. The challenges faced by the relations between Hindus and Muslims obviously continue to be of great concern for India.

Hinduism has had a significant influence around the world.
Right and far right: Hare Krishna devotees participate in ritual and celebration.

Hinduism Outside of South Asia

The vast majority of Hindus still live in India and Nepal (in both nations the Hindu population exceeds 80 percent), but during the modern period enough people have left India to give rise to significant Hindu populations throughout the world, especially in cities.

Hinduism has also moved outside of South Asia in the form of sects and philosophical societies that, though based on the teachings of Hinduism, have often been adopted and advocated by non-Indians. Beginning in the 1960s, such movements as the International Society for Krishna Consciousness (the Hare Krishna movement) and the transcendental meditation movement became very popular in the West, especially among young people.

Swami Vivekananda and the Parliament of Religions

A follower of Shri Ramakrishna, Swami Vivekananda (1863 to 1902) took up his master's teaching on the unity of religions and established the Ramakrishna Mission, which is a significant organization within Hinduism today. Vivekananda also became the first Hindu missionary, and he achieved fame in 1893 by explaining the teachings of Hindu Vedanta to the Parliament of Religions in Chicago. He went on to found Vedanta societies in New York, San Francisco, and many other cities. Owing largely to Ramakrishna and Vivekananda, Hinduism is alive and flourishing in the Western world today.

The Ever Changing Currents of Hinduism

The many rivers of Hindu belief and practice are more numerous today than ever. Along with the diversity that has always come so naturally, the modern world presents a vast new set of challenges, alternatives, and opportunities.

Hinduism is in the midst of a great coming together of old and new. In many villages of India, the traditional ways have changed little. The temples are still in place; the festivals occur as they always have; and *brahmins* perform ancient rituals. In the high-rise offices and apartment buildings of the cities, on the other hand, the typical features of modernity, including televisions, are present. And on television on most any Sunday morning, viewers can watch the ancient story of the *Ramayana* unfolding amid this modern world.

And so these many rivers—ancient and modern, rural and urban—continue to flow toward the distant ocean of salvation, finally merging the millions of Hindus in the harmony that unites their religion.

Glossary

artha. Material success and social prestige, one of the four goals of life.

ascetic. One who renounces physical pleasures and worldly attachments for the sake of spiritual advancement; common in Hinduism and many other religious traditions, most notably Jainism.

Atman (aht'muhn). The eternal self, which the Upanishads identify with Brahman; also used (often in lowercase) to signify the eternal soul of an individual that is reincarnated from one body to the next and is ultimately identified with Atman.

avatar. An incarnation, or living embodiment, of a deity, generally of Vishnu, who is sent to earth to accomplish a divine purpose; Krishna and Rama are the most popular *avatars*.

Bhagavad-Gita (buh'guh-vuhd gee'tah; Sanskrit: "The Song of the Blessed Lord"). A short section of the epic poem *Mahabharata* in which the god Krishna teaches the great warrior Arjuna about the Path of Devotion *(bhakti marga)* and other ways to God; Hinduism's most popular sacred text.

Brahman (brah'munh). The eternal essence of reality and the source of the universe, beyond the reach of human perception and thought.

brahmin (brah'min). The highest of the four castes, made up of priests.

castes. Traditional social categories dividing Hindu society into four main classes: *brahmin, kshatriya, vaishya,* and *shudra;* each class contains numerous subcastes, resulting in more than three thousand categories.

dharma (dahr'muh). Ethical duty based on the divine order of reality; one of the four goals of life.

kama (kah'muh). Pleasure, especially of sensual love; one of the four goals of life.

karma (Sanskrit: "action"). The moral law of cause and effect of actions; determines the nature of one's reincarnation.

kshatriya (kshuht'ree-yuh). The second of the four castes, made up of warriors and administrators.

maya (mah'yah). Cosmic illusion brought about by divine creative power.

moksha (mohk'shuh). Liberation or release of the individual self, atman, from the bondage of *samsara;* salvation; one of the four goals of life.

monism. The doctrine that reality is ultimately made up of only one substance and that all things share a common essence.

Path of Devotion (Sanskrit: *bhakti marga* [buhk'tee marguh] or *bhakti yoga*). The most popular of the three Hindu paths to salvation, emphasizes loving devotion to one's chosen god or goddess.

Path of Knowledge (Sanskrit: *jnana marga* [nyah'nah] or *jnana yoga*). One of three Hindu paths to salvation, emphasizes knowing the true nature of reality through learning and meditation.

Path of Works (Sanskrit: *karma marga* or *karma yoga*). One of three Hindu paths to salvation, emphasizes doing right actions according to *dharma*.

Rig Veda (rig vay'duh). A collection of 1,017 Sanskrit hymns composed about 1500 B.C.E. or earlier; Hinduism's oldest sacred text.

samadhi (suh-mah'dee). A trance-like state in which self-consciousness is lost, and the mind is absorbed into the ultimate reality; the culmination of the eight steps of Yoga.

samsara (samh-sah'ruh). The wheel of rebirth or reincarnation; the this-worldly realm in which rebirth occurs.

Sankhya (sahng'kyuh). A system of Hindu philosophy and one approach within the Path of Knowledge, which asserts that reality is composed of two distinct categories: matter and eternal selves.

sannyasin (sun-yah'sin). A wandering ascetic who has advanced to the fourth and highest stage of life.

sati (suh'tee). The traditional practice of burning a widowed wife on her husband's funeral pyre; outlawed in 1829, though still occurs rarely.

shudra (shood'ruh). The lowest of the four castes, made up of servants and laborers.

Upanishads (oo-pah'ni-shuhdz; Sanskrit: "sitting near a teacher"). A collection of over two hundred texts composed between 900 and 200 B.C.E. that provide philosophical commentary on the Vedas.

vaishya (vish'yuh). The third of the four castes, made up of producers, such as farmers, merchants, and artisans.

Vedanta (vay-dahn'tuh). A system of Hindu philosophy and one approach within the Path of Knowledge, which holds that all reality is essentially Brahman; most notable advocate is the medieval Hindu philosopher Shankara.

Yoga. A system of Hindu philosophy and one approach within the Path of Knowledge, which seeks to free the eternal self from the bondage of personhood, culminating in the experience of *samadhi.* When the word *yoga* is lowercased, it refers generally to physical and psychological techniques for spiritual advancement.

PAKISTAN

NEPAL

Lumbini

Ganges

Varanasi
(Benares)

Gaya

I N D I A

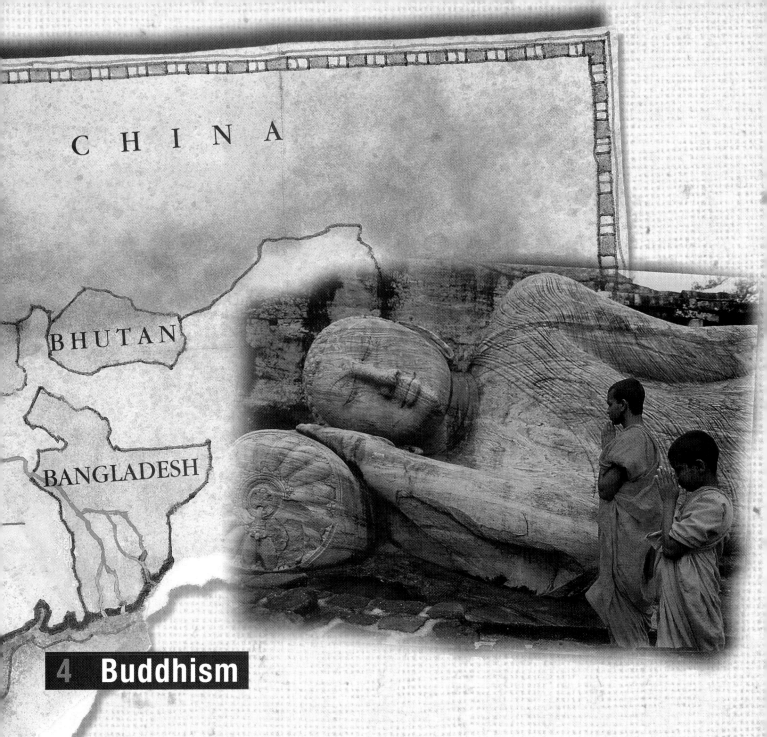

4 Buddhism

A Therapy for Living from One Who "Woke Up"

Buddhism, like Hinduism, arose in ancient India. But in stark contrast to Hinduism, with its streams of traditions converging from various sources of India's past, Buddhism began with one man. He was merely a man—not a god or other super-natural being—but he was an exceptional man who underwent an extra-ordinary experience. Briefly put he "woke up" (and hence the name **Buddha,** which is derived from *budh,* "to awaken"). He awoke to full awareness of the nature of the human condition, and to the means of transcending it. The religion of Buddhism teaches the discoveries attained by this man, Gautama, through this experience of awakening.

Fundamental to Gautama's discoveries is that human beings are by nature prone to suffer. In other words we are in a state of dis-ease, and we need treatment. In a manner very much like that of a physician, proceeding rationally and empirically, Gautama diagnosed the human condition and prescribed a cure. One way of understanding Buddhism, then, is as a therapy for living.

Having begun with just one man, Buddhism gradually developed into a religious tradition that includes varying interpretations of the Buddha's teachings. We will explore the major divisions within Buddhism at the end of this chapter. First, let us examine the foundations—Gautama the Buddha and his teachings—which are of central significance for all forms of Buddhism.

The Life of Gautama

As with most founders of great religious traditions, the life of Gautama is known more through legend than through verifiable fact. Any attempt to produce an accurate life history of Gautama is doomed to some degree of failure. Full accounts of the Buddha's life were not written down until hundreds of years after his death, by which time legendary elements had long been established. Nevertheless, the story of Gautama is meaningful and instructive, reflecting in vivid form the issues and ideals that lie at the heart of Buddhism.

From Pampered Prince to Starving Ascetic

Born in about 563 B.C.E., the future Buddha was given the name Siddhartha. His family's name was Gautama, and so his full name is Siddhartha Gautama (though he is most commonly referred to simply as Gautama). His family belonged to the warrior caste, and his father was the ruler of a small region in northern India.

Gautama was thus born into a position of worldly power. According to traditional Buddhist belief, he was destined to become either a universal king (that is, a ruler over all peoples) or a Buddha, an awakened one who would offer the world salvation. The accounts of his birth are filled with miraculous events befitting the arrival of such a great one. Said to have come out of his mother's side, Gautama at once strode seven paces and declared that in this lifetime he would gain enlightenment. A sage, upon seeing the boy's perfect form, affirmed that this child would indeed gain enlightenment and become a savior.

Gautama's father would have had it otherwise, preferring that Gautama instead become a universal king. He pampered the young prince with all the comforts of the palace. Gautama grew up in luxury, safe from the sufferings of the outside world.

He was surrounded by thousands of beautiful dancing girls, and servants who provided for his needs. Eventually he married the finest maiden of the kingdom, and they had a son. It would seem that Prince Siddhartha was living a life of complete satisfaction.

The Four Passing Sights

Soon Gautama was to discover that such satisfaction would not endure forever. In spite of his father's attempts to shield him from the harsh realities of the world, Gautama encountered them firsthand in the famous episode known as the Four Passing Sights. While on a pleasure excursion in the countryside, his chariot passed by a decrepit old man. Never before having seen old age, Gautama brooded over the implications of this sight—that such a fate was in store for everyone, himself included. On a second ride, the prince saw a diseased man, and again was dismayed and deeply disturbed. How could people enjoy life when disease threatened them all? On a third trip, Gautama saw a corpse for the first time. He was now more devastated than before, for with this sight he learned of death. Was it not senseless for people to go on living as if oblivious to the certainty of death?

These first three sights were penetrating lessons about the reality of suffering and the impermanent nature of life's pleasures. Having seen them, Gautama knew that he would never again find contentment in the luxuries of the palace. Nor could he again feel safe, now that he had learned the truths of old age, disease, and death. He mounted his horse and rode out from the palace, grieving as he observed the toil of peasants plowing the fields, and the destruction of living things uprooted by the plows. Eventually Gautama saw a religious mendicant, one who had chosen to lead a homeless life of solitude. The man explained that he was in search of salvation from this world of suffering, and then he continued on his way.

The mendicant, the fourth of the passing sights, filled Gautama with elation and hope: here was a means of overcoming his despair. Soon he would leave the palace once and for all, to embark on the homeless life.

The Great Going Forth

At the age of twenty-nine, Gautama gave up his life as prince, secretly leaving his family and palace by horseback in the dark of night. Gautama removed his jewels and dismissed his servant, sending him back with a message for the king: Gautama did not leave out of resentment or lack of affection. Rather, his purpose was to put an end to old age and death. Gautama renounced a life of power and sensual enjoyment for the austere rigors of a religious mendicant's life. This event in Gautama's life is known as the Great Going Forth, and is revered by Buddhists as the triumph of the spiritual over the worldly life.

1
How are the facts of old age, disease, and death given meaning within your religious tradition or within the religious tradition with which you are most familiar?

Left: This image of the Buddha in meditation was created during the medieval period in India. *Above:* Schoolchildren visit a statue of the Buddha in Sri Lanka.

A Chinese painting depicts Mara's assault on Gautama as he sat beneath the fig tree seeking enlightenment.

2

Imagine yourself in Gautama's place, a pampered prince or princess with all of life's worldly joys available at your beck and call. What would it take for you to leave it all, as Gautama did?

3

How might the doctrine of the Middle Way be of relevance for your life? Reflect on the ways you follow (or do not follow) the Middle Way.

Gautama came upon other mendicants who taught him their versions of meditation. Quickly he learned their methods, but he was not satisfied with their results. Salvation, he believed, lay beyond the meditative accomplishments of these teachings. Soon he joined a group of five mendicants who practiced asceticism (rigorous self-denial) in order to win salvation. Gautama excelled in the practice of fasting, spending the next several years on the brink of starvation. The tradition tells of meals consisting of one piece of fruit, one sesame seed, one grain of rice. In the belief that reduction of the body would increase his spiritual powers, Gautama was physically reduced to skin and bone.

The Middle Way

Starvation did not lead to salvation. And so, six years after leaving the palace, in another famous episode, Gautama accepted a simple meal of rice and milk. He quickly regained his strength, and was thereby enabled to proceed on his quest for salvation. His five companions left him, disgusted that he had abandoned asceticism.

Gautama thus discovered the central Buddhist doctrine of the **Middle Way.** Having earlier rejected a lifestyle of sensual indulgence in the palace, he now rejected the other extreme of asceticism. A healthy spiritual life depends on a healthy physical life. Though indulgence in bodily pleasure is rejected, the body itself is not. In general, the doctrine of the Middle Way embraces the idea that contentment is a good thing. Spiritual happi-

ness implies complete happiness—in body, in mind, and in spirit.

The Enlightened One

Now Gautama, contented and strong in body, was prepared to devote all his effort to attaining salvation. Sitting down in the lotus position beneath a fig tree, he resolved not to leave the spot until he had found complete and perfect fulfillment.

Traditional accounts of Gautama's enlightenment begin by depicting his encounters with the basic human shortcomings of fear and passionate desire. Mara, the god of death, noted Gautama's resolution, and was alarmed at the prospect that he might succeed. Attempting to defend his realm, Mara desperately tried to frighten Gautama from his spot. But Gautama could not be frightened away. Then Mara sent forth his three daughters—the goddesses Discontent, Delight, and Desire—hoping to move Gautama through an appeal to his passions. Again Gautama was unmoved, touching the earth to call it to be a witness to his resolve. Defeated, Mara and his hosts departed.

Enlightenment

Gautama had overcome the distractions of fear and passion, represented in the legend by Mara and his hosts. Now he turned his focus inward and entered a meditative trance. He ascended through levels of ever deepening awareness, until he could perceive with perfect clarity the true nature of the human condition.

During the portion of the night traditionally called the First Watch, from evening until midnight, Gautama perceived his own previous lifetimes. He observed his long passage from rebirth to death to another rebirth and so on, a continuous journey of suffering. During the Second Watch (from midnight until four in the morning) he acquired the "divine eye," the ability to perceive the deaths and rebirths of all living beings. Nowhere in this world was there any safety, nowhere an escape from death. During the Third Watch, Gautama discovered the Four Noble Truths, the perfect summation of the human condition and the means for transcending it. We will consider the Four Noble Truths in detail shortly.

By discovering the Four Noble Truths, Gautama had attained enlightenment, and thus had won salvation. Now Gautama had become the Buddha, the Awakened One.

Founding the *Sangha*

Gautama the Buddha remained for many days in his spot beneath the fig tree (referred to ever since as the *bodhi,* or "wisdom," tree). In a state of perfect tranquility and infinite wisdom, he was forever freed from the sufferings of the human condition. He was tempted to leave his body and pass once and for all into **nirvana,** the state of eternal bliss

4

Gautama discovered the truths of Buddhism solely by looking inward, through meditation. Take a few minutes to look inward, contemplate who you are. What truths regarding your own nature are you able to discover?

The *bodhi* tree, where Gautama attained enlightenment, continues to be revered by Buddhists.

Buddhist monks in Thailand in a procession near their monastery

5
As one of the Three Jewels, the Sangha obviously plays an important role in Buddhism. Describe a community (religious or otherwise) in which you participate. What is the role of community togetherness and organization? What is the relationship between community and learning?

6
"Work out your salvation with diligence." Based on what you now know of the Buddha's religious quest, elaborate on the meaning of these, his final words.

that is ultimate salvation. His depth of compassion, however, compelled him to remain in the world and to share his discoveries with his fellow humans. True, his doctrines would be quite difficult for others to understand. Yet if just one person could understand them and thereby gain salvation, it would be well worth his effort.

The Buddha wondered, to whom should he offer his teachings? His five former companions would perhaps understand them, he thought, and so he set off to find them. When the five first saw Gautama, they decided to ignore him, convinced he was no longer worthy of their company because he had abandoned asceticism. But his spiritual presence overcame their intentions. Soon they sat listening as the Buddha, perfectly calm and radiant in his wisdom, set forth the momentous First Sermon, preached at the famous Deer Park near the city of Benares. He taught the doctrines of the Middle Way and the Four Noble Truths. Gradually the five mendicants grasped his teachings and attained enlightenment, thereby becoming *arhats* (saints). Thus the Buddha had gained his first followers. Buddhism as a religious tradition was born.

For the remaining forty-five years of his life, the Buddha continued to teach, attracting an ever growing following. The Buddhist community, or **sangha,** was formed, consisting of men and women from all walks of life.

Gautama's son is said to have been among those earliest Buddhists. The *sangha* was carefully organized, with specific roles for monks, nuns, and laypeople. For the three months of the monsoon season, the entire *sangha* remained together in retreat. During the remaining nine months, the Buddha and his followers traveled about the land teaching.

To this day, being a Buddhist means to "take refuge" in the Three Jewels: the Buddha, the Dharma (the Buddha's teachings), and the Sangha. The act of taking refuge amounts to a formal acknowledgment of the authority of the Three Jewels.

Death and Final *Nirvana*

At the age of eighty, in about 483 B.C.E., the Buddha became seriously ill after eating a meal of spoiled food. Amid a gathering of monks and nuns, Gautama spoke his final words: "'All the constituents of being are transitory; work out your salvation with diligence'" (quoted in *Buddhism in Translations,* page 109). In this last message the Buddha affirmed the hope of salvation for subsequent Buddhists. The physician was leaving his patients, but his prescription was to remain available for all.

After ascending through the stages of meditation to a state of perfect tranquility, Gautama died, passing forever into *nirvana.*

The Dharma: Buddhist Teachings

The Buddha was an exceptional man who underwent an extraordinary experience. Most Buddhists revere Gautama and look to his life and enlightenment as the model for their own religious aspirations. But the Buddha's teachings, rather than the Buddha himself, play the predominant role in defining the religious life of Buddhism.

The teachings, or **Dharma** (not to be confused with the related Hindu doctrine of *dharma,* or "ethical duty"), are in some respects difficult to understand. They are born not of mental reflection but of insight gained through a profound meditative experience. Thus full understanding of Buddhist teachings requires an equal degree of insight gained directly through meditation. Gautama himself questioned whether anyone would comprehend his teachings, and all along he seems to have advocated Buddhism only for the few who considered themselves fit for the task.

But Buddhist teachings also have a simple aspect: they are the insights of a mere human being. Unlike many religions, Buddhism does not depend on a revelation from the divine for its truths. Buddhist truths were discovered through the inward reflections of a man, and are therefore potentially understandable for anyone. Rather than relying heavily on faith, Buddhism emphasizes the development of wisdom, or insight into the human condition. Buddhism is thus the most psychologically oriented of all the great religions.

Buddhism and Hinduism: The Indian Context

Buddhism arose in India during the period when the Upanishads were being written, so Buddhism naturally shares many ideas with Hinduism. But whereas Hindus have regarded Buddhism as being a close relative of their own religion (many Hindus even consider the Buddha to be an incarnation of the god Vishnu), the Buddha himself in many ways reacted against the Hinduism of his day.

A Shared Cosmology

Buddhism and Hinduism both regard time as cyclical. They maintain that the universe is eternal, with ages of creation and destruction following one after the other. Due to this eternal time scheme, both Buddhism and Hinduism are regarded as "eternal" religions. In cyclical fashion they have come to be and passed away over and over again, along with the rest of creation. For Buddhists, then, Gautama the Buddha is not the first or only Buddha. In fact, countless Buddhas preceded him, and countless Buddhas will follow him.

Amid this eternal cyclical time scheme, many worlds exist. Various heavens are inhabited by gods and goddesses, and hells are inhabited by demons. Between them are the middle realms, including those of animals and humans. This scheme of multiple worlds has much in common with the Hindu universe.

Basic to this cosmology for both traditions is the doctrine of **samsara,** the "wheel of rebirth," which holds that the inhabitants of all these realms are generally destined to continue being reborn in one realm or another. The ongoing cycle of rebirth can only be escaped through liberation from *samsara,* usually referred to as *moksha* in Hinduism and as *nirvana* in Buddhism. For both traditions, liberation is the final goal.

The Buddha's Reaction Against Early Hinduism

The Buddha was discontented with many of the religious features of his day, especially the speculative philosophy and the sacrificial rituals that were the domain of the *brahmin* caste. As the Upanishads illustrate, early Hinduism embraced philosophical speculation regarding the nature of the world, the human self, and the divine. The Buddha dismissed such speculation as being useless for the task of winning salvation. He insisted, instead, on direct inward observation of the human condition. Equally useless, he thought, were the sacrificial rituals designed to offer devotion to the gods. Although Buddhism accepts the existence of gods, it holds that salvation must be won through the efforts of the human mind.

7

"The essence of Buddhism is, there is no essence." Discuss the meaning of this saying.

8

As you observe the natural world, do you tend to perceive things as being permanent or impermanent? Could the things that you perceive as being permanent really be impermanent? Give some specific examples.

Gautama also rejected the institutional structure of Hinduism, in which the sacrificial rituals and sacred texts were controlled solely by males of the *brahmin* caste. The Buddha, himself born into the powerful warrior caste, explicitly rejected the Hindu caste system. And, though apparently with some reluctance, he allowed women to join the *sangha* and to become nuns.

Buddhism's tendency to accept all people is also apparent in that its earliest texts are written in **Pali,** a local dialect spoken by the common people. At this time the sacred texts of Hinduism were all written in Sanskrit, which only the *brahmins* were expected to know. The teachings of the Buddha, though difficult to understand, were made available to everyone.

Individuals and Their Destiny

Buddhist teachings focus on the predicament of individuals and their destiny. This focus contributes greatly to the simple aspect of the teachings, for it confines their subject matter to one thing, the individual. Everything the Buddha discovered is discoverable in oneself. The difficult aspect of the teachings lies mainly in this paradox: To examine completely the inner realm of self leads to the discovery that the self *does not exist*. Let us attempt to make some sense of this paradox.

Three Marks of Existence: No-Self, Impermanence, Suffering

The main discovery of the Hindu Upanishads is that Atman, the eternal self that resides deep within everyone, is identical to Brahman, the ultimate reality. To find Atman within and to be absorbed in it is the final aim for the Hinduism of the Upanishads.

Gautama looked deeply within, but his discovery led him to a radically different conclusion. In a word, Gautama discovered *change.* Everything, within and without, is changing, in a constant state of flux, impermanent. He summarized this changing nature of reality by noting **Three Marks of Existence.**

Anatta. Rather than finding Atman (*atta* in Pali), the Buddha found *anatta,* "no-self." *Anatta* means there is no ultimate reality within, no essence underlying existence, no eternal substratum that is truly real, enduring beyond the present moment. This paradox, central to Buddhist teachings, can thus be summarized: The essence of Buddhism is, there is no essence.

Let us try to draw on the simple aspect of Buddhism—that it is based on the insights of a mere human being—to gain understanding of the doctrine of *anatta*. Consider your own situation. Where were you ten years ago? It may be tempting to answer, "grade school," or this or that place. But the Buddha would answer that "you" simply did not exist ten years ago. The "you" that exists now is the result of a long sequence of change. And you continue to change, literally from moment to moment. You hear a new idea from a friend or teacher, and suddenly your outlook has changed; you are left with a different self. You eat a meal, and the nutrients affect the makeup of your body. Modern physiological science would generally agree with the Buddha, for not a single molecule of the body we inhabit was part of us more than seven years ago. Our body, like our self, is continually changing.

Anicca. The second mark of existence defined by the Buddha is *anicca,* which means "impermanence." (*Anicca* is so closely related to *anatta* that much of what has been said about *anatta* applies here as well.) The world is constantly changing. Consider this example: Often we speak of a river flowing. The Buddha, always insistent on the precision of speech, would correct us. It is not really the river that is flowing; rather, the

The second mark of existence is *anicca,* or impermanence. We may see the waterfall as an unchanging thing, but it is actually an ongoing flow.

flowing *is* the river. A river is a dynamic process, not a static entity. We may think we see a river, a real and unchanging thing, but the river is merely an appearance—in actuality, a river is an ongoing flow, a constant sequence of change. The same understanding applies to the self. It appears that the self is real and unchanging, but it too is an ongoing flow—of thoughts, perceptions, fears, hopes, and so on—that is constantly changing.

Dukkha. The third mark of existence is *dukkha,* which is usually translated as "suffering." *Dukkha* is a natural result of *anicca* and *anatta.* We will consider *dukkha* in more detail in our discussion of the Four Noble Truths.

Samsara: Buddhist Rebirth

The paradoxical doctrine of *anatta* presents a difficult problem regarding belief in rebirth, or *samsara.* If there is no self, what is reborn? In Hinduism this is not a matter of concern, because the eternal Atman resides within everyone. Death, as the analogy in the Bhagavad-Gita demonstrates, is similar to taking off one's clothes at night. The atman will simply put on a new body in its next birth.

Because Buddhism denies the existence of a self, the question of what is reborn is important. In an attempt to explain this issue, Buddhism also turns to analogies. For example, if a flame is passed from one candle to another, is the second candle burning with the same flame as the first? A flame, like a river, is not a static entity, but a dynamic process. It is an ever changing bundle of energy, and the passage from one candle to another is, most precisely, a transference of energy. The same can be said of rebirth from one body to the next. It is the transference of a bundle of energy, which is patterned according to one's *karma.*

Karma:
Buddhist Morality and Personal Identity

The Buddhist doctrine of ***karma*** generally has the same meaning as the Hindu version: the moral law of cause and effect. *Karma*

functions hand in hand with *samsara,* in that the nature of one's rebirth depends on the status of one's *karma.* Indeed, because Buddhism denies the transference of any self or soul, personal identity depends entirely on *karma.* When an individual dies, his or her *karma* continues on its particular trajectory, as it were, eventually bringing about rebirth. At conception the new person is possessed of this particular status brought on by the *karma* of the previous life.

Because *karma* is constantly affected by the moral adequacy of one's actions, morality is of central concern for all Buddhists. The moral life requires observance of the **Five Precepts:**

1. Do not take life.
2. Do not take what is not given.
3. Do not engage in sensuous misconduct.
4. Do not use false speech.
5. Do not drink intoxicants.

The Five Precepts apply to all Buddhists. The following precepts are added for monks and nuns:

6. Do not eat after noon.
7. Do not watch dancing or shows.
8. Do not use garlands, perfumes, or ornaments.
9. Do not use a high or soft bed.
10. Do not accept gold or silver.

The emphasis in Buddhist morality is on intention. The degree to which an act is immoral depends on the individual's intention to commit the act, rather than on the actual outcome. For example, intentionally shooting at a deer and missing would clearly be considered immoral by a Buddhist. However, a Buddhist would be unlikely to consider as immoral the accidental killing of a deer with a car.

Buddhist precepts emphasize respect for life

9
The analogy of the flame being passed from one candle to another is the most famous one used to describe Buddhist rebirth. Invent a second analogy to help explain this doctrine.

10
Some systems of morality, such as the Buddhist one, emphasize the intention of an action; other systems emphasize the outcome of an action. Explain which you consider to be of greater moral significance: intention or outcome?

Young Buddhist monks in Burma engage in the daily tasks of monastic life.

The Four Noble Truths

During the Third Watch of the night of his enlightenment, upon reaching the most profound level of insight, Gautama perceived the **Four Noble Truths:**

1. To live is to suffer.
2. Suffering is caused by desire.
3. Suffering can be brought to cessation.
4. The solution to suffering is the Noble Eightfold Path.

These were the foundational discoveries through which Buddha, the physician (to follow our earlier analogy), could go about applying his therapy to humankind: diagnosis of the disease, determination of its cause, the prognosis, and the prescription for a cure. The Buddha taught the Four Noble Truths in his momentous First Sermon, preached in the Deer Park near Benares. They are the central teachings of Buddhism.

Diagnosis of the Disease: *Dukkha*

Because of the difficulties involved in translating the Four Noble Truths into single English words, it is helpful to learn the original Pali terms. The first is **dukkha,** which is translated variously as "suffering," "frustration," "dislocation," or "discomfort," to name only a few possibilities. The word originally referred to disjointedness, as a wheel not perfectly centered on its axle, or a bone slightly ajar in its socket. Generally speaking, to assert that life is *dukkha* is to imply that things are not quite as they should be, but are somehow out of joint and in need of repair.

That life is *dukkha* is obvious to anyone who is experiencing pain, be it physical or emotional. When we hurt or are ill, even to a slight degree, it is all too clear that things could be better. But what about the good times, when health and contentment prevail? What about those moments when we feel a deep happiness and yearn that life could continue this way forever? The problem, the Buddha would say, is that such happiness will not continue. Human life is finite, and all our experiences are of limited duration. Life's best times hasten to their end. The ordinary times, even if not hampered by illness or injury, are never quite as good as they could be.

In his First Sermon, the Buddha provided a practical list of specific life experiences during which suffering is most readily apparent. He began by citing stages of the life process: birth, old age, disease, and death. Birth entails suffering simply because it marks the beginning of life in human form, another round of existence in *samsara*. Recall that among the Four Passing Sights that prompted Gautama to leave his palace life were an old man, a diseased man, and a corpse. Although Gautama's life as a prince may have seemed ideal at the time, these sights prompted him to acknowledge the suffering that was in store even for him. As it is for all human beings, his life was finite, of limited duration. He too would grow old, experience disease, and die.

The Buddha went on to cite three day-to-day experiences. In spite of all their efforts, people continually come into contact with unpleasant things. At the same time, people have to continually endure separation from pleasant things, along with harboring unfulfilled wishes. The problem common to these last two experiences, and a term that is highly relevant to understanding Buddhism, is *attachment*. It is our attachment to pleasant things that sets us up to suffer when we are separated from them. What is a wish other than a mental attachment to some object or event that is not yet ours to enjoy?

The Buddha was severe in his condemnation of attachment, denouncing even such commonly cherished bonds as those between family members. In the following story, retold by Buddhist monk Thich Nhat Hanh, a woman called Lady Visakha visits the Buddha in the city of Savatthi. She is grieving over the death of a child:

The Buddha asked her, "Visakha, where have you been? Why are your clothes and hair so wet?"

Lady Visakha wept. "Lord, my little grandson just died. I wanted to come see you, but in my grief I forgot to take my hat or parasol to protect me from the rain."

"How old was your grandson, Visakha? How did he die?"

"Lord, he was only three years old. He died of typhoid fever."

"The poor little one. Visakha, how many children and grandchildren do you have?"

"Lord, I have sixteen children. Nine are married. I had eight grandchildren. Now there are only seven."

"Visakha, you like having a lot of grandchildren, don't you?"

"Oh yes, Lord. The more the better. Nothing would make me happier than to have as many children and grandchildren as there are people in Savatthi."

"Visakha, do you know how many people die each day in Savatthi?"

"Lord, sometimes nine or ten, but at least one person dies every day in Savatthi. There is no day without a death in Savatthi."

"Visakha, if your children and grandchildren were as numerous as the people of Savatthi, your hair and clothes would be as soaked as they are today every day."

Visakha joined her palms. "I understand! I really don't want as many children and grandchildren as there are people in Savatthi. The more attachments one has, the more one suffers. You have often taught me this, but I always seem to forget."

The Buddha smiled gently. (*Old Path White Clouds,* page 407)

Dukkha would seem to be unavoidable. All of life's experiences are of finite duration, and we are constantly bombarded by opportunities to become attached. Indeed, the Buddha concluded in his First Sermon that human life itself, by its very nature, is unavoidably wrapped up in *dukkha.* Bodies, personalities, thoughts—all are finite, all are constantly changing. All are subject to *dukkha.* This is a grave diagnosis.

Determination of the Cause: *Tanha*

Despite this diagnosis, the Buddha did not stop here, abandoned to the hopelessness of the diseased human condition. Instead he proceeded to determine its cause. He identi-

fied the second noble truth as **tanha,** which is translated variously as "desire," "thirst," or "craving."

It is helpful to think of *tanha* as implying selfish desire, for it seems impossible not to desire anything. Did not the Buddha himself desire to lead others on the path to enlightenment? The distinguishing characteristic of *tanha* is its selfish orientation. It is desire for individual attainment, for private fulfillment.

Just as *dukkha* is seemingly unavoidable, so too is *tanha,* its cause. How can an individual refrain from desiring her or his own fulfillment? The Buddha himself would likely answer that a person cannot refrain from such desire. Individuals are destined to be selfish; *tanha* is an unavoidable aspect of being an individual. But recall what the Buddha taught about individuality. He taught the doctrine of *anatta,* no-self. That which we regard as our "self," our individuality, is not part of any ultimate reality. We are in fact changing from moment to moment. Yet we imagine that we exist as individuals, each of us unique and endowed with a self that is real and abiding and significant. But this is a falsehood. It is also another form of attachment. Attached to our false idea of being an individual self, we tend to care for ourself diligently, all the while only adding fuel to the fire of *tanha,* and tightening the grip of *dukkha.* A British-born Buddhist teacher who went by the pen name of Wei Wu Wei puts it like this:

Why are you unhappy?
Because 99.9 percent
Of everything you think,
And of everything you do,
Is for yourself—
And there isn't one.

(*Ask the Awakened,* page 1)

It is a vicious circle! It is precisely this fictitious self that goes on thinking of itself as real. How can such a circle be broken? It is the profound difficulty of this challenge that suggests that the Buddha was not an ordinary physician, but an ingenious one who

11

Reflect on the Buddha's teaching to the woman whose grandson had just died. How do you feel about this teaching? How does it compare with your perspective on family ties? How might you deal with such grief?

12

Have you ever performed a truly selfless act? Is such an act, completely free of any selfish motivation, even possible? (According to Buddhism it would only be possible after attaining enlightenment.) Explain.

Two views of a serene Buddha in Sri Lanka

prescribed a radical cure that would change forever the world's religious landscape.

Is Buddhism a Pessimistic Religion?

Before examining the Buddha's cure in detail, let us pause and consider one of the persistent criticisms of the Buddha's diagnosis of the human condition. Critics of Buddhism often point out that focusing on suffering is an unnecessarily pessimistic approach. Surely there are alternative perspectives on life. The adage "Eat, drink, and be merry, for tomorrow you may die" calls to mind one such alternative. But even if blatant indulgence in bodily pleasure is not the focus of other perspectives, it is common for philosophies and religions to place more emphasis on the joys of life than on the sorrows.

To gain a fair opinion of Buddhism's emphasis on suffering, it is important to note that the overwhelming impression one gets from reading the accounts of Buddhists is of a deep joy and contentment that comes from practicing their religion. Rather than characterizing Buddhism as pessimistic, it is perhaps more accurate to label it as *realistic*. People *do* suffer. Even happiness is yoked to suffering. Life, it would seem, can be better than it is. The Buddha understood the extreme importance of first being aware of the disease and its cause before proceeding. And he believed wholeheartedly that the disease and its cause can be rooted out from each of us. His prognosis can only be described as optimistic.

The Prescription for a Cure: The Noble Eightfold Path

In light of the pervasiveness of suffering and its cause, it is appropriate that the cure set out in the **Noble Eightfold Path** encompasses all aspects of life. In keeping with the doctrine of the Middle Way, though, the Noble Eightfold Path sets forth a life of moderation,

13
Make a short list of "truths" that summarize the human condition. Describe your reasons for making the list that you did.

14

Consider the steps of the Eightfold Path. The final three tend to be specifically Buddhist, whereas the first five are similar to teachings of other religions. What aspects of these first five steps strike you as being familiar? What aspects are strange to you, and how do you think they relate to Buddhist teachings in general?

not of extreme religious practices. Also, the eight steps constitute ongoing practices, not stages to be mastered and then left behind.

1. *Right views.* Learn the content of the Buddha's teachings, especially the Four Noble Truths.

2. *Right intentions.* Abandon the evil attitudes of greed, hatred, and delusion. Nurture the good attitudes of generosity, friendship, and insight.

3. *Right speech.* Avoid vocal wrong deeds such as gossip, lying, abusive talk, and idle talk.

4. *Right conduct.* Obey the Five Precepts, or ten for monks and nuns (recall the discussion of the precepts earlier in this chapter).

7. *Right mindfulness.* Through careful attention to helpful topics, develop the mental focus needed for meditation.

8. *Right meditation.* Ascend through the four levels of trance (different versions describe eight or nine levels), ultimately reaching a point of perfect tranquility, in which the sense of individual existence has passed away. This is the state of *nirvana.*

Together the eight steps embrace the primary focal points of Buddhist training: wisdom (1 and 2), morality (3, 4, and 5), and concentration (6, 7, and 8). Though all three focal points are essential, the heart of Buddhist practice lies in concentration, and specifically in the practice of meditation. The Buddha's primary teachings derive from his

5. *Right livelihood.* Abstain from occupations that harm living beings, such as selling weapons, selling liquor, butchering, hunting, or being a soldier.

6. *Right effort.* Maintain mental alertness so as to control the effect of the senses, and to discriminate between wise and unwise mental activity.

own meditative experience; their truths can be fully understood only when an individual attains the same level of insight through meditation. The centrality of meditation can also be observed in Zen (a division of Buddhism so important that we shall devote a separate chapter to it). *Zen* is Japanese for "meditation."

Enlightenment and *Nirvana*

To follow the steps of the Eightfold Path to its end is to reach *nirvana*. Just as for the Buddha, though, final *nirvana* awaits the death of the body. In the meantime the life of the **arhat** (the "saint" who has become awakened) is forever transformed, having experienced a foretaste of the final *nirvana*.

All Buddhists look forward to the same experience of salvation as that of their model, Gautama the Buddha. Buddhas are distinct from their followers, however, in that they do not need a model to provide teachings leading to their awakening. Buddhas are able to accomplish this on their own. Gautama the Buddha, then, though merely human and not

of *tanha,* and thus free from *dukkha.* The *arhat* has fully realized the truth of the doctrine of *annata,* or no-self, and has let go of any sense of individual existence. Still engaged in the affairs of this world but no longer attached to them, the *arhat* is perfectly compassionate toward all living things.

With the inward experience of enlightenment, the outward virtues of compassion, friendliness, joy, and evenmindedness are simultaneously perfected. Although the focus of Buddhist teachings is mainly on the perfection of one's inner nature, the development of socially oriented virtues is also essential.

The ideal of compassion is especially emphasized. It is vividly illustrated in Buddhist

Far left: Monks in Thailand prostrate during morning prayer.
Left: A wall painting in Sri Lanka depicts an incident from one of the Buddha's former lives.

above his followers in terms of the ultimate experience of salvation, has a special status.

Compassion: The Enlightened *Arhat*

Having become awakened, the *arhat* is "enlightened," fully aware of the truth of the Buddha's teachings. With this perfect wisdom, the *arhat* is now free from the imprisonment

stories, many of which depict the Buddha in former lives. One such story, originally told by Gautama, is presented here as retold by storyteller Rafe Martin:

Once, long, long ago, the Buddha came to life as a noble prince named Mahasattva, in a land where the country of Nepal exists today.

One day, when he was grown, he went walking in a wild forest with his two older brothers. The land was dry and the leaves brittle. The sky seemed alight with flames.

Suddenly, they saw a tigress. The brothers turned to flee, but the tigress stumbled and fell. She was starving, and her cubs were starving too. She eyed her cubs miserably and, in that dark glance, the prince sensed her long months of hunger and pain. He saw, too, that unless she found food soon, she might even be driven to devour her own cubs. He was moved to compassion by the extreme hardness of their lives.

"What, after all, is this life for?" he thought.

Stepping forward, he calmly removed his outer garments and lay down before her. He tore his skin with a stone and let the starving tigress smell the blood. Mahasattva's brothers fled.

Hungrily, the tigress devoured the prince's body and chewed the bones. She and her cubs lived on, and for many years, the forest was filled with a golden light.

Centuries later, a mighty king raised a pillar of carved stone on this spot, and pilgrims still go there to make offerings even today.

Deeds of compassion live forever. (*The Hungry Tigress,* page 130)

15
Contemplate the story of the prince Mahasattva and the tigress. What does it tell you about the nature of Buddhist compassion?

This extreme example of compassion is fitting for the Buddha, who presents a role model for all Buddhist ideals. This story also illustrates that it takes many lifetimes to nurture the degree of compassion suitable for a Buddha.

Nirvana

When the life of the *arhat,* characterized by perfect compassion, ends, he or she enters into the state called *nirvana.* The word *nirvana* literally means "blowing out." This is helpful, in one sense, for we may apply this to our earlier analogy of the flame being passed from one candle to another. For rather than being reborn, the life energy of the *arhat* is "blown out" upon the passage into *nirvana.* Having extinguished all selfish desire, including desire for continued existence, the *arhat* has attained freedom from *samsara.*

To describe the state of *nirvana* precisely has always been impossible for Buddhists to do. Not even the Buddha could come up with words that could sufficiently describe this state. *Nirvana* cannot be understood until it is experienced. It is as difficult to understand *nirvana* as it would be for an unborn child to understand life outside the womb. Those still in *samsara* have never experienced anything that can even approximate the experience of *nirvana.* The most that can be said is that *nirvana* is the total cessation of suffering, and thus is absolute peace.

But if *nirvana* is total cessation, does the *arhat* experience "life after death"? Because enlightenment is precisely the abandonment of one's sense of individual existence, who (or what) is left to experience the absolute peace of *nirvana?* The Buddha specifically refused to say whether a person exists or does not exist in *nirvana.* He only insisted that *nirvana* is the cessation of suffering. And this, together with the Buddha's radiant happiness born of his enlightenment, suggest that if anything is experienced in *nirvana,* it is indescribably joyful.

Three Rafts to Cross the River: Divisions of Buddhism

Buddhists often invoke the crossing of a river as an analogy of the quest for salvation. On this side is the realm of *samsara,* the ordinary world of suffering. On the farther shore lies *nirvana,* impossible to know until it is experienced, but beckoning all Buddhists as their final destiny of absolute peace. The process of crossing the river is the task of religion. And so Buddhism thinks of itself as a raft, a means for crossing.

In fact, over the centuries Buddhism has divided into three great rafts, or "vehicles" *(yanas):* Theravada, also referred to by the somewhat derisive name of Hinayana (the Lesser Vehicle); Mahayana (the Great Vehicle); and Vajrayana (the Vehicle of the Diamond). Some of the differences among the three vehicles are a result of regional variations, for Buddhism has spread far beyond its original homeland and is now present throughout most of Asia. Interestingly, it disappeared almost entirely from India a long time ago.

Theravada: "The Way of the Elders"

Theravada Buddhism is now the prevalent form in the countries of Sri Lanka, Myanmar (formerly Burma), Thailand, and Kampuchea (formerly Cambodia). *Theravada,* which means "the way of the elders," follows the earliest texts, and thus tends to agree with the original teachings of the Buddha. Theravada regards the Buddha first and foremost as he who experienced enlightenment and then taught others how to accomplish the same. The Buddha is forever beyond the reach of humans, having passed into the eternal peace of *nirvana.* The teachings of Buddhism, not the figure of the Buddha, are central.

And so Theravada focuses on the teachings: the cultivation of wisdom through knowing the Four Noble Truths, and practicing the Noble Eightfold Path, especially meditation. The final aim, of course, is to enter *nirvana.* Those who succeed are the *arhats,* which for Theravada are the ideal types whom all strive to imitate (much as saints are the ideal types in Catholicism).

Theravada's focus on meditation has led naturally to an emphasis on monastic life, because monks and nuns, unlike the laity, have sufficient time for meditating. This emphasis has resulted in a religious hierarchy in most Theravada regions, such that the roles of laity and of monks and nuns are differentiated. Even among the ordained, the roles differ. Monks, who outnumber nuns by more than ten to one, have always held the most prominent position within Theravada Buddhism. It is also notable that in some Theravadin countries, it is common for men to enter a monastery only temporarily. A term as a monk lasting for at least three months is seen as a required step toward becoming an adult.

A Theravadan depiction of the Buddha in Sri Lanka

Mahayana: "The Great Vehicle"

By naming themselves the Great Vehicle, **Mahayana** Buddhists are only in part asserting their superiority over Theravada Buddhists, whom they named Hinayana (the Lesser Vehicle). Mahayana is indeed the largest division of Buddhism, claiming well over half the world's Buddhists. Today Mahayana is the dominant form of Buddhism in China, Korea, and Japan. But the name also indicates something of the nature of Mahayana. Whereas Theravada emphasizes the

Far left: A Chinese depicition of the *bodhisattva* Kuan-Yin
Left: A Japanese sculpture of the *bodhisattva* Avalokiteshvara

individual's path of meditation (and hence can suffice with a lesser vehicle, or raft), Mahayana is Buddhism for the masses.

For one thing, rather than concentrating on the Buddha's teachings, Mahayana focuses on the Buddha himself, celebrating him as a divine savior. This has potent popular appeal because it opens the doors to religious devotion and prayer. Rather than depending on the cultivation of wisdom through meditation on difficult teachings, this form of Buddhism offers salvation through the infinite grace of the compassionate Buddha.

And Mahayana does not stop with Gautama the Buddha, but recognizes the salvific grace of all the Buddhas of the past. More important, Mahayana reveres *bodhisattvas.* In its most general definition, **bodhisattvas** are those who are dedicated to attaining enlightenment. They are "Buddhas in the making." More specifically, the term *bodhisattva* is used

to describe persons who are capable of entering into *nirvana* but, motivated by compassion, stop short of this goal so as to help others achieve it. Mahayana accepts these definitions but adds another in which *bodhisattvas* take on mythical qualities. These *bodhisattvas* exist beyond the earthly realm and are believed to dwell in one of the Buddhist heavens, from which they provide divine assistance to those who worship them. Owing to the infinite depth of their compassion, the mythical *bodhisattvas* are believed to transfer merit of their *karma* to their devotees. On occasion they appear in the world as human beings. Several *bodhisattvas* are prominent in Mahayana, including Maitreya, whom Buddhists expect some day to be reborn into the world as the next Buddha.

For Mahayana Buddhists, the *bodhisattva,* rather than the *arhat,* is the ideal type. And compassion, which is perfectly embodied by the *bodhisattvas,* is the supreme virtue, regarded more highly even than wisdom. Mahayana Buddhists see Gautama's decision to preach the Dharma rather than enter immediately into *nirvana,* as proof for the primacy of compassion. They look to the *bodhisattvas* as embodiments of compassion, because the *bodhisattvas* have vowed that they will wait to enter *nirvana* so that they may assist others, even until "the last blade of grass" becomes enlightened.

Vajrayana: Fighting Fire with Fire

When Mahayana Buddhists elevated the figure of the Buddha to that of divine savior, the Buddha was depicted holding the *vajra,* a diamond scepter. The Vehicle of the Diamond bears this name as a result of its unique application of Buddhist teachings, resembling in their energetic rigor the strength and clarity of a diamond.

Vajrayana comprises but a small minority of Buddhists, and yet it is of special interest. This is due both to its unique form and to the situation of its homeland, Tibet. Now claimed as a part of the People's Republic of China, Tibet has endured much religious persecution by China's communist government. Many Vajrayana Buddhists have been killed; many others are now living in exile in India and elsewhere. But for centuries the high mountain plateaus of Tibet sheltered Vajrayana from the rest of the world. The relatively pristine state of this form of Buddhism has also attracted special interest.

The uniqueness of Vajrayana centers on the notion of fighting fire with fire. In general, Buddhist teachings prescribe shutting off the energy of desire to accomplish the cessation of suffering. Vajrayana harnesses this energy and turns it against itself. The end goal of *nirvana* remains the same, but the means of reaching it are remarkably unique.

By harnessing the sensual energies of life, Vajrayana attempts to propel the individual toward enlightenment. Prominent among the practices used to achieve this are **mandalas**, patterned icons that visually excite; **mudras**, choreographed hand movements that draw on the energies of movement; and **mantras**,

16
From the perspective of your own upbringing, which form of Buddhism—Theravada or Mahayana—seems more familiar to you? What specific characteristics of that form are familiar to you?

Exiled Tibetan Buddhists perform a ritual in India.

A Pure Offering, Every Day

Tsechang Gonpo is a Tibetan (or Vajrayana) Buddhist living in Minneapolis. Although he and his wife, Sonam, are far from their people's native homeland of Tibet, Buddhism continues to be central to their lives. Writing on behalf of both of them, Tsechang explains what their religion means to them, and why.

Buddhism plays a very big part in our day-to-day life. It is even more important than family. A main reason for this is our belief in life after death and the wheel of rebirth, or *samsara*. When I die, I have to leave behind those who are near and dear to me, and travel on to the next life alone. It would be bad to be too attached to the things of this life, even my family.

The nature of my next life depends on the deeds I have done during this lifetime and previous lifetimes. If I have practiced Buddhism well and accumulated lots of good *karma*, then maybe I can take on a good life form, such as a human. If not, maybe I will become a bird, or even worse, I may have to go to hell. My next life is therefore very important to me, as is the ultimate goal of escaping from the pain and suffering of *samsara* to a state we call *nirvana*. When we are enlightened, we can become a Buddha. All of us have this chance, depending on our level of practice. One can even get to Buddhahood or *nirvana* in this lifetime, if one is willing to sacrifice all worldly things and follow the tough way of intense meditation and other practices. This was proved by Milarepa, one of the great Tibetan Buddhists of the past. In his youth he accumulated many bad deeds by killing many living beings. But later he regretted his actions. He found a great teacher and worked so hard that he ultimately attained *nirvana* in his lifetime.

Milarepa is a good inspiration for Sonam's father, who was a Khampa warrior and killed many Chinese soldiers during the Chinese invasion of Tibet. He now very much regrets those bad deeds, and he prays a lot. He has made pilgrimages to all the important Buddhist sites in India and Nepal, and while there has given offerings to the temples and monasteries. In this way he thinks he may be able to reduce some of his bad *karma*.

The reincarnation of *lamas* illustrates our beliefs in life after death. Many high lamas who maintain exceptional practice and meditation are reincarnated in their next life as previous *lamas*. The basic difference between such *lamas* and ourselves is based on the level of Buddhist practice. They can remember their previous life form, whereas we do not remember anything because of our relatively low level of practice and our ignorance.

My father was a reincarnation of a previous *lama*. He was from the eastern part of Tibet, but came to central Tibet to master Buddhism and then to return to his people. Unfortunately he was not able to return home because of the Chinese invasion. He escaped to India, and for his own self-defense he took a weapon. Because of that he had to give back the vows of *lama,* and he became an ordinary man.

Another example of a reincarnated *lama* is His Holiness the Dalai Lama. We believe that he is the *bodhisattva* Avalokiteshvara in human form. The present Dalai Lama, Tenzin Gyatso, is fourteenth in the succession of reincarnations. He is both the temporal and spiritual leader of Tibet, and is an important figure for the Tibetan people. He had to take over the leadership at a very young age, during our most difficult period. Tibet lost its independence to communist China in 1959. Nearly two million Tibetans died during the occupation, and six thousand monasteries, temples, and other cultural and historic buildings were destroyed and their contents pillaged. But fortunately His Holiness the Dalai Lama and about eighty thousand Tibetans escaped to India.

Upon arriving as a refugee in India, the Dalai Lama requested that the Indian government build schools for Tibetan children. He believes that the children are the future seeds for Tibet. I attended one of those schools in Pathlikhul, which is in northern India. At first the conditions at the school were really poor. We did not have enough to eat. Our parents could not help much because most of them worked in road construction and earned minimum wages. Many kids my age died of malnutrition at that time. Fortunately help came from Western countries, including the

United States. I still remember the oil tin with the two hands shaking and the American flag printed on it. We kids liked that oil because it tasted like butter. Slowly our living conditions improved, and the Indian government helped us with new, qualified teachers. Later on when we had grown up, we found even better opportunities for higher studies like medicine and engineering. I was fortunate to get one of the engineering scholarships. All of this is possible because of our great leader the Dalai Lama, my father's encouragement, and lastly my generous sponsor from Germany whom I consider as a second mother provided by God.

The Dalai Lama also started a Tibetan government in exile based on the principles of democracy. The Tibetan people elect their representative to the parliament every five years. The Dalai Lama also stressed the importance of Tibetan Buddhist culture and set up various institutions. He believes that we should get back our independence through nonviolent means. This approach is much appreciated by people all around the world, and ultimately he won the Nobel Peace Prize in 1989. He is one of the best-known people in the world.

The Dalai Lama's kindness and his help for the Tibetan people is so much that it is difficult to express in words. In my daily prayer, I always pray for his long life and well-being. I believe that we Tibetans are unfortunate to have lost our country, but fortunate to have a leader like His Holiness to take us through this difficult moment. I hope that we will get our country back during his lifetime, and once again Buddhism will be practiced and spread all over Tibet.

In our hearts the Dalai Lama is like a true Avalo-kiteshvara, but he always claims himself to be a simple Buddhist monk. In today's world it is difficult to find a great leader like him who is so humble.

Although he is very busy, he finds time to meet with people once a week whenever he is not traveling or meditating. He resides at the palace at Dharamsala in northern India, where I was born and lived for many years.

When we make an important decision, like beginning a business venture or setting a date for a marriage ceremony, we always get advice from a higher *lama*. This is because, according to our system of astrology, there are some good days and some bad days in a week, depending on each person's calendar.

Tibetans have their own form of medicine, which is very different from Western medicine. When taking a pill, some of it must be taken only after meditation, and on that particular day, no meat or dairy products are to be eaten.

I start each day with prayer. I pray for the well-being of all sentient beings and for the long life of His Holiness the Dalai Lama, and that I might accumulate some good *karma* during the day. Our deities are also in my prayers. Belief in deities is common among Tibetans. The majority of us believe in Nechung and Palden Lhamo, deities who give advice to us through oracles. After prayer I offer seven bowls of water to the gods, and then I burn incense. Water is offered because it is cheapest and therefore there is no sense of loss. If I felt loss due to attachment, my offering would not be pure. I then go to work, and during the day I always try to think about the most simple Buddhist teaching: "If you cannot help anybody, at least try never to harm anyone." This is really good for a common layperson like me as it is very simple and easy to follow. When the day is done and before I go to bed, I think about how I have done during the day. If I have done something bad, then I regret that and ask for forgiveness in my prayers to the Three Jewels: the Buddha, his teachings and the scriptures, and the community of monks and nuns. I meditate sometimes, but being in America it is difficult to find time to meditate every day.

resonating chants that harness the spiritual potency of sound. Together these practices invoke sound, movement, and sight, capitalizing on the sensual energies as a way to achieve the goal of spiritual enhancement.

Another of Vajrayana's unique practices involves the harnessing of one of life's basic energies, that of sexuality. Whereas most Buddhists target sexual desire as being especially problematic and in need of being controlled, Vajrayana regards sex as being all the more potent as an energy for furthering spiritual progress. In a carefully guarded set of practices known as Tantrism, some Vajrayana Buddhists engage in ritualized sex. Far from being sex merely for its own sake (it is not motivated by a desire for pleasure), Tantrism is regulated by masters, and is engaged in solely for the purpose of enhancing spiritual energies.

Another important feature of Vajrayana is its institution of *lamas,* a hierarchy of clergy headed by the **Dalai Lama.** The present Dalai Lama, who won the 1989 Nobel Peace Prize for his efforts on behalf of regaining Tibetan freedom, is the fourteenth in a direct line of succession. But rather than being based on descent by natural birth, this line of succession is through rebirth. Originating with the

Top: His Holiness the Dalai Lama, the leader of Tibetan Buddhism
Bottom: Mandalas are used to propel people toward enlightenment.

incarnation of a prominent *bodhisattva* (Avalokiteshvara), the lineage is believed to continue through the reincarnation of one Dalai Lama into the next. Whenever a Dalai Lama dies, his successor is sought out through various means, some supernatural, and others more mundane (such as noting a likely child's attraction to the former Dalai Lama's possessions).

The Enduring Wisdom of the Buddha

Each raft of Buddhism charts its own course, but ultimately reaches the same shore, delivering its adherents into *nirvana.* A famous Buddhist mantra invokes the end of the crossing: "Gone, gone, gone beyond, completely gone beyond, enlightenment hail!" (Robinson and Johnson, *The Buddhist Religion,* page 94). *Nirvana,* the ultimate goal of all Buddhists, is beyond every experience of this life. In typically paradoxical fashion, it is even beyond Buddhism itself. The raft that has ferried the adherent across the river to the shore of salvation must then be abandoned lest the journey remain unfinished.

In other ways, too, Buddhism is paradoxical. It is indeed a unique case among the world's religions. Buddhism focuses on the spiritual condition of the human being, not on the supremacy of a divinity. Even more uniquely, it denies the existence of a self, or soul.

Buddhism relies instead on features that are strikingly akin to the ways of the modern, scientific view of life. In fact, modern scientific theory has much to say that is in close agreement with the observations of Gautama the Buddha regarding the nature both of the universe and of the human psyche.

This is not an accident, for the Buddha, skilled physician that he was, proceeded scientifically—empirically investigating the nature of what it is to be human. People suffer. A life of moderation, as exemplified by the doctrine of the Middle Way, helps to alleviate suffering. And meditation, the Buddha's favored method of therapy, nurtures the wisdom that leads to transcendence.

Glossary

arhat (ahr'huht). One who has become enlightened; the ideal type for Theravada Buddhism.

bodhisattvas (boh-dee-saht'vahs). Future Buddhas. As the ideal types for Mahayana Buddhism, those beings who have experienced enlightenment but, motivated by compassion, stop short of entering *nirvana* so as to help others achieve it.

Buddha (bood'duh; Sanskrit and Pali: "awakened one"). The title applied to Siddhartha Gautama and all others who have by their own insight attained perfect enlightenment.

Dalai Lama (dahl'ee lahm'ah). The spiritual leader of Vajrayana (Tibetan) Buddhism, believed to be an incarnation of the *bodhisattva* Avalokiteshvara (ah-wah-loh-ki-tesh'-wah-rah).

Dharma (dahr'muh). The teachings of the Buddha, and one of the Three Jewels of Buddhism.

dukkha (dook'huh; Pali: "suffering," "frustration," "dislocation," or "discomfort"). The first of the Four Noble Truths, the basic Buddhist insight that suffering is part of the human condition. *See also* Three Marks of Existence.

Five Precepts. The basic moral requirements that are binding for all Buddhists.

Four Noble Truths. The central teachings of Buddhism: to live is to suffer; suffering is caused by desire; the cessation of suffering can be achieved; the solution is the Noble Eightfold Path.

karma (Sanskrit: "action"). The moral law of cause and effect of actions; determines the nature of one's rebirth.

Mahayana (mah-hah-yah'nah; Sanskrit: "Great Vehicle"). The largest of Buddhism's three divisions, prevalent in China, Korea, and Japan; encompasses a variety of forms, including those that emphasize devotion and prayer to the Buddhas and bodhisattvas.

mandalas (mahn'duh-luhs; Sanskrit: "circle"). Patterned icons that visually excite; used in Vajrayana Buddhism to enhance meditation.

mantras (mahn'truhs). Phrases or syllables chanted in order to evoke a deity or to enhance meditation; used in Hinduism and Buddhism, especially in Vajrayana.

Middle Way. A basic Buddhist teaching that rejects both the pleasures of sensual indulgence and the self-denial of asceticism, focusing instead on a practical approach to spiritual attainment.

mudras (mood'rahs). Choreographed hand movements used in the rituals of Vajrayana Buddhism.

nirvana (Sanskrit: "blowing out"). The ultimate goal of all Buddhists, the extinction of desire and any sense of individual selfhood, resulting in liberation from *samsara* and its limiting conditions.

Noble Eightfold Path. The fourth of the Four Noble Truths, defines the basic practices of Buddhism that lead to *nirvana*.

Pali (pah-lee). An ancient language of India, similar to Sanskrit but more commonly understood, and used in the writing of the earliest Buddhist texts; most important for Theravada Buddhism.

samsara (samh-sah'ruh). The wheel of rebirth or reincarnation; the this-worldly realm in which rebirth occurs.

sangha (sahn'guh; Sanskrit and Pali: "assemblage"). The Buddhist community of monks, nuns, and laity; when the word *Sangha* is capitalized, it refers to one of the Three Jewels of Buddhism.

tanha (Pali: "desire," "thirst," or "craving"). The second of the Four Noble Truths, selfish desire, which causes *dukkha*.

Theravada (thai-ruh-vah'duh; Pali: "The Way of the Elders"). Prevalent form of Buddhism in Sri Lanka, Myanmar (Burma), Thailand, and Kampuchea (Cambodia); focuses on the earliest texts and emphasizes monastic lifestyle.

Three Marks of Existence. Characteristics that summarize the changing nature of reality: *anatta* (no-self), *anicca* (impermanence), and *dukkha* (suffering).

Vajrayana (vuhj-ruh-yah'nuh; Sanskrit: "The Vehicle of the Diamond"). Named for the *vajra*, the Buddha's diamond scepter; prevalent form of Buddhism in Tibet; emphasizes the harnessing of sensual energies to attain *nirvana*.

PAKISTAN

NEPAL

Delhi

Vaisali

Ganges

Indus

Ahmadabad

Calcutta

INDIA

Bombay

Madras

SRI
LANKA

N

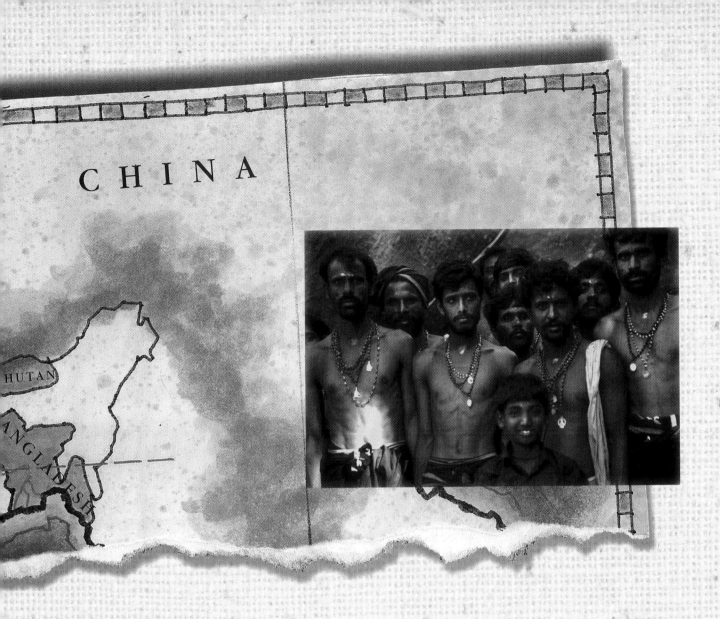

5 Jainism

All breathing, existing, living, sentient creatures should not be slain, nor treated with violence, nor abused, nor tormented, nor driven away.

This is the pure, unchangeable, eternal law, which the clever ones, who understand the world, have declared. (Acaranga Sutra, book 1, lecture 4, lesson 1.1–2)

Ahimsa and Asceticism: Jainism's Ideals

Like Hinduism and Buddhism, Jainism originated in India, where today almost all of its adherents live. Jainism shares many of the basic doctrines of Hinduism and Buddhism. Worlds arise and decay in an infinite series of cycles. Human

beings are on the wheel called *samsara,* the long sequence of rebirths. The specific nature of each rebirth is determined by **karma,** the moral law of cause and effect. The ultimate religious goal of salvation consists of liberation (called *moksha* by Jains and Hindus alike) from *samsara.*

The ethical principle of **ahimsa,** "nonviolence," is important to Hinduism and Buddhism; this is evident in the prevalence of vegetarianism among their adherents. For Jainism, however, *ahimsa* is the central principle, the "pure, unchangeable, eternal law." For all Jains, religious life is first and foremost the avoidance of doing injury to their fellow "sentient creatures," a broad category that includes humans and animals (including insects). For Jain monks and nuns, whom the laity revere as ideal types, the principle of *ahimsa* is expanded to include all life forms, even the atomic particles thought to be alive in such substances as wind, water, earth, and fire. This strenuous practice of *ahimsa* can only be accomplished through a lifestyle of rigorous self-denial, or **asceticism**.

These two features—*ahimsa* and asceticism—are the defining characteristics of Jainism. And though Jainism is a relatively small tradition (having only about three million followers), these features assure its place as an important and enduring contribution to the religious landscape of the world.

Makers of the River Crossing

The name Jainism is derived from **jina,** which means "conqueror." The spiritual conquerors of the past, those who have attained salvation, are referred to as **tirthankaras,** "makers of the river crossing." Like other Indian religions, Jainism regards rivers as being symbolic of the spiritual quest. The river crossing, or ford, is especially significant. It symbolizes a means of crossing over the realm of *samsara* to salvation beyond. According to Jain belief, in the present turning of the world cycle, twenty-four persons have established a river crossing, enabling their fellow Jains to seek salvation. Jains acknowledge the authority of these *tirthankaras,* "conquerors" who have exemplified the practice of *ahimsa* and the discipline of the ascetic life.

Jains believe that the sequence of world cycles is without beginning or end. Throughout this eternal process, *tirthankaras* have appeared, so there is an infinite number of them. Jainism reveres all the *tirthankaras.* The twenty-four of the present turning of the world cycle are each known by name and by specific symbols. Detailed stories tell of their earthly lives. However, scholars regard only the last two as historical persons. Parshva, the twenty-third *tirthankara,* lived in the eighth century B.C.E., and continues to be a popular object of Jain devotion. Today there are more statues and other images of Parshva than of any other *tirthankara.* By far the most important *tirthankara,* though, is the last one, Mahavira. His life story has provided the predominant role model for Jains through the centuries.

Mahavira, the Twenty-fourth *Tirthankara*

Mahavira (which means "great hero") lived, according to tradition, from 599 to 527 B.C.E., and was a contemporary of Gautama the Buddha. The two have much in common. The Jain biography of Mahavira, like the Buddhist biography of Gautama, is clearly legendary, serving to set forth an example of the required lifestyle and essential events of a perfect religious life.

Like Gautama, Mahavira was born into a family of the *kshatriya* caste of warriors and administrators. (Like Buddhism, Jainism rejected the Hindu caste system; unlike Buddhism, Jainism replaced it with a caste system of its own.) Mahavira's father was a *rajah,* or ruler, of a territory in northeastern India, not far from the home of Gautama. Mahavira grew up, married, had a daughter, and lived amid the many luxuries of the palace. But by his middle twenties, he was restless with this lifestyle, desiring instead to leave it all behind and join a group of Jain ascetics, followers of Parshva. At age twenty-eight the future *tirthankara* gave away all that he possessed, said farewell to his family, and began the rigorous life of a Jain monk.

Shortly after joining the ascetics, Mahavira went off on his own. He discarded his robe (as a symbol of total departure from society) and wandered naked about the land for more than twelve years. He practiced the most extreme forms of asceticism. When ridiculed or physically abused by others, Mahavira passively endured the attacks. He frequently went without sleep and fasted for long periods. When not fasting, he ate sparingly, begging for food and accepting only that which had been prepared without causing violence. When insects crawled on his body, he endured their bites rather than cause injury by brushing them off.

People make offerings in a Jain temple in northern India.

Right: The birth of Mahavira is celebrated in this miniature painting from fifteenth-century India.
Far right: Parshva, the twenty-third tirthankara

1

As the last *tirthankara* to have appeared on Earth, Mahavira is the most important person for Jainism. Still, he is only one *tirthankara* among countless who have appeared before and who will appear in the future. From your point of view, how does the fact that Mahavira is one of many *tirthankaras* affect his status as a religious figure? In your answer try to draw on comparisons with other religious figures, such as Jesus Christ or Gautama the Buddha.

Two other important contrasts between Jainism and Buddhism should be noted. First, whereas Gautama rejected asceticism in favor of the Middle Way, Mahavira held fast to the most extreme form of asceticism. Jains have always regarded this distinction with pride. Second, whereas Gautama discovered on his own the true practices of Buddhism while seeking enlightenment, Mahavira learned the true practices of Jainism from others. Gautama and Mahavira thus play different roles as "founders" of these religions.

Eventually Mahavira's asceticism led him to the supreme goal of enlightenment. After fasting without water for two and a half days in the hot sun, Mahavira squatted on his haunches in meditation, near a tree but intentionally not in its shade. (Again we note a contrast with Gautama, who *sat* in the lotus position *under* a fig tree.) Here Mahavira attained **kevala,** Jain enlightenment, which is perfect and complete knowledge, or omniscience. Like Buddhist enlightenment, *kevala* marks the point at which one is free from the negative effects of *karma,* and thus has gained release from the earthly bondage of *samsara.*

Mahavira spent the rest of his life preaching to his followers, especially to his eleven principal disciples, Hindu *brahmins* who had converted to Jainism when they heard Mahavira's teachings. These disciples formed the basis of the Jain community that survives to this day.

At the age of seventy-two, Mahavira undertook his final ascetic act, voluntarily starving himself to death. Jains believe that Mahavira's pure soul was finally freed from his physical body, and that it ascended to its rightful place at the top of the universe, where it dwells in supreme bliss for eternity.

Knowing the Universe: Cosmology and Salvation

Gautama the Buddha spoke very little about cosmology; such discourse, he felt, did not serve the real concern of finding salvation. Mahavira took the opposite approach. He described the universe in abundant detail. Through the omniscience of *kevala,* he knew everything regarding the makeup of the universe. Such knowledge has always been esteemed by Jainism, which maintains that salvation of the soul depends on understanding its predicament. And the soul's predicament is based in the makeup of the universe, which is composed both of eternal souls and of infinite particles of matter.

The Jain Universe

Jains understand the universe to be a vast yet finite space called the **loka.** It is almost indescribably vast, in fact. By one account, if a god were to fly at the speed of ten million miles per second, it would take him seven years to travel from the top of the *loka* to the bottom. (Note the similarity between this unit of measurement and the "light year" used in modern astronomy; such points of similarity between Jainism and science are striking.) Within this space are all things, both living and nonliving. Outside the *loka* is nothing but strong winds. The *loka* is eternal: it was never created and will never come to an end.

The *loka* is often depicted as having the shape of a giant man. In the center is the small but very significant Middle Realm, home to several worlds (including our own) inhabited by human beings. The soul has the opportunity to move closer to salvation in only one of these worlds. Below the Middle Realm are hells inhabited by hell beings, and above are heavens inhabited by deities.

Many of the gods and goddesses of Hinduism are also acknowledged by Jains. To some extent they are believed to provide certain forms of material welfare, such as cures for illnesses, or good weather for growing crops. For this reason some Jains worship these deities. In no way, though, can the deities assist with the quest for salvation. They too are bound to *samsara* and must first be reborn as human beings in order to have any hope for release. Both deities and hell beings, then, are destined to experience rebirth; the torments endured by the hell beings, and the bliss enjoyed by the deities are both temporary conditions.

At the very top of the *loka* is a roof in the shape of an umbrella, the "slightly curved place." This is the realm of liberated souls, such as those of Mahavira and the rest of the *tirthankaras*. These souls are eternally liberated, never again to be reborn.

Upward and Downward Cycles

The Jain universe passes through cycles that are depicted as turnings of a wheel. As the wheel turns upward, the quality of each world improves. As the wheel turns downward, all things gradually decay, eventually reaching a state of utter destruction. At this point the next cycle begins, and the world gradually improves. The wheel continues turning like this forever.

Each upward and downward turning of the wheel is divided into six ages, each lasting twenty-one thousand years. According to Jains, this world is presently in the fifth age, nearing the end of a downward turn. Due to the rampant state of decay, people are meaner now, and their physical stature is smaller. Even more important is that people now lack the moral or spiritual competence to attain salvation. In each of the six ages, twenty-four *tirthankaras* appear. Mahavira is the last of this cycle; he and his eleven disciples are the last humans of this world to attain salvation. Until conditions improve significantly, the best that Jains of this world can hope for is a good rebirth, optimally as a human in a different world, one in which salvation is presently a possibility.

The Human Predicament: Clean Souls in Dirty Matter

The *loka* is inhabited by two distinct types: living things, which are **jivas**, or souls; and the nonliving **ajiva**, which consists of space, time, motion, rest, and all forms of matter. *Jivas* are perfectly pure. Matter is impure. For reasons that are beyond explanation, souls have become entwined with matter, and are thus tarnished and no longer pure. The religious

2
Jains depict the universe in a highly visual manner, envisioning the *loka* to be in the shape of a giant man. Draw a visual representation of your own view regarding the makeup of the universe. Use your imagination (it need not be a technically accurate depiction).

3
Compare the Jain concept of upward and downward cycles with your own understanding of time and the cycles of growth and decay of the universe.

4

Jainism holds that animals, and even some plants, can participate to some degree in religious life. In your opinion, might animals possess any form of spirituality? Offer some specific examples.

quest for salvation is for the *jiva* to make itself clean. Before we investigate this quest, let us examine more closely the nature of these two categories of reality.

In contrast to the predominant Hindu perspective of monism, in which all reality is essentially one thing, Jainism understands reality as being a pluralism, asserting that reality is ultimately many things, an infinity of *jivas* and an infinity of particles of matter. All these entities are eternal, and all can be said to exist on their own. In simplified form, though, Jain cosmology can correctly be thought of in terms of two categories: the soul and matter. The entire process of human destiny is based on this duality; salvation consists of liberation of the soul from the matter in which it is entwined.

All *jivas* are, in their original purity, equal in size and quality. The soul of an ant, for instance, is identical to that of an elephant. Only the bodies they inhabit, the forms of matter in which they are entwined, differ.

Jainism is famous for its extensive classification of these various bodies, or life forms. The basic classification divides them into two categories: stationary, such as plants, and moving, such as insects, animals, and so forth. A more complex scheme categorizes life forms according to the number of senses they have: animals, humans, deities, and hell beings are all classified as five-sensed (they can see, hear, taste, touch, and smell); flying insects are four-sensed (they lack hearing); insects such as ants and fleas are three-sensed (they lack hearing and sight); shellfish and certain insects such as worms are two-sensed (they lack hearing, sight, and the sense of smell); and plants and microbes (the simplest form) are one-sensed (they possess only the sense of touch).

Much more elaborate systems further classify these life forms according to the details that distinguish one from another. The essential point in terms of the religious life of Jainism, though, is this: All life forms, by virtue of being inhabited by a soul, are to be regarded as fellow creatures worthy of respect and care.

Most life forms are capable of some degree of participation in religious life. Plants can express feelings; for example, they can desire nourishment and feel fear. Animals are able to learn simple forms of religious disciplines (lions, for instance, can learn to fast). Even some microbes, which do not have bodies but group together in the bodies of more complex life forms, are believed to have the potential for spiritual advancement. To have the possibility of attaining salvation, all souls must eventually be reborn as humans.

The Religious Quest: The Rise of the Fallen Soul

The Jain quest for salvation can be understood by again picturing the *loka* as a giant man. The pure, liberated souls reside at the "umbrella" at the very top of the head, while all other life forms reside below, weighed down by the matter in which their souls are entwined. Salvation is attained when the soul cleans all matter from itself and regains its original state of purity. It is then free to bubble upward to its eternal home.

Karma is central to the destiny of the soul, just as it is in Hinduism and Buddhism. However, Jainism understands *karma* in a purely materialist sense. All actions are believed to involve the various forms of matter. Whenever the soul acts, it is tarnished by matter of some kind. Immoral actions, such as injuring other life forms, dirty the soul with thick, heavy matter. Highly virtuous actions cause only light, fleeting bits of residue, and eventually lead toward purity. The moment in which total purification of the soul is accomplished is called *kevala*. Once one has attained *kevala*, the soul is no longer subject to the tarnishing effects of *karma*. Like Mahavira, who attained *kevala* long before he died, an enlightened Jain can go on experiencing life in the body. The actual moment of death, which is carefully approached through rituals, results in the complete liberation of the soul.

For Jains of this world, in this era of continuing decline, salvation is not attainable. Under these circumstances the immediate goal of the

religious life is to achieve a good rebirth. This goal, like the goal of eventually attaining salvation, is dependent on *karma,* so living a good life remains essential. Rebirth itself is believed to occur immediately upon death, and a person can be reborn into any of the various life forms. The result depends on the status of the soul—whether *karma* has made it heavy or light with matter.

The Religious Life

The religious life of Jainism is divided into two categories: that of the laity, and that of monks and nuns (collectively known as ascetics). These two styles of religious life differ greatly from each other. The vast majority of Jains remain as laypersons. Among the roughly three million Jains in the world today, the ascetics number only in the hundreds. Still, the monks and nuns set forth an ideal type for all Jains. Famous for their rigorous self-denial and deliberate detachment from all aspects of everyday society, the ascetics are revered by the laity as heroic role models. Laypersons remain members of Indian society, and typically are not nearly as involved with ascetic practices. The principle of nonviolence, *ahimsa,* is the central standard of conduct for both lifestyles.

White-Robed and Sky-Clad: Jain Sects

Like all major religious traditions, Jainism is divided into different sects. The two largest are the **Shvetambaras,** "those whose garment is white," and the **Digambaras,** "those whose garment is the sky." The Digambara monks, as their name suggests, go about naked, or "sky-clad" (the nuns do not). This practice is intended to help the monks abolish any ties to society. The Shvetambaras use bowls when begging for food and eating; the Digambaras use only their hands.

Beyond these differences in practice, the sects also have certain important doctrinal differences. Although both sects include nuns, only the Shvetambaras, who are generally more liberal, believe that women can attain *kevala.* The Digambaras, who are more conservative contend that a woman must first be reborn as a man before *kevala* can be a possibility. Another difference involves beliefs concerning the physical needs of one who has attained *kevala.* The Shvetambaras believe that once one has attained *kevala,* one continues to need food to go on living; the Digambaras deny this.

The Digambaras also reject the authority of Shvetambara scriptures, and hence the two sects rely on slightly different accounts of the life and teachings of Mahavira and the other *tirthankaras.* Yet despite these differences,

the religious lives of Jains are not determined so much by sectarian distinctions as by the choice between remaining among the laity or becoming an ascetic.

Monks and Nuns: The Ascetic Life

Jains believe that the extreme difficulty of completely purifying the soul can only be achieved through an ascetic life. Because Jainism denies the existence of any deity who can offer divine assistance, monks and nuns must accomplish everything through their own human efforts. The *tirthankaras* are also entirely beyond contact; their souls are in a state of complete liberation from the material world. Their life stories and their teachings are left behind to point the way, but they cannot provide any direct assistance. The only way out of the human predicament is to set off on the arduous path of a wandering ascetic.

Once an individual has reached the minimum age requirement (eight for the more lib-eral Shvetambaras; young adulthood for the more conservative Digambaras), she or he is free to decide to become an ascetic. It is a drastic decision. Family ties are severed almost completely (although Shvetambara nuns are sometimes allowed to be visited by relatives). The initiation ceremony that marks the transition is intentionally designed to resemble a marriage, only in this case one is joined (for life) to the ascetic lifestyle itself. Generally a teacher oversees the ceremony. The young ascetic then remains with that teacher. The ceremony involves several ritual acts: repeating the vows that are binding for all Jain ascetics; receiving an alms bowl (though this does not apply to Digambaras) and a whisk, which is used to clear insects from one's path lest any be stepped on; pulling out five tufts of hair, which signifies renunciation of sexual life; and fasting.

Once initiated, the ascetics own nothing, and receive all their food through begging. Today they tend to wander in groups. To set out alone, as Mahavira did, is now regarded as being especially heroic, and it rarely occurs. During the rainy season, ascetics stay with communities of lay Jains. This is due not only to the difficulty of traveling on soggy paths but also to the increase of life forms on the paths during the rainy season. The principle of nonviolence dictates that the ascetics try to avoid walking during this time.

Five Great Vows

The vows that are binding for all ascetics define their lives in terms of both outward behavior and inward conviction. The **Five Great Vows** are these:

1 Do not injure other life forms.
2. Avoid lying.
3. Do not take what has not been given.
4. Renounce sexual activity.
5. Renounce possession.

Ahimsa

The first vow contains subclauses that indicate the all-encompassing nature of *ahimsa*, the principle of nonviolence. These subclauses require that ascetics be careful when walking and when laying down the begging bowl, that they inspect their food and drink before consuming them, and that they search their mind and their speech so as to avoid negative thoughts and evil words.

The centrality of *ahimsa* can also be seen in the relation of each of the other four vows to this one. For instance, the vow of not taking what is not given means, on the most profound level, not to take the life of another. The fifth vow, renouncing possession, rids oneself of the passion that comes from attachment to possessions; passion, in turn, is thought to be the primary cause of violence.

Despite the rigors of *ahimsa*, Jains acknowledge some important practical concessions. For instance, *ahimsa* is considered to be violated only when the injury is accompanied by lack of care. In other words, intention matters. If a nun is carefully sweeping the path before her and yet steps on a bug, she has not violated the vow of *ahimsa*. The classification of life forms also plays a practical role; injuring a lower life form, such as a microbe, is considered to be less immoral than injuring a higher one. Closely related to this concession is the notion that violent action damages the status of the soul to the same extent as the violence inflicted. Killing a microbe might taint a person's soul with a small amount of matter, while killing a mammal would severely dirty the soul with impurities. Finally, Jain nonviolence does not imply complete pacifism; Jains are generally not required to "turn the other cheek" if violence is done to them, whether by humans or by some other life form. For example, if a tiger attacks a group of ascetics, they are allowed to kill the tiger in self-defense.

Asceticism

Through minimizing the bad effects of *karma*, ascetic practices serve to purify the soul. The close relationship of asceticism and the vow of *ahimsa* can be readily observed in most of these practices. The rigorous vegetarianism of Jains (ascetics and laity alike) is extended well beyond avoidance of meat to include any vegetable or other food thought to contain life forms. For example, fruits with an abundance of seeds are avoided because of the lives residing in the seeds themselves. In keeping with the rules requiring the inspection of food, water, and pathways, the ascetic is not allowed to build fires or to dig in the ground, because such actions almost inevitably injure life forms. Likewise for bathing, which is carefully regulated in part to prevent injuring any microbes residing in the water.

In the midst of these many practical concerns, most of which involve avoidance of injury, the ascetic focuses on certain religious obligations. Along with regular periods of fasting and meditation, these obligations include devotional disciplines. The ascetic offers hymns of praise to the *tirthankaras*, and pays formal acts of respect to his or her teacher. A ritual of standing in silent meditation (usually for forty-eight minutes) helps the ascetic nurture an attitude of benevolence.

5

Imagine you are a young Jain who has decided to become an ascetic. As the day of your initiation ceremony arrives, what aspects of your former life will you miss the most? In what ways might being an ascetic improve your life?

6

Identify some ways in which something similar to the Jain ideal of *ahimsa* is applied in our society. Do you think these forms of nonviolence stem from religious motives or from something else?

Vegetarianism, a Jain Ideal

Although Jainism does not attempt to gain converts, it does promote ahimsa *(nonviolence), in part through advocating the universal practice of vegetarianism. A series of international conferences have given Jain participants opportunities to present their perspectives on vegetarianism and other aspects of* ahimsa, *such as disarmament and world peace. At the Third International Jain Conference in New Delhi, India, one of the presenters was Shri Nitin Mehta of the Young Indian Vegetarians of the United Kingdom. Here is his perspective on vegetarianism:*

Violence against defenceless animals remains the greatest indictment of the human race. Our so-called modern civilization has perfected the most abominable and despicable ways of exploiting the Animal world. At no time in [the] history of [the] world have animals been treated as cruelly as they are today.

Just one example is sufficient to prove my point—as if there was not enough to eat, people in certain parts of the world have developed a love of frog's legs—and until recently India was a willing supplier of this "delicacy." In this terrible situation who else can be expected to take up this fight against barbarism but the followers of Lord Mahavira?

It is well known that in this land of Dharma and Ahimsa, meat eating is spreading fast. Our youths are being brain-washed in to ape-ing all that is negative in [the] western way of life. Jains must mobilise their *resources* and drive back this horror of violence towards defenceless animals. Let the Jains "buy out" those involved in the frog trade and re-employ them usefully somewhere else. Let the whole fish-killing industry be re-employed somewhere else. Let the slaughter of cows be stopped immediately throughout India. I am told that even during the time of Akbar, Jains managed to halt the slaughter of the cow for a certain time.

The meat industry in the West is extremely rich and powerful. Indian people should expect the international "fast-food" chains to come to India very soon—if they are not there already. Money without morals is the motto of many involved in [the] meat trade. The Jain Community should be vigilant and try to ensure that the Indian people do not "get hooked" on Western "fast foods." . . .

Millions of people in the West are giving up their meat diet, and a growing number of them are working day and night to reduce the suffering of animals. I call them the "practising Jains." Many are even sent to prison when they are caught rescuing animals from laboratories where painful experiments are carried out on them. They need our moral and material support which, at present, is not available.

For those who are ignorant of God's Laws, punishment is not as severe as it is to those who know it and break it. The Jains and the Hindus who eat meat are knowingly and willingly breaking God's Laws and so the punishment will be severe.

For our own sake we should re-establish the teachings of Lord Mahavira. India can set the example for the world, but time is running out.

I end with a quotation from Gandhiji [Mahatma Gandhi]:

"The greatness of a nation and its moral progress can be judged by the way it treats its animals." (*Perspectives in Jaina Philosophy and Culture,* pages 45–46)

The central ritual is that of repentance. Performed twice daily in the presence of one's teacher, this ritual involves acknowledgment of wrongdoing, and ends with the recitation of this famous statement from the Jain scripture known as the Avashyaka Sutra: "'I ask pardon from all living creatures. May all creatures pardon me. May I have friendship for all creatures and enmity towards none'" (quoted in Dundas, *The Jains,* page 148).

All Jain ascetics pattern their lives after that of their great role model, Mahavira. Naturally, over the centuries certain variations have become established as normal. Thus very few Jains now practice the act of voluntary starvation undertaken by Mahavira. Occasionally it still occurs, but only rarely. Jains do, however, fervently defend the practice, insisting that it is not a form of suicide because it does not involve passion and violence. Quite to the contrary, Jains hold that voluntary starvation is the avoidance of the act of eating, which prevents any further accumulation of *karma.* It is thus the ideal method of dying.

Jain Laity

Jainism is famous for the asceticism of its monks and nuns, but because they make up only a small percentage of Jains, it is essential also to consider the religious life of the laity. The laity regard the ascetics with honor and respect, acknowledging their authority and tending to their needs. To a limited extent, both groups share an ascetic lifestyle. All Jains are rigorously vegetarian, and fasting is a common ritual among the laity, especially women.

For the most part, though, the Jain layperson is concerned with leading a prosperous and moral life. The ultimate aim of salvation, with its extreme ascetic requirements, is seen as a distant possibility. A good rebirth brought about through improving one's *karma* is the present concern. One of the central aspects of such a lifestyle is the act of giving food (and shelter, during the rainy season) to ascetics. Carefully based on codes for proper conduct, such acts of giving are the primary means of improving the status of a person's *karma.*

7
Jain ascetic practices tend to be directly related to the ideal of *ahimsa.* Make a list of ways in which denying yourself of physical and material things might help to prevent violence toward other life forms.

A Jain worker stands outside a temple in northern India.

8
Carefully consider the Twelve Vows taken by members of the Jain laity. Which strike you as being similar to your own religious and moral principles and practices? Which are foreign to you? Can you think of some benefits that might be derived from following the principles that seem foreign to you?

Jains today are among India's wealthiest citizens, engaging primarily in trade.

Other means include living in accordance with certain vows and performing acts of worship. The Twelve Vows for Jain laity include the Five Lesser Vows (milder parallels to the ascetic vows):

1. Do not intentionally injure a sentient life form (that is, one having two or more senses).
2. Avoid lying.
3. Do not take what has not been given.
4. Avoid unchastity.
5. Avoid greed.

The next three vows supplement the Five Lesser Vows:

6. Avoid excessive travel.
7. Avoid excessive indulgence in things such as food or clothing.
8. Avoid any unnecessary harmful behavior (such as self-indulgence or excessive complaining).

The final four vows prescribe religious practices:

9. Restrict one's activities to a certain place for a period of time.
10. Regularly perform the standing meditation (as required of the ascetics).
11. Fast on certain days.
12. Give to ascetics and to charitable causes.

Jain worship takes on various forms, including annual festivals, pilgrimages to holy places, and acts of devotion before small domestic shrines. The most visible form is the temple-centered worship of images of the *tirthankaras*. Some of India's most striking architectural monuments consist of Jain temples, typically coated in marble, along with gigantic statues of the *tirthankaras*. The most common act of worship involves simply gazing reverently at a statue. Another is the anointing of statues with various ritual substances. Such worship is believed to produce good *karma* due to the attitude of devotion required. In no way does it reflect a belief in the actual assistance of the *tirthankaras,* who are forever beyond contact with the worshipers.

Jains in Today's World

In light of the rigorous asceticism of Jain monks and nuns, one might expect lay Jains not to be involved in the normal economic and social affairs of India. The situation is quite the opposite. Jains today tend to be among the country's wealthiest citizens, and are actively involved in such philanthropic endeavors as environmental and peace movements. Indeed, though they make up only about 2 percent of India's population, contributions by Jains to national philanthropic efforts have been known to exceed 50 percent of the total amounts contributed.

Such involvement is based, like all other aspects of the religion, in Jainism's emphasis on the principle of nonviolence. Through the centuries Jains have avoided traditional forms of agriculture, especially those involving livestock. Instead they have engaged primarily in trade, and this has proven successful. Jains generally do not seek converts, though they do advocate the principle of nonviolence, including the universal practice of vegetarianism. True to this spirit, helping other people through philanthropic efforts also comes naturally. All life forms are, at their most basic level, equal.

Glossary

ahimsa (ah-him'suh; Sanskrit: "nonviolence," "not desiring to harm"). Both the avoidance of violence toward other life forms and an active sense of compassion toward them; a basic principle of Jainism, Hinduism, and Buddhism.

ajiva (uh-jee'vuh). Nonliving components of the Jain universe: space, time, motion, rest, and all forms of matter.

asceticism. The renouncing of physical pleasures and worldly attachments for the sake of spiritual advancement; common in many religious traditions, most notably Jainism.

Digambaras (dig-ahm'buh-ruhz; Sanskrit: "those whose garment is the sky"). The second largest Jain sect, whose monks go about naked so as to help abolish any ties to society; generally more conservative than the Shvetambaras.

Five Great Vows. The vows that are binding for Jain ascetics: do not injure other life forms; avoid lying; do not take what has not been given; renounce sexual activity; renounce possession.

jina (ji'nuh; Sanskrit: "conqueror"). Jain title for one who has "conquered" *samsara;* synonymous with *tirthankara.*

jivas (jee'vuhs; Sanskrit: "souls"). The finite and eternal life-monads, or souls.

karma (Sanskrit: "action"). The moral law of cause and effect of actions; determines the nature of one's reincarnation; for Jainism, purely materialistic, such that all actions involve various forms of matter.

kevala (kay'vuh-luh). The perfect and complete knowledge that is Jain enlightenment; marks the point at which one is free from the damaging effects of *karma* and is liberated from *samsara.*

loka (loh'kah). The Jain universe, often depicted as having the shape of a giant man.

Shvetambaras (shvayt-ahm'buh-ruhz; Sanskrit: "those whose garment is white"). The largest Jain sect, whose monks and nuns wear white robes; generally more liberal than the Digambaras.

tirthankaras (teert-hahn'kuhr-uhs; Sanskrit: "makers of the river crossing"). The Jain spiritual heroes, such as Parshva and Mahavira, who have shown the way to salvation; synonymous with *jinas.*

KASHMIR

Islamabad

Lahore   Amritsar

P U N J A B

Delhi

P A K I S T A N

Karachi

I N D I

6 Sikhism

Understanding Sikhism

Sikhism, though numerically not a large tradition, stands out in the religious landscape of the world. Fewer than twenty million Sikhs exist today, the majority of them living in the state of Punjab in northwestern India. Still, the figure of a bearded Sikh with a colorful turban is a familiar sight to many. Some have seen Sikhs in the movies or on television; others have seen Sikhs in the streets and cafes of their neighborhood. A disproportionately large percentage of Sikhs have emigrated to Western countries. Sikh communities can be found today in most of the large cities of the West.

Sikhs pay homage to Guru Nanak in Lahore, Pakistan.

Together with their physical visibility, Sikhs stand out because of the reputation, both good and bad, of their tradition. Sikhism has long been admired as a religion that tries to reconcile the great differences between Hinduism and Islam, the two religions of medieval India, where Sikhism arose. (Islam, the subject of chapter 14, is a monotheistic religion that has much in common theologically with both Judaism and Christianity.) Sikhism is based primarily in Hinduism, but it also agrees with certain fundamental aspects of Islam. Most significantly, Sikhism is monotheistic. Like Islam, Sikhism insists that there is only one God, creator of the world and sovereign ruler over all. And yet human salvation for Sikhism depends on a mystical union with God, the same sort of experience that is central to most forms of Hinduism.

In light of this reputation for reconciliation, it is ironic that Sikhism has also acquired a reputation for being a militant religion. Over the centuries Sikhs have on occasion engaged in violent conflicts with both Muslims (adherents of Islam) and Hindus. When Sikhism was founded nearly five centuries ago, Muslims ruled northern India. After years of skirmishing, in 1799 Sikh military prowess overcame the Muslims, and an independent Sikh kingdom endured for nearly half a century. Much more recently, Sikh conflicts with Hindus culminated in 1984 with the assassination of Indian Prime Minister Indira Gandhi by members of her Sikh bodyguard. The struggle for Sikh independence that led to that incident continues today, and Sikhism maintains an uncomfortable relationship with India's Hindu majority.

In this chapter we will attempt to understand Sikhism by going beyond mere reputations and outward images. What is the actual place of militancy within the Sikh religion? What is Sikh theology, such that it bridges the seemingly irreconcilable differences between Hinduism and Islam? Why do Sikh men wear turbans and refuse to shave their beards? In answering such questions, we will get to the heart of the matter: Beyond its reputations, beyond what is most visible to the outside world, what is Sikhism?

The Development of Sikhism: From Guru Nanak to the Guru Granth Sahib

By the time Guru Nanak (1469–1539), the founder of Sikhism, had come on the scene, the important role of the guru had long been established within Hinduism. A **guru** is a spiritual teacher. The literal meaning of the term is popularly explained by referring to its parts: *gu* means "darkness," *ru* means "enlightenment." The guru, then, is one who delivers people from the darkness of ignorance to a state of enlightenment.

Guru is an important concept for Sikhism. The word *sikh* literally means "learner" or "disciple"—that is, one who learns and follows the teachings of the Guru. *Guru* itself is used in three slightly different ways. For one, it is the title of Guru Nanak and his successors, the ten historical leaders of Sikhism. It also refers to the sacred text of Sikhism, the **Adi Granth,** which is commonly referred to as the Guru Granth Sahib. Finally, it is used as a name for God, often in the form "True Guru." In each case the guru functions as the revealer of Truth, or God's will. (In Sikhism God lovingly reveals the divine will to humans; God, too, thus functions as Guru.)

The ten historical Gurus of Sikhism were revealers of truth. They are considered to have been linked to one another through sharing the same divine essence. This made them spiritually more adept than ordinary people, but they still were not divine incarnations of God. Hence they are not to be worshiped by Sikhs, though they are greatly revered. Guru Nanak constantly stressed his human limitations, humbly referring to himself as God's slave. All the Gurus were highly prestigious persons. They were revered for their spiritual gifts, and acquired much worldly prestige as well. The Muslim emperors who ruled northern India knew the Gurus personally and tended to respect them, in some cases developing strong friendships with them.

The Life of Guru Nanak

Nanak was born in 1469 in a small village near Lahore (in present-day Pakistan). His family was Hindu and of the warrior caste, though of relatively low economic standing. He married in his teens and had two sons.

The legendary accounts of Nanak's early life emphasize his dissatisfaction with typical forms of employment, and his general rejection of traditional forms of Hindu worship. It seems that he sought out the company of a variety of holy men, both Hindu and Muslim. His spiritual searching led him to a religious outlook that asserted the oneness of God, and the need to move closer to God. This, Nanak believed, could best be accomplished through meditation and singing hymns of praise to God. Eventually Nanak began composing his own hymns with his friend Mardana, a Muslim musician.

According to tradition Nanak was a spiritual leader even at this early stage of his life. He would rise before dawn and bathe in the river, meditate, and then lead others in singing hymns of praise. The crucial experience leading to the founding of Sikhism, though, occurred when Nanak was about thirty years old.

1

Guru Nanak spent about twenty years journeying from place to place and developing his spiritual perspective. In your view, how might travel to distant places and encounters with foreign forms of religion nurture spiritual growth?

Receiving God's Revelation

One morning Nanak did not return from bathing in the river. He was presumed drowned, and yet his body was not found. Three days later Nanak returned to the village, but remained silent for a day. When he finally spoke, he proclaimed:

"There is neither Hindu nor [Muslim] so whose path shall I follow? I shall follow God's path. God is neither Hindu nor [Muslim] and the path which I follow is God's." (Cole and Sambhi, *The Sikhs,* page 9)

When he explained what had happened to him, Nanak said that he had been escorted to the court of God, who gave him a cup of nectar and told him:

"This is the cup of the adoration of God's name. Drink it. I am with you. I bless you and raise you up. Whoever remembers you will enjoy my favour. Go, rejoice in my name and teach others to do so. I have bestowed the gift of my name upon you. Let this be your calling." (Cole and Sambhi, *The Sikhs,* page 10)

The Journeys of Guru Nanak

Deeply moved by this revelation, Guru Nanak spent the next stage of his life, from age thirty to about age fifty, on a series of travels. The traditional account depicts four long journeys, reaching as far as Mecca and Baghdad. Although the distances and remarkable incidents that occurred along the way are probably exaggerated, the general nature of Nanak's travels are made clear. He visited holy sites and encountered a wide variety of religious people. He also proclaimed and practiced his own teachings, sometimes in the face of a hostile audience.

Several incidents during Guru Nanak's travels shed light on the new message he proclaimed. On one occasion, while visiting a famous Hindu shrine, he found himself among *brahmins* throwing water toward the rising sun as an offering to their dead ancestors. Nanak turned and threw water the other way, explaining, "'If you can send water to your dead ancestors in heaven, surely I can send it to my fields in the Punjab'" (quoted in Singh, "Sikhism," *Encyclopedia of Religion,* volume 13, page 316). Such stories illustrate Nanak's consistent rejection of traditional rituals, along with his concern for the practical things in life. The fields of the Punjab needed rain.

Founding the Sikh Community

It is not likely that Guru Nanak intended to create a new religion. Rather, drawing from his revelation experience and years of journeying, he continued proclaiming his own understanding of the truth. In doing so he attracted a large following. At about the age of fifty, Nanak built a new township called Kartarpur (abode of the creator). Here he and his followers formed the first Sikh community, and established the lifestyle that has characterized Sikhism to this day.

Above right: The Golden Temple at Amritsar provides Sikhs with a geographical center.
Right: A priest at the Golden Temple

Guru Nanak erected a special building for worship, therefore providing the model of the **gurdwara,** which is the central structure of any Sikh community. He also built a hostel to accommodate the many visitors to Kartarpur. Nanak, though in most respects a regular member of the community, sat on a special seat when teaching. Followers recognized the nature of the Guru as merely human and yet also spiritually advanced. Today the Adi Granth, Sikhism's sacred text, occupies the role once held by the Gurus. The Adi Granth sits on a special seat within the *gurdwara.*

In 1539, after leading the Kartarpur community for about twenty years, Guru Nanak died. The tradition tells us that the Guru, aware of his approaching death, settled a dispute regarding the proper disposal of his body. In keeping with their respective traditions, his Hindu followers intended to cremate him; the Muslims, to bury him. Nanak instructed them that when he died, the Hindus should lay flowers at his right side, and the Muslims at his left. Those whose flowers were still fresh in the morning were to do as they wished with his body. The Guru covered himself with a sheet in preparation for death. When the sheet was removed, the body was gone, and the flowers on both sides were still fresh. Even with his death, Guru Nanak helped to settle the differences between Hinduism and Islam. (Today Sikhs generally cremate their dead; burial, though, is also permissible.)

Sikhism Evolves: Contributions of Nanak's Successors

Guru Nanak has remained the most prominent and revered of the ten Gurus of Sikhism. Yet his successors, each in his own way, have contributed significantly to the development of the religion.

The contributions of Guru Arjan (Guru from 1581 to 1606), the fifth successor, deserve special mention. For one thing, he compiled the Adi Granth, thus giving Sikhism its sacred scripture. He also constructed the great Temple of God (commonly called the Golden Temple) at Amritsar, which provided the Sikhs with a geographical center. In contrast to Hindu temples, which typically have only one door, Arjan designed the Temple of God with four doors, representing Sikhism's openness to people of all four castes.

2
Although he probably did not intend to found a new religion, Guru Nanak's life and leadership proved so inspirational that his followers united to form Sikhism. Which three or four characteristics of Guru Nanak or events in his life do you think were most responsible for the establishment of Sikhism? Describe how these events or characteristics might have inspired his followers.

The role of the Guru was also forever altered during Arjan's time. He was a worldly leader as well as a spiritual one, on very friendly terms with the great Muslim Emperor Akbar. Eventually, though, Arjan's worldly ambitions resulted in his imprisonment and death by torture. Arjan's involvement in political affairs had a lasting effect on Sikhism, which to this day is very politically oriented. Arjan's political concerns also led to another major change: Sikhism now took on a military dimension. That, too, has endured in various forms to the present day. Before Arjan died he presented his son, his successor, with two swords, representing spiritual and worldly power, saying, "'Let him sit upon the throne and maintain an army to the best of his ability'" (quoted in Singh, "Sikhism," *Encylopedia of Religion,* volume 13, page 319).

3
Guru Arjan initiated a long history of Sikh involvement in political and military affairs. As you consider the world today, what similar relationships between religion and political or military involvement do you observe? Describe two such relationships.

Guru Gobind Singh: The Last of the Ten Gurus

The tenth Guru, Gobind Singh (Guru from 1675 to 1708), is revered as the greatest Guru after Nanak. His strength of character and spiritual adeptness made him a successful and memorable leader. Guru Gobind Singh contributed significantly to the growth of Sikh militarism. He engaged in many armed conflicts during a period when revolts against the Muslims were common, and the Sikhs had a realistic possibility of establishing independent rule.

Most notably, Guru Gobind Singh brought about two innovations that forever changed the structure of Sikhism. He instituted the Khalsa, which would redefine the Sikh community; and he installed the Adi Granth, the sacred scripture, as Guru, which radically altered the nature of leadership.

Instituting the Khalsa, the "Pure Ones"

In the midst of a period of great unrest and violent confrontations between Sikhs and Muslims in 1699, the Sikhs had gathered to

Above: Members of the Khalsa display the five Ks (see page 113).
Right: Sikh teachers review the Adi Granth in its place of honor in the *gurdwara.*

celebrate an annual festival. Guru Gobind Singh perceived a desperate need for loyalty and cohesion among the Sikhs, so he addressed the multitude. Raising his sword, he challenged any Sikh who was willing to die for him to come forward. An uncomfortable silence followed. Then one man stepped out of the crowd and followed Guru Gobind Singh into his tent. The stunned crowd heard the thud of a falling sword. Then the Guru emerged alone, with bloodstained sword in hand. Another man stepped forward, and the process was repeated. Three more men followed in turn. The crowd waited in silence. Eventually Guru Gobind Singh emerged with all five men, alive and well. The bodies of five decapitated goats lay beside them.

These men forever afterward have been known as the beloved five. They were the original members of the **Khalsa,** the "Pure Ones," an order within Sikhism based on the principle of loyalty exhibited by these men. The Guru had the five men initiate him into the Khalsa, and soon thousands more joined. All the men were given the additional name Singh, meaning "lion." All the women were named Kaur, which means "princess." To this day, most Sikhs belong to the Khalsa, and hence bear the name of Singh or Kaur.

Guru Gobind Singh's Successor

Guru Gobind Singh was mortally wounded by an enemy sword. Before dying, he is said to have officially installed the Adi Granth as the next Guru. This was obviously a significant step in the development of Sikhism. Leadership of the Sikh community passed from human hands. From that time forward, the earthly center of the religion has been the scripture.

The Adi Granth: Sikhism's Greatest Attraction

Ever since Guru Gobind Singh installed it as Guru in 1708, the Adi Granth has been regarded just as the Gurus had been. Whereas the Gurus once occupied a special seat amid Sikh disciples, the Adi Granth now occupies the same type of seat in the middle of any place of worship. Whereas the Gurus were once the authorities on religious matters, now Sikhs consult the Adi Granth.

Adi Granth literally means "first book." Sikhs commonly express their reverence for the scripture by referring to it as the Guru Granth Sahib (*sahib,* like guru, is a title of

4
Imagine yourself as a Sikh in a crowd that gathered to celebrate an annual festival in 1699. Suddenly your leader, Guru Gobind Singh, challenges anyone who is willing to die for him to come forward. What are your thoughts as you decide whether to step from the crowd?

respect). Every copy is identical in both script and page number. Partly due to this traditional consistency in form, the Sikhs have been hesitant to translate their scripture from Punjabi. Most English translations are only partial versions.

In addition to its profound theological content, the Adi Granth is remarkable for its poetic and musical brilliance. It is made up of hymns composed by six of the Sikh Gurus, along with several other religious figures of medieval India. Most notable among these others is the poet Kabir (1440 to 1518), whose religious perspective was very similar to that of Guru Nanak.

It is difficult to capture the brilliance of the Adi Granth without hearing it put to music and in its original language of Punjabi. Beyond this, it is worth noting the description of one commentator: "The poetic excellence, the spiritual content, and the haunting, lilting melodies of the hymns of the Adi Granth are Sikhism's greatest attraction to this day" (Singh, "Sikhism," *Encylopedia of Religion,* volume 13, page 319).

Religious Teachings: God, Humans, and Salvation

The religious teachings of Guru Nanak and his successors, as conveyed through the Adi Granth, present a rare combination of monotheism, the predominant theology of Western religions, and mysticism, which is so prevalent among religions of the East. As a result the teachings of Sikhism provide the student of religion with a fascinating subject of inquiry.

In brief, Sikhism teaches that the ultimate purpose of life is to attain complete union with God, and thus to escape *samsara,* the cycle of death and rebirth. (Sikhism adopted, with no major alterations, the concept of *samsara* from Hinduism.) The experience of union with God is eternal bliss, and is indescribable; it is beyond the reach of human thought and language.

Such a brief overview obviously requires some detailed consideration of the nature of God, of the human being, and of the union that leads to salvation.

God: Formless One, Creator, True Guru

Guru Nanak's understanding of the nature of God is the center from which all Sikh teachings evolve. It is fitting that the Adi Granth begins with a concise summary of Sikh theology. This summary is known as the Mool Mantra:

There is one God,
Eternal truth is his name,
Creator of all things and the all-pervading
    spirit.
Fearless and without hatred,
Timeless and formless.
Beyond birth and death,
Self-enlightened.
By the grace of the Guru he is known.
    (Cole and Sambhi, *The Sikhs,* page 69)

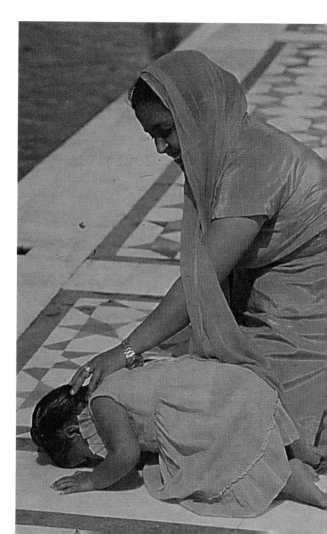

Much of this description should sound familiar to adherents of the monotheistic traditions of the West: Judaism, Christianity, and Islam. God is one, eternal, beyond time, and beyond spatial constraints ("formless"). The latter description is frequently used in the Adi Granth: God is the Formless One, beyond all attributes that humans use to describe reality. The fact that God is referred to as "he" in Sikhism is because of the limitations of language; there is no neuter pronoun in Punjabi. Sikhs actively strive to avoid assigning such human attributes to God.

For reasons beyond the grasp of human comprehension, God decided to create the world and all that is in it, including human beings. In addition to being the Creator, he is also the Preserver and the Destroyer. Sikhism here draws from the important Hindu triad of gods: Brahma (Creator), Vishnu (Preserver), and Shiva (Destroyer). The Sikhs, though, reject Hindu polytheism, insisting that their God is one. These three functions are thus different aspects of the one God.

In God's primary state, to which the Gurus refer when they use the name Formless One, God is distinct from his creation in much the same way that an artist remains distinct from her or his artwork. And yet God dwells within creation—within nature and within human beings. God is thus said to be **immanent,** or indwelling (as opposed to transcendent, or beyond creation, which is the prevalent view of Western theology). In this state of immanence, God is personal and approachable through loving devotion. Because of God's immanence in creation, it is possible for humans to make contact with God and come to know him. To extend our analogy, one can know something of an artist by seeing her or his works. So too can one come to know God through experiencing his creation. Indeed, part of the ongoing purpose of creation is that God, through his loving grace, might reveal the divine self to human beings. It is in this capacity that God is referred to as Guru, for in this manner God delivers humans from darkness to enlightenment.

Sikh Ritual, Sikh Homeland

Bhai Dhanna Singh is a devoted Sikh who is engaged in the struggle to establish a Sikh homeland, to be called Khalistan. In this interview Dhanna Singh describes the ritual of initiation, or baptism, into the Khalsa.

"In the morning on which a Sikh is to be baptized he is to bathe completely, including washing of his hair. And then he has to have the five articles of faith on his body when he comes to the place where the baptism is to happen. Baptism is done in the presence of the Guru Granth Sahib, and in the presence of five beloved ones *[panj piaras]*, who are already there. All of them are wearing the five articles of faith. There we express our desire, standing before those five beloved ones, to be baptized. Then we are asked about certain principles and commitments which a Sikh has to have to be baptized. Those commitments have to be met even if it comes to sacrificing oneself for the value of truth. Then the five beloved ones ask, 'Are you ready for that?' and when it is nodded yes, then the Sikh is baptized. In a bowl [made] of iron, water and some sugar crystals are stirred with the double-edged sword by the five beloved ones, one by one, and as they are stirring they are reciting a hymn. Then those five hymns which are recited during the baptism ceremony become the prayer that the Sikh recites in the morning, afternoon, and night. After the *amrit* [the nectar mixed in the iron bowl] is ready the Sikh goes before the five beloved ones in a special posture, having his right knee on the ground, and one of the beloved ones takes the *amrit* and gives him five drinks, puts the *amrit* on his head five times, and sprinkles it on his eyes five times. All the time the seeker who is being baptized says 'Waheguru ji ka Khalsa, Waheguru ji ki Fateh' (Khalsa belongs to God and Victory belongs to God).

"After a Sikh is baptized he is told that from now on all Sikhs are brothers and sisters and there should not be any distinction on the basis of caste, color, or creed. You are all brothers and sisters, they say, and from now onwards you all belong to one Father, Guru Gobind Singh, and you will all believe in one Almighty God who is formless. Never worship any idols or anything else, never bow before graves or pseudo-saints. Guru Granth Sahib will be your holy Guru. A Sikh must say his prayers every morning and evening. A Sikh is supposed to earn his bread through the sweat of his brow, and give one-tenth of his earnings to the needy and poor. Those are the ideals of Guru Nanak which are reinforced during the baptism ceremony, which reminds the Sikh that his duty is to obey them throughout his life." (Quoted in Mahmood, *Fighting for Faith and Nation,* pages 144–145)

Bhai Dhanna Singh envisions the Sikh homeland, Khalistan, as an ideal state directly based on the following message of Guru Nanak:

"What I enshrine in my soul along with most of the Sikhs is a Khalistan that is an ideal state which the world has not seen before. A place where without distinction of caste, color, or creed all the citizens will have equality. Everybody will have the right to worship as they please. Citizens of Khalistan will be prosperous, and we will contribute toward the promotion of world peace. We will see that the whole world becomes a just place to live for the people of the Lord." . . .

"We don't have any malice or animosity toward the common Hindu or toward anybody. Of course there is no question that some Sikhs will take revenge on the Hindus or other innocent people, but the people who have committed heinous crimes on the Sikhs will be punished not on the street but according to the law of the land. They will be tried in the courts of Khalistan, and after their guilt is proved they will be punished according to the law. . . .

"Guru Nanak's message is based on love, equality, and justice, and as Sikhs we won't be great if we don't live up to this love, equality, and justice. It's our moral duty. We can't be close-minded people. We will have to hear the viewpoints of others." (Page 150)

Humans:
Self-Centered and Bound to *Samsara*

Human beings are especially near to God. Though Sikhism advocates kindness to living things, it also holds that other creatures are here to provide for us. (Unlike Hindus, therefore, Sikhs are not opposed to eating meat.) More important, God dwells within all human beings, and is actively concerned about their spiritual welfare. Humans, however, tend to neglect the need to center their lives on God.

Rather than being God-centered, humans are inclined to be self-centered. Our primary shortcoming is expressed in the Sikh term *haumai,* which is difficult to translate accurately into English. Various possibilities include "self-reliance," "pride," and "egoism." *Haumai* is humans' insistence to make do on our own rather than to acknowledge dependence on God. When life is dominated by *haumai,* its five accompanying vices—lust, anger, greed, attachment, and pride—tend to run rampant. *Haumai* and its vices increase the distance between the person and God.

This distance from God is compounded through ignorance. The world and its charms are mistaken for being the true object of attention. Rather than seeking the Creator, humans in their ignorance seek God's creation. In this manner, creation itself can be a pitfall because it presents the vices with countless attractions. Lust and greed for the world, anger and pride regarding the world, and attachment to the world: these are the evil workings of *haumai.* As long as ignorance, *haumai,* and the other vices persist, humans are destined to remain in *samsara,* the ongoing cycle of death and rebirth.

Salvation: Union with God

Despite the problem of human attachment to the things of creation while ignoring the Creator, God's creation ultimately is good and necessary for salvation. Creation offers us the potential to move closer to God. God's immanence in creation is perceivable in **hukam,** the divine order. Through *hukam* God asserts his will on the world and communicates truth to the human heart. Under these circumstances the quest for salvation is a constant struggle between the self-centeredness to which humans are naturally inclined, and the call to live in accordance with the will of God.

God plays an essential role in determining the outcome of this struggle, for it is through God's grace that humans acquire the potential for perceiving God. Having received God's grace, the task is to respond in loving devotion through meditation on the nature of God. Different terms are used to refer to the object of meditation: *the Name of God, the Word, Truth, the Divine Order.* These are all ways of expressing the immanence of God in creation.

Salvation, in Sikhism, amounts to moving beyond all human shortcomings to a state of complete union with God. This state is eternal, infinitely blissful, and forever beyond the cycle of death and rebirth.

The Religious Life:
Worship, Ritual, and Lifestyle

A primary aspect of Guru Nanak's teachings was the rejection of much of the traditional religious life of Hinduism and Islam. Focused as he was on seeking the indwelling God through meditation on God's nature, Nanak regarded the external forms of religion as useless.

Still, Guru Nanak himself instituted certain practices that amounted to a Sikh way of life. His successors continued to define this way of life, with the most notable innovations coming from the last successor, Guru Gobind Singh. The Khalsa, the order of the Pure Ones, is especially rich in symbolism and ritual practice.

6
A detailed description of Sikh theology requires the use of some difficult terms and concepts (such as *immanent* and *hukam*). Make sure you have read this section carefully ("God: Formless One, Creator, True Guru"). Now, without referring back to the section, describe the Sikh God in your own words.

7
In Sikhism, God's creation can be a hindrance because of human attachment to it, but it is also necessary for salvation because it reveals God's will, or *hukam.* Reflect on your own beliefs regarding creation. How does creation relate to your spiritual life? Is creation completely good? Or does it present some problems?

Sikh Worship in the *Gurdwara*

8
Compare Sikh worship in the *gurdwara* with the forms of worship that are familiar to you. What are the similarities? What are the differences?

Gurdwara literally means "doorway of the Guru." Any building that contains a copy of the Adi Granth is, technically speaking, a *gurdwara,* a Sikh house of worship. Most *gurdwaras* have a characteristic Sikh style, with minarets and chalk-white paint. Aside from the presence of the Adi Granth, which usually sits atop cushions and under a canopy, there are no specific requirements regarding the interior.

The *gurdwara* serves mainly as a place for Sikhs to congregate for worship. This they do frequently, on no particular day of the week. Usually worship takes place in the evening, though the early morning is also a popular time. Worship in the *gurdwara* is preceded by bathing, and consists of singing the Gurus' hymns, reading from the Adi Granth, or telling a story about one of the Gurus. No formal requirements govern the exact nature of worship. It generally ends, though, with a sharing of a special cake made of wheat and honey. This act is symbolic of the unity of the Sikh community.

The sharing of food is central to another Sikh institution. Each *gurdwara* generally has within it a community kitchen, where Sikhs gather at various times to share in the preparation and consumption of a meal. Again, this ritual symbolizes the unity of the community, regardless of the caste status of its individual members. It also provides food for the needy.

The Khalsa:
Entry into the Community of Pure Ones

Perhaps the most vivid ritual of Sikhism is the ceremony of initiation into the Khalsa. The initiate should be at least fourteen years old. He or she must possess the "Five Ks" (so named because of the Punjabi terms for these requirements, each of which begins with a *k*): uncut hair, a comb, a steel wrist guard, a sword or knife, and a pair of shorts. Although it is difficult to determine the precise symbolism of each of the Five Ks, their primary purpose is to strengthen Sikh identity.

The ritual is performed by five people, recalling the original initiation of Guru Gobind Singh by the beloved five. The Adi Granth is opened, and one of the five explains the basic principles of Sikhism to the initiates, who are asked if they are willing to accept them. The initiates are then served nectar made from water and sugar, which has been mixed in an iron kettle and stirred with a two-edged sword. The Mool Mantra of the Adi Granth is recited, and the initiates are instructed about the ethical requirements of the Khalsa. These include prohibitions against adultery, the cutting of one's hair, and the use of tobacco. The initiation ends with the sharing of honey cake.

Like most aspects of Sikh religious life, the Khalsa strengthens the social identity of the community. Although it is not required that one belong to the Khalsa, the majority of Sikhs today choose to be members.

9

The Five Ks of the Sikh Khalsa serve primarily to strengthen Sikh identity. As you consider your own religious tradition or the traditions of people around you, what similar sorts of symbols do you observe? How do you think these symbols serve to strengthen the sense of identity among those belonging to that religion?

Sikhism   113

Work, Worship, and Charity: Sikhism's True Identity

Let us once again consider the well-known figure of the Sikh with colorful turban and beard. As one of the Five Ks, we can now recognize the beard as a sign of membership in the Khalsa, and hence as a symbol of Sikh identity. The turban, the wearing of which is almost universal among male Sikhs, is another important symbol of Sikh identity. In places like the United Kingdom, motorcycle helmet laws have even been modified to suit the insistence of Sikhs regarding this custom.

That the turban causes Sikhs to stand out in the world is no accident, nor is it regretted. Such ease of recognition nurtures social identity, a hallmark of Sikhism. But for such a relatively small religious community to be so easily recognized also makes it vulnerable to being misunderstood by outsiders. Sikhism has the reputation of being militant, which has sometimes led to discrimination against law-abiding Sikhs. On the other hand, as mentioned earlier, Sikhism is famous for providing a degree of reconciliation between Hinduism and Islam.

Both of these reputations are partially accurate. But from the Sikh point of view, other aspects of their tradition are primary. Though Sikhism provides a theology that reconciles Hinduism and Islam, for Sikhs themselves it is the uniqueness, coherence, and effectiveness of their own path to God that is most important. As for the reputation for being militant, yes, this is part of the Sikh tradition (just as it is part of virtually every other religious tradition). But the militant aspect is secondary to the Sikh commitment to justice. From its beginnings, Sikhism has been on the side of religious freedom and justice for oppressed people. Justice is carried out partly through the regular donation of one-tenth of one's income to charitable causes.

The three guiding principles of Sikh life are work, worship, and charity. As a tradition that effectively provides for the spiritual nourishment of the individual, while at the same time nurturing material and social welfare, Sikhism does indeed deserve to stand out on the religious landscape of the world.

Glossary

Adi Granth (ah'dee gruhnth; Punjabi: "first book"). Sikhism's most important sacred text and, since it was installed as Guru in 1708, Sikhism's earthly center and authority; also called the Guru Granth Sahib.

gurdwara (goor'dwah-ruh; Punjabi: "doorway of the Guru"). A special building for Sikh worship that houses a copy of the Adi Granth and is the central structure of any Sikh community.

guru (goo'roo). A spiritual teacher and revealer of truth, common to Hinduism, Sikhism, and some forms of Buddhism. When the word *Guru* is capitalized, it refers to the ten historical leaders of Sikhism, to the sacred text (the Guru Granth Sahib, or Adi Granth), and to God (often as True Guru).

haumai (how'may; Punjabi: "self-reliance," "pride," or "egoism"). The human inclination toward being self-centered rather than God-centered, which increases the distance between the individual and God.

hukam (huh'kahm). The divine order of the universe.

immanent. Indwelling; Sikh theology maintains that God dwells within nature and within human beings in such a way that God is personal and approachable through worship.

Khalsa (khal'sah; Punjabi: "pure ones"). An order within Sikhism to which the majority of Sikhs belong, founded by Guru Gobind Singh in 1699.

PART 3
East Asia

大成殿

MONGOLIA

NORTH KOREA

SOUTH KOREA

Beijing

Yellow

LU

Shanghai

CHINA

Yangtze

Chongqing

TAIWAN

Guangzhou

INDIA

BURMA

LAOS

THAILAND

VIETNAM

7 Confucianism

The Ethical Foundation of East Asia

Religion in the lands of East Asia (China, Japan, and Korea) has typically involved a variety of traditions, including various strands of folk tradition. The great traditions of Confucianism, Taoism, Buddhism, and, in Japan, Shinto have formed an interwoven fabric. This fabric, rather than any one particular tradition, has typically provided for the religion of the individual. As we investigate each of the great traditions forming this fabric, it is therefore crucial to understand them as parts of a larger whole.

Throughout this fabric of East Asian religion, the threads of Confucianism show prominently. For centuries Confucianism has provided the ethical foundation of East Asia, defining proper behavior from early childhood to death. In the words of one scholar, "East Asians may profess themselves to be Shintoists, Taoists, Buddhists, Muslims, or Christians, but seldom do they cease to be Confucians" (Tu Wei-ming, "Confucianism," *Our Religions,* page 149).

As a religion that features ethics, or moral values and principles, Confucianism naturally focuses on human relationships. How should individuals behave so that families might flourish, governments may thrive, and humanity as a whole might progress toward an ever more healthy and happy state? Confucianism's answers are derived from a central project: learning to be human. When an individual learns more deeply what it is to be human, then families, governments, and humanity itself are improved. At the same time, the individual moves closer to realizing the full potential of human happiness.

Great Master K'ung: The Life and Legacy of Confucius

Confucianism got its start, appropriately, with China's "First Teacher," Confucius (551 to 479 B.C.E.). His steadfast eagerness to learn to be human, and his expertise at teaching others his views, have defined the lifestyle of East Asia for over two thousand years. This vast influence, affecting about one-fourth of the world's population, makes Confucius one of the most influential people ever to have lived.

Confucius

K'ung Fu-tzu (Master K'ung) is better known throughout the English-speaking world as Confucius (from an attempt to render his name in Latin). He was born in eastern China in 551 B.C.E. The few details that we know of his life hardly suggest the eventual extent of his influence worldwide. On the surface, in fact, Confucius appears to have been a failure.

Life and Career

Confucius's family, though of noble lineage, was poor. His father died while Confucius was still a baby, leaving his mother to attend to his early education. For this she became a role model through the centuries for Chinese mothers, who generally are the primary nurturers of their children.

Confucius was an exceptional student, and was famously eager to learn. Among his favorite subjects were poetry and history. As a young man, he began a career of teaching others, and quickly gained a following of loyal disciples. Along with teaching the literary and historical classics from the past, Confucius strove to apply the lessons of the ancients to the problems of his own day, including the problem of government.

And so, at about age fifty, Confucius became a public official, securing a minor cabinet position with the Duke of Lu, his home state. He apparently grew frustrated with his inability to apply his ideas in Lu, and so he soon left. For the next thirteen years, Confucius wandered from state to state, trying to put his theories into practice. Eventually he gave up and returned to Lu to devote his time to teaching and study. He died in 479 B.C.E., an apparent failure. History would prove otherwise.

Eager Student, Diligent Teacher: Confucius's Character

Confucius's vast influence obviously stems from something beyond his meager accomplishments as a government official. One major factor is the strength of his character. That Confucius is remembered at all is due to the enormous influence he had on his disciples. It was they who, probably within a generation after Confucius's death, assembled his many teachings into the collection known as the **Analects.** Learned during childhood by countless Chinese and other East Asians, the sayings in the Analects are the most important source we have for the actual teachings of Confucius.

Confucius's character shines through in the Analects. Modest regarding his own talents and abilities, yet highly inspirational to his disciples, Confucius seems most of all to have been an eager student and diligent teacher, who lived a full and joyful life. That he is usually referred to simply as "the Master" further illustrates how deeply his disciples respected him.

The Master said, "How dare I claim to be a sage or a benevolent man? Perhaps it might be said of me that I learn without flagging and teach without growing weary." (Analects 7.34)

The Master is cordial yet stern, awe-inspiring yet not fierce, and respectful yet at ease. (Analects 7.38)

A disciple of Confucius once found himself at a loss to describe the Master. Upon hearing of the incident, Confucius said to his disciple:

"Why did you not simply say something to this effect: he is the sort of man who forgets to eat when he tries to solve a problem that has been driving him to distraction, who is so full of joy that he forgets his worries and who does not notice the onset of old age?" (Analects 7.19)

China's Problems and Confucius's Solutions

Along with Confucius's strength of character, another reason for his eventual influence is the brilliance of his ideas. Though Confucius's ideas were not accepted initially, history has shown that they provided potent solutions for China's problems.

Even from Confucius's vantage point in the sixth century B.C.E., China was an ancient civilization with a glorious past. But things had begun to decline rapidly. States were warring against one another. Rulers were oppressing their subjects. Society was falling into disarray.

At roughly the same time that Confucius was teaching, others were setting forth theories as solutions to China's problems. The Legalists advocated a stern rule of law enforced by very severe punishments. The Mohists, following the lead of their founder, Mo Tzu (480 to 390 B.C.E.), taught universal love, even toward one's enemies. (Mo Tzu's teachings on love are very similar to Jesus' teaching to love one's neighbors as one's self.) The Taoists (the

subject of the next chapter) placed more emphasis on the individual than on society. They believed that the path to human happiness lay in the individualistic pursuit of harmony with nature.

Confucius took a markedly different approach. Deeply dedicated to restoring society, he embraced a vision of humanity that centered on human relationships. He thus differed greatly from the individualistic Taoists. Though he advocated the need to love one another, Confucius did not go as far as the Mohists. He argued that justice, not love, should be the primary response when dealing with an enemy. As for the Legalists, Confucius regarded punishment as an ineffective means of nurturing lasting improvement in people. Rather than being punished for making mistakes, people should be inspired by good examples.

Confucius derived his examples from the past, from rulers and sages of ancient times who so perfectly embodied the ethical principles on which a healthy society must be based. Confucius was therefore more concerned with transmitting traditional ways than with inventing new theories: "'I transmit but do not innovate; I am truthful in what I say and devoted to antiquity'" (Analects 7.1).

One important aspect of Chinese tradition that Confucius helped to transmit was the worship of ancestors. According to archaeological evidence, for centuries before Confucius's time the Chinese had believed that their deceased ancestors could influence the welfare of the living, for good and for ill. Through regular offerings of prayer and sacrifice, ancestor worship assured that the dead were satisfied.

Confucius had little to say about life after death, but he advocated the continuation of ancestor worship as part of the traditional rites of the people:

"When your parents are alive, comply with the rites in serving them; when they die, comply with the rites in burying them; comply with the rites in sacrificing to them." (Analects 2.5)

By transmitting traditions such as ancestor worship, Confucius sought to provide the fundamental ethical ideas with which to improve Chinese society. He believed that the power of tradition would ensure their acceptance. And though he claimed he was merely a transmitter, Confucius made profound contributions in developing these ideas. We will investigate his contributions in a later section of this chapter.

Confucius's Legacy: The Confucian Tradition

The enduring reputation of Confucius's character and the brilliant content of his teachings continued to inspire new generations of disciples. All of them respectfully sought to understand the Master's original meaning in the teachings. Inevitably, however, different followers offered differing interpretations, some with brilliant innovations of their own. It would thus be a mistake simply to equate Confucianism with the teachings of Confucius.

One such brilliant innovator was Mencius (390 to 305 B.C.E.), who is revered as the second founder of Confucianism. He claimed that human beings are naturally good, and that evil actions are done in violation of our true nature. This eventually became accepted as a basic teaching of Confucianism. Mencius's teachings are set forth with clarity and sophistication in the **Book of Mencius,** one of the central texts of Confucianism.

For a few centuries, Confucianism was confined to philosophers and teachers like Mencius, with hardly any effect on society at large. Gradually these philosophers began to have an influence on government officials. And in 136 B.C.E., the state established a school of Confucian scholars. Soon anyone training to become an official was required to learn the Confucian texts. Since that time, almost without interruption until the beginning of the twentieth century, a formal Chinese education has included a thorough study of Confucian teachings.

An important chapter in the continuing saga of Confucianism's influence is the philosophical tradition known as **Neo-Confucianism.** Arising around 1000 C.E., Neo-Confucianism was largely a response to the challenges facing Confucianism from the popular religions of Taoism and Buddhism. Its most famous figure, and one of the world's greatest philosophers, is Chu Hsi (1130 to 1200). Chu Hsi's

2
Confucius believed strongly in the power of tradition as a means of improving Chinese society, and history has often proved him correct. In our society does the power of tradition play a part in improving life? Or does tradition get in the way of improvement?

A Chinese painting from the nineteenth century depicts Confucius and his disciples.

The Teacher's Place

The Confucian emphasis on learning has always implied a special respect for teachers. In this excerpt from A Chinese Childhood, *by Chiang Yee, the author tells of his gratitude toward his teacher, despite the teacher's sometimes "tyrannical" ways.*

Our teacher held a very high position in our family life in my childhood. A Chinese proverb, *I-jih-ch'ih-Ssu, Chung-sheng-wei-fu,* states that he who becomes the teacher of a child for one day is the "father" of that child's lifetime. This proverb always rang in my ears when I listened to the serious talk of my elders. In the middle of our ancestral shrine we had a big red tablet painted with five golden characters representing Heaven, Earth, Nation, Parents and Teacher. . . . The position of "Teacher" was the fifth and last, but it stood next to that of "Parents." Twice a month, on the first day and fifteenth, one of my elders burned incense in front of the shrine and knelt down to pay respect on behalf of the family. . . .

The importance attached to the teacher's position is testified to by the fact that he stood side by side with our parents on these occasions. Confucius taught that children should be filial to their parents and respect their elders. I do not know whether the idea of setting up the tablet to Heaven, Earth, Nation, Parents and Teacher originated with him or not. If it did, he must have been an odd man—afraid, perhaps, that his own disciples might not respect him as highly as he expected!

Theoretically speaking, young people in China have always gone in awe of their elders. In my house I felt there were already enough elders to be respected without a most tyrannical teacher as well. . . .

I do not know why my elders always gave way to the teacher's tyranny. Whenever they saw him look distressed or annoyed they would ask us whether any of us had offended him or had not been working

well. Then they would apologize to him for us and endeavour to soothe him. This made us very careful of our behaviour in the family school, and also encouraged the teacher to be more tyrannical than ever. The elders seemed to think that he could not be too tyrannical. They often told us that without strict training in youth, one could not expect to achieve anything in later life. They also said that parents could not train their own children well, being influenced by affection for them: we had, therefore, to have a good teacher; and they went on to emphasize how fortunate we were to have *this* good teacher. . . . (Pages 79–80)

The teacher adopted different methods for each of us, according to our age and mentality. There were two sets of simple books, used for both girls and boys, composed of lines of three characters and lines of four characters with rhymes. They were universally used in China for teaching children to recognize the characters. We all learned them by heart without necessarily knowing their meaning. Then we began to read the "Four Books," with Confucius' Analects as the first book. We had to be proficient in each book before we could proceed to the next, so some of us got on faster than others. At first we were taught only to read and recite them over and over again. We could not question the "by rote" method and in those days we did not think of doing so. When we could recite the whole four books without a mistake the teacher explained the meaning of them to us passage by passage for an hour or two every day. Then we began to read the commentaries on each book by well-known Confucian scholars. . . . (Page 83)

How strict [our teacher] was! I do not agree with his way of teaching, but I am glad that I was trained under his tyrannical rule, for otherwise I might not remember Confucius' classics as well as I do. (Page 86)

interpretations have since then defined the nature of Confucianism. Among his other contributions, Chu Hsi determined the "Four Books" from among the Confucian texts that to this day are considered most important. Along with the Analects and the Book of Mencius, these include The Great Learning and The Doctrine of the Mean. We shall be drawing from all of the Four Books throughout our investigation of Confucian ideas.

Learning to Be Human: Confucianism's Central Project

The sayings in the Analects clearly convey Confucius's deep commitment to learning:

The Master said, "In a hamlet of ten households, there are bound to be those who are my equal in doing their best for others and in being trustworthy in what they say, but they are unlikely to be as eager to learn as I am." (5.28)

Along with being steadfast in his own eagerness to learn, Confucius expected no less of his students:

The Master said, "I never enlighten anyone who has not been driven to distraction by trying to understand a difficulty or who has not gone into a frenzy trying to put his ideas into words." (Analects 7.8)

Confucius's deep commitment to learning arose from his understanding of the nature of learning itself. Rather than being a mere gathering of information, learning for Confucius provided a means of discovering *what it is to be human*. Only through learning to be human can one possibly mature toward greater well-being. In a famous statement from the Analects, Confucius charts the ongoing nature of his maturation through ever deepening degrees of learning:

Confucius said, "At fifteen my mind was set on learning. At thirty my character had been formed. At forty I had no more perplexities. At fifty I knew the Mandate of Heaven. At sixty I was at ease with whatever I heard. At seventy I could follow my heart's desire without transgressing moral principles." (2.4)

In the rest of this chapter, we will try to make sense of Confucius's discoveries as he advanced in his lifelong project of learning. We begin in the present section by investigating his perspective on specific qualities of being human: what it is to be mature, what the pinnacle of human virtue is, how best to behave, how to be a cultured person, and how to govern. First let us consider a concept basic to all forms of Chinese religion: the Tao.

Tao: The "Way" of Chinese Philosophy

The Taoist religious tradition, as the name suggests, elaborates extensively on the meaning of Tao; we will therefore devote more time to it in the next chapter. However, Tao is also of basic significance for Confucianism.

Tao literally means "way." In Confucianism Tao generally refers to the moral order that permeates the universe, and is thus the Way that should be followed. If one can learn to know the universal Way, then one can come into harmony with it. For Confucius, learning to know the Tao was of fundamental importance: "'He has not lived in vain who dies the day he is told about the Way'" (Analects 4.8).

The Human Ideal: *Chun-tzu*

The Analects devotes more than eighty passages to describing the ideal human being, the **chun-tzu.** A *chun-tzu* is a person with perfect moral character, a "mature person" or "gentleman." Ancient China was a patriarchal society, organized according to male lines of descent, and Confucius seems to have assumed that only a man could become a *chun-tzu*. "Gentleman" is therefore an accurate translation, though in principle the concept of the ideal human certainly can be applied to all, male and female.

3
Carefully reread Confucius's words regarding his own lifelong process of learning (Analects 2.4). In China these words have long served as a model for lifelong learning. Are people in Western society encouraged to continue to learn more and more deeply as they grow older? Discuss similarities and differences between these societies' attitudes toward learning.

Along with being patriarchal, the concept of the *chun-tzu* is somewhat elitist. Confucius frequently contrasts the gentleman with the "small man," assuming all along that it is the gentleman's role to lead, the small man's role to follow, and so forth. Yet Confucius must also be acknowledged for making a great contribution toward social equality. Until his teachings took hold, the status of gentleman, or noble, was simply acquired at birth if a man's father happened to be of the nobility. According to Confucius, one becomes a gentleman through steadfast learning. Once Confucianism was established as the official tradition, nobility was bestowed by merit rather than by birth.

Confucius's numerous references to the *chun-tzu* describe a person with such abundant virtues that he is able to contribute to the improvement of society. Like all Confucian ideals, becoming a *chun-tzu* depends first of all on learning.

The Master said, "The gentleman seeks neither a full belly nor a comfortable home. He is quick in action but cautious in speech. He goes to men possessed of the Way to be put right. Such a man can be described as eager to learn." (Analects 1.14)

The Master said of Tzu-ch'an that he had the way of the gentleman on four counts: he was respectful in the manner he conducted himself; he was reverent in the service of his lord; in caring for the common people, he was generous and, in employing their services, he was just. (Analects 5.16)

The Supreme Virtue: *Jen*

Confucianism advocates several virtues. Wisdom, courage, trustworthiness, reverence, uprightness—all these are encouraged in the Analects and elsewhere. But the supreme virtue is **jen**. *Jen* is often translated as "goodness," "love," or "benevolence." In passages like the following, Confucius emphasizes the fundamental importance of *jen*:

Elderly Confucian men converse during a ceremony at the Sun Kyung Kwan Temple in Korea.
Far right: Lanterns decorate a Confucian temple in Nanjing, China.

"If a man sets his heart on benevolence, he will be free from evil." (Analects 4.4)

"If the gentleman forsakes benevolence, in what way can he make a name for himself? The gentleman never deserts benevolence, not even for as long as it takes to eat a meal. If he hurries and stumbles one may be sure that it is in benevolence that he does so." (Analects 4.5)

We gain a more precise understanding of *jen* when we note its two primary components: doing one's best, and reciprocity (*shu* in Chinese).

Fan Ch'ih asked about benevolence. The Master said, ". . . When dealing with others do your best." (Analects 13.19)

Tzu-kung asked, "Is there a single word which can be a guide to conduct throughout one's life?" The Master said, "It is perhaps the word *'shu.'* Do not impose on others what you yourself do not desire." (Analects 15.24)

The notion of **shu** is especially intriguing, for it is essentially identical to the reciprocity taught by the Golden Rule—"Do unto others as you would have them do unto you"—a central ethical teaching in Judaism and Christianity. Yet Confucianism does not go as far as Christianity, which teaches, "Love your enemies." For Confucius, reciprocity works along these lines:

Someone said, "What do you think of repaying hatred with virtue?" Confucius said, "In that case what are you going to repay virtue with? Rather, repay hatred with uprightness and repay virtue with virtue." (Analects 14.36)

4
Confucius taught that one becomes a *chun-tzu*—a person of perfect moral character—through steadfast learning. Explore the relationship between learning and the development of moral character. Focus on agreeing or disagreeing with this statement: It is possible to "learn" to be a better person.

5
Compare the Confucian doctrine of *shu,* or reciprocity, with the Christian teaching to love one's enemies.

The importance of *jen* cannot be overemphasized. It is a perfect form of benevolence—doing one's best to treat others as one would wish to be treated. It is the central component of a perfect moral perspective.

Proper Behavior as Sacred Ritual: *Li*

Confucianism's emphasis on human relationships goes hand in hand with a deep concern for proper behavior. Behaving properly is as important as having the right moral perspective, and the two are closely related. The individual who demonstrates the right moral perspective will naturally behave properly.

rules of behavior that constitute *li.* This vast store of traditional rules sets forth a complete guide to personal behavior.

The Analects contains detailed accounts of Confucius's attention to *li.* Note how carefully he regulated his own behavior, as if performing an ongoing ritual:

In the local community, Confucius was submissive and seemed to be inarticulate. In the ancestral temple and at court, though fluent, he did not speak lightly.

At court, when speaking with Counsellors of lower rank he was affable; when speaking with Counsellors of upper rank, he was

A person bows before a Confucian temple in Ch'u-Fou, China, the birthplace of Confucius. *Right:* A student practices the art of calligraphy.

The Chinese term for proper behavior is **li.** *Li* has two definitions. It means "rite," or sacred ritual, and "propriety," behaving properly given the situation at hand. Confucianism combines both definitions of *li.* Behaving properly, even when performing apparently mundane routines, carries at all times the significance of a sacred ritual. Because he always admired the ancient ways, Confucius looked to China's past in determining the

frank though respectful. In the presence of his lord, his bearing, though respectful, was composed.

When he was summoned by his lord to act as usher, his face took on a serious expression and his step became brisk. When he bowed to his colleagues, stretching out his hands to the left or to the right, his robes followed his movements without being disarranged. (Analects 10.1–3)

This account illustrates a significant aspect of *li:* proper behavior is largely dependent on one's place in society. Confucians refer to this as the rectification of names. He who is called emperor ought to behave in a manner befitting of the name emperor; counselors ought to behave as proper counselors, and so on for every level of society. The rectification of names helps define the nature of human relationships within Confucian society.

A Human Being Is Cultured: *Wen*

Along with the ritualized rules of behavior that constitute *li,* learning to be human involves acquiring skills of behavior that are broadly categorized as **wen,** the cultural arts. Mainly these are the arts of poetry and music, for which Confucius had deep admiration. He frequently refers to his love of music and to the *Book of Odes,* an anthology of Chinese poetry that preserved works from centuries before Confucius's time. But *wen* also includes other skills, of which Confucius is said to have been a master: archery, charioteering, calligraphy, and mathematics.

The cultural arts play a vital role in assuring unity and continuity in society. For Confucianism the arts accomplished this and much more. Confucius praised art not only for its beauty but also for its moral goodness. Becoming a cultured human being—a person who appreciates and participates in the arts and skills that make up *wen*—is, in actuality, a moral education. Individuals become better people through contact with the cultural arts, and society, in turn, is improved.

Leading by Power of Moral Example: *Te*

Learning to be human nurtures people's well-being. It also helps them develop the ability to lead others. Good government is a primary goal of Confucianism, as we have seen in Confucius's own attempt to put his theories into practice in government service.

Good government comes about through the cultivation of *te.* **Te** means "virtue" or, more specifically, "virtue as shown through the power of example." It is one of the attributes of the gentleman *(chun-tzu),* and it is both the product of a life of learning and the means of educating society through example. Confucius remarks that *te* is extremely potent, with a sort of gravitational pull:

"A ruler who governs his state by virtue is like the north polar star, which remains in its place while all the other stars revolve around it." (Analects 2.1)

Confucius deemed *te* a far more effective tool of leadership than laws and punishments. Laws and punishments may restrict bad behavior for the short term, but *te* has the long-term effect of nurturing moral conscience, which Confucius refers to in this passage as "shame":

"Guide them by edicts, keep them in line with punishments, and the common people

6

According to Confucianism, the cultural arts, or *wen,* play an important role in assuring the unity and continuity of East Asian society. Explore the role of the cultural arts in our society. First identify several art forms that you consider most relevant. Then explain how these art forms help maintain the unity and continuity of our society.

Confucius believed that *te,* virtue as shown through the power of example, is a more lasting means of improving society than mere punishment of bad behavior. If you agree with Confucius, reflect on two situations you have observed in which the power of moral example has proved to be more effective than punishing bad behavior. If you disagree with him, reflect on two situations in which punishment has been more effective than moral example.

will stay out of trouble but will have no sense of shame. Guide them by virtue, keep them in line with the rites, and they will, besides having a sense of shame, reform themselves." (Analects 2.3)

Self, Family, Nation, Heaven: Confucian Harmony

The men of old who wished to make their virtue shine throughout the world first put in order their own states. In order to put in order their own states they first regulated their own families; in order to regulate their own families they first disciplined their own selves. (The Great Learning, quoted in Thompson, *Chinese Religion,* page 12)

This famous passage from The Great Learning (one of the Four Books of the Confucian canon) illustrates the Confucian vision of the grand harmony among human relationships.

The self, the family, the nation, and the entire world of humanity are all intimately related to one another. The health of each depends on the others. The role of relationships in the vision of harmony is emphasized by the doctrine of the **Five Constant Relationships.** This doctrine is summarized in the Book of Mencius as consisting of "love between father and son, duty between ruler and subject, distinction between husband and wife, precedence of the old over the young, and faith between friends" (Book 3, part A).

Self

Confucianism has a unique understanding of selfhood. Rather than emphasizing the individuality of the self, Confucianism regards the self first and foremost as a center of human relationships. This is readily observed in the doctrine of the Five Constant Relationships. Self-identity is determined primarily by one's status as parent or child, ruler or subject, and so on.

In this Japanese print entitled *The Moon of the Filial Son,* Ono no Takamura, a model of the filial son, collects firewood on a hillside but realizes his mother needs him in the cottage below.

The Confucian self, furthermore, is thought to be constantly changing. Through learning to be human, one continues to grow, attaining deeper and more fulfilling levels of maturity. The individual is thus engaged in an ongoing process of self-cultivation.

Learning to be human takes place with the world as classroom. The self is not withdrawn from the world, but engaged in it. And as the self is cultivated, society is improved. The realm of society that receives foremost attention from every Confucian is the family.

Family

The significance of the family in Chinese religion can hardly be overemphasized. Confucianism emerged at a time when the family was already the center of Chinese society, and Confucianism has fortified this significance. Three of the Five Constant Relationships involve family. The following passage, taken from a Confucian classic on *li* (rites and propriety), elaborates on these relationships:

"The father is merciful, the son filial; the elder brother is good, the younger brother submissive; the husband is upright, the wife complaisant; the adult is kind, the child obedient." (*Records of Rituals,* quoted in Thompson, *Chinese Religion,* page 11)

The primary virtue in relating to one's elders is to be "filial," or to act in a way suitable to a son or daughter. This virtue plays a central role in Confucianism, extending to the subject-ruler relationship as well. In the Analects, Confucius pays particular attention to being filial, pointing out that being filial is even more important than correcting one's parents when they are wrong:

"In serving your father and mother you ought to dissuade them from doing wrong in the gentlest way. If you see your advice being ignored, you should not become disobedient but remain reverent. You should not complain even if in so doing you wear yourself out." (Analects 4.18)

One's relationships with family members are defined throughout life in Confucian society. In theory this provides a clear sense of place and of purpose. In practice it is subject to abuse. The "complaisant" wife, obligated to consent to her husband's wishes, could fall victim to a domineering husband if he abandoned his duty to be "upright." The "obedient" child could be unjustly treated, and so on. Confucians themselves are fully aware of such potential abuse, and have, especially lately, maintained a critical perspective on their own system.

In any event, one aspect of the Confucian family is prominent—deep respect for elders. The older people get, the more they are respected. Contemporary Western society, which tends to regard old age negatively, could perhaps learn from Confucianism on this point. Rather than having to dread the aging process, Confucians can look forward to increased social standing and to greater opportunities to share the wisdom that they, through their lifelong learning, have acquired.

Nation

Good government has always been of central concern to Confucian thought. The nation is thought of as being one great family. Within the grand harmony of human relationships, the ruler plays a decisive role. The ruler is a gentleman *(chun-tzu),* one who has acquired the necessary moral perfection so that he might lead by power of example *(te).* The subjects, in turn, are to be filial toward their ruler. In its entirety, Confucian government offers the best for all, ensuring the happiness of the people and the ongoing improvement of society.

Chi K'ang Tzu asked Confucius about government, saying, "What would you think if, in order to move closer to those who possess the Way, I were to kill those who do not follow the Way?"

Confucius answered, "In administering your government, what need is there for you to kill? Just desire the good yourself and the

8
Consider carefully the two passages quoted in the text about the relationships within the Confucian family. Critique this structure. Be sure to comment on both the Five Constant Relationships and the virtue of being filial. Is this a good way of structuring family relationships? Is there a potential for abusing this structure?

9
In Chinese society, the older people get, the more deeply respected they are. Answer the following questions:

- What differences do you see between the Confucian attitude toward aging and the attitudes of North American society?
- In both societies, what are the consequences for the elderly and for the rest of society?
- Which perspective on aging do you prefer?

common people will be good. The virtue of the gentleman is like wind; the virtue of the small man is like grass. Let the wind blow over the grass and it is sure to bend." (Analects 12.19)

The harmonious relationship between the government and individuals can be further observed in the following passage. Confucius, who at the time of this remark was not officially working within the government, explained that individuals and governments nurture each other:

Someone said to Confucius, "Why do you not take part in government?"

The Master said, "The *Book of History* says, 'Oh! Simply by being a good son and friendly to his brothers a man can exert an influence upon government.' In so doing a man is, in fact, taking part in government. How can there be any question of his having actively to 'take part in government'?" (Analects 2.21)

Heaven

Confucianism seems to say little regarding Heaven or other forms of divinity, leading some to wonder whether it is actually a religion at all. Confucius himself seems to have had little to say on such matters, as some passages in the Analects indicate:

Chi-lu asked how the spirits of the dead and the gods should be served. The Master said, "You are not able even to serve man. How can you serve the spirits?"

"May I ask about death?"

"You do not understand even life. How can you understand death?" (11.12)

Having little to say regarding typically religious concepts, however, is not the same thing as having no interest in them. As the following passages show, Confucius clearly understood Heaven to be a vital aspect of reality:

The Master said, "Heaven is author of the virtue that is in me." (Analects 7.23)

"When you have offended against Heaven, there is nowhere you can turn to in your prayers." (Analects 3.13)

"If I am understood at all, it is, perhaps, by Heaven." (Analects 14.35)

We should also recall Confucius's famous statement, cited earlier in this chapter, in which he declares, "'At fifty I knew the Mandate of Heaven'" (Analects 2.4).

During the time of Confucius, Heaven was in fact China's principal deity. For Confucius, though, it seems to have represented a universal moral force, similar, if not equivalent to, the Tao, or Way. The workings of the human world are believed to affect Heaven. In turn, Heaven, as the ultimate moral force, guides and nurtures humanity. Confucianism's grand harmony of relationships thus extends beyond humanity, involving Heaven itself.

A Legacy for East Asia, Lessons for the World

Various forms of upheaval have gripped the nations of East Asia in recent times. China, except for the small island state of Taiwan, is ruled by a communist government that officially opposes the practice of traditional religion, including Confucianism. Korea is divided between the communist North and the westernized South. Japan, also strongly influenced by Western culture, has achieved remarkable economic success, challenging traditional ways of life.

Still, Confucianism shows signs of being a legacy that will far outlast the temporary currents of government or economics. Whatever might be declared in official decrees or encouraged by motives of the marketplace, deeply imbedded Confucian attitudes, especially those that affect the ways of the family, seem destined to endure.

Turning our sights westward, Confucianism offers ideas that have exciting prospects for improving society. Many in the West mourn the loss of traditional "family values." In this realm Confucianism has always excelled. Confucius himself understood his society to be decaying largely because of a loss of such traditional values. He set about consciously applying the ways of the past to remedy the ills of the present, establishing rules of behavior and ideals of moral virtue to fortify the ethical foundations of his society. Could such ideas supply solutions for the West? Could a renewed widespread effort to "learn to be human" lead to improvements in self-cultivation, family togetherness, national prosperity, and harmony with Heaven?

Whatever prospects Confucianism might have for improving society, its insights on what it means to be human will remain a precious contribution to humanity. We close with a few more gems of wisdom from the great Master K'ung.

The Master said, "Yu, shall I tell you what it is to know. To say you know when you know, and to say you do not when you do not, that is knowledge." (Analects 2.17)

"If one is guided by profit in one's actions, one will incur much ill will." (Analects 4.12)

"Men of antiquity studied to improve themselves; men today study to impress others." (Analects 14.24)

"Can you love anyone without making him work hard? Can you do your best for anyone without educating him?" (Analects 14.7)

"Not to mend one's ways when one has erred is to err indeed." (Analects 15.30)

"The gentleman agrees with others without being an echo. The small man echoes without being in agreement." (Analects 13.23)

"Do not worry because you have no official position. Worry about your qualifications. Do not worry because no one appreciates your abilities. Seek to be worthy of appreciation." (Analects 4.14)

Glossary

Analects. The collected sayings of Confucius, one of the Four Books of Confucianism.

Book of Mencius. The collected teachings of Mencius, one of the Four Books of Confucianism.

chun-tzu (jin-dzuh; Chinese: "gentleman"). The mature person, an ideal human being with perfect moral character.

Five Constant Relationships. A doctrine summarizing the proper ethical principle for each basic human relationship, such as duty between ruler and subject.

jen (ruhn; Chinese: "goodness," "love," or "benevolence"). The supreme human virtue, doing one's best to treat others as one would wish to be treated.

li (lee; Chinese: "rite" and "propriety"). Proper behavior in any given social circumstance, as if performing a sacred ritual.

Neo-Confucianism. A major philosophical and religious tradition that developed around 1000 C.E. as a response to challenges facing Confucianism from Taoism and Buddhism; Neo-Confucianism's most important figure is Chu Hsi.

shu (shoo; Chinese: "reciprocity"). A basic principle of Confucian ethics that says not to do to others what you would not want them to do to you.

Tao (dow; Chinese: "Way"). For Confucianism, the moral order that permeates the universe, the Way that should be followed. Sometimes the word tao is lowercased to refer more generally to an individual tao, or "way."

te (day; Chinese: "virtue"). Virtue as shown through the power of example, an attribute of the mature person.

wen. The cultural arts, skills of behavior valued by Confucius as being of moral benefit and as befitting the mature person.

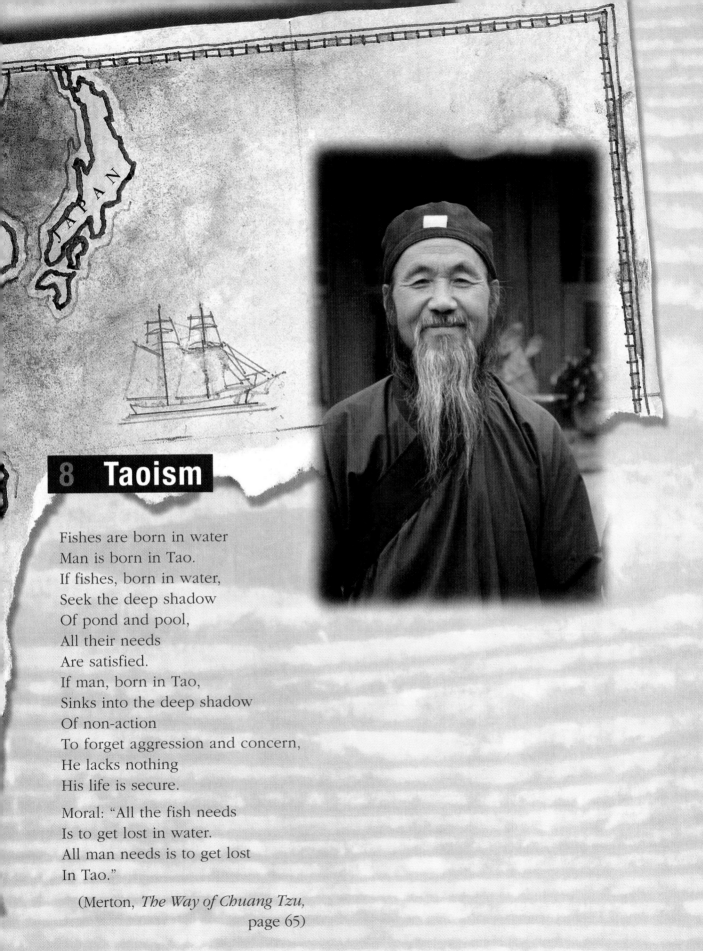

8 Taoism

Fishes are born in water
Man is born in Tao.
If fishes, born in water,
Seek the deep shadow
Of pond and pool,
All their needs
Are satisfied.
If man, born in Tao,
Sinks into the deep shadow
Of non-action
To forget aggression and concern,
He lacks nothing
His life is secure.

Moral: "All the fish needs
Is to get lost in water.
All man needs is to get lost
In Tao."

(Merton, *The Way of Chuang Tzu,*
page 65)

Living in Harmony with the Way of Nature

East Asian religion is an interwoven fabric of various traditions. All incorporate to some extent this fundamental idea of Eastern culture: All aspects of the universe are in harmony, each part nurturing and balancing the whole. Human beings, usually regarded by Western religions as somehow distinct from the rest of nature, are considered part of this grand harmony. Taoism places special emphasis on this fundamental idea of the harmony of the universe. It teaches living in harmony with **Tao,** "the Way" of nature.

Over the centuries Taoism has functioned in complementary fashion with Confucianism, Buddhism, and (in Japan) Shinto to form the fabric of East Asian religion. Taoism is actually made up of two distinct strands. The first strand, philosophical Taoism, is based almost entirely on classic texts like the **Tao Te Ching** and the **Chuang Tzu** (both of which we will consider shortly). Philosophical Taoism focuses on the great mysteries of Tao and its implications for living. This is presently a subject of much interest well beyond the religion's original land of China; currently there are over eighty different English translations of the *Tao Te Ching* alone.

The other strand is popular, or "religious," Taoism. Followers of this strand of Taoism strive to achieve physical longevity and, ultimately, immortality. Popular Taoism combines its own interpretation of the classic texts with various beliefs and practices of folk tradition, and has derived a fascinating array of techniques to aid the adherent in the pursuit of immortality. These techniques include meditation, breathing exercises, and the eating of certain herbs and minerals.

This chapter focuses on the teachings of the classics—the *Chuang Tzu* and the *Tao Te Ching*. Along with being the basic teachings of philosophical Taoism, they also provided the foundations for the growth of popular Taoism.

Lao Tzu and Chuang Tzu: Legendary Sages, Mystical Texts

The origins of Taoism are ancient, dating back to about the time of Confucius (551 to 479 B.C.E.). They are also shrouded in mystery. In fact, we cannot even be certain of whether the traditional founder of Taoism, Lao Tzu, ever existed. Nor is much known about its other great founding figure, Chuang Tzu. However, we do have the texts attributed to each of them. We also have traditional accounts of the lives of Lao Tzu and Chuang Tzu which, though almost entirely legendary, tell us a good deal about the mystical character of early Taoism.

Lao Tzu, the "Old Master"

The legendary flavor of the story of Lao Tzu is evident in his name, which in Chinese literally means "old master." Supposedly born in the year 604 B.C.E., he is said to have been conceived by a shooting star. When his mother finally gave birth to him, Lao Tzu was already eighty-two years old, a wise man with flowing white hair. (In Chinese culture old age is highly respected; it is a mark of wisdom.)

Tradition has it that Lao Tzu worked as a government archivist. More notably he was a venerated sage whose wisdom was sought by many. Even Confucius is said to have come seeking advice. One story tells of Lao Tzu chiding Confucius for his arrogance and misguided ambition. Confucius, much impressed by the venerable Lao Tzu, withdrew and told his disciples:

"I know a bird can fly; I know a fish can swim; I know animals can run. Creatures that run can be caught in nets; those that swim can be caught in wicker traps; those that fly can be hit by arrows. But the dragon is beyond my knowledge; it ascends into heaven on the clouds and the wind. Today I have seen Lao Tzu, and he is like the dragon!" (Ssu-ma Ch'ien, *Shih Chi*)

Eventually Lao Tzu became disenchanted with the rampant corruption of government, and left his career and his home. When he arrived at the Han-ku Pass in the western mountains separating China from Tibet, the keeper of the pass convinced him to write down his wisdom before leaving. Three days later Lao Tzu handed him the *Tao Te Ching* and proceeded on his way.

The *Tao Te Ching*: Taoism's Foundational Text

Regardless of how much historical truth is preserved in the legend of Lao Tzu, it is convenient to think of him as being the author of the *Tao Te Ching*. In fact, the work was originally called the *Lao Tzu,* and it is still frequently referred to by that title. Whatever its origins, the final form of eighty-one short chapters dates to about the third century B.C.E. Brief and yet profound, the *Tao Te Ching* can be read in an afternoon, but its ideas can be pondered rewardingly for a lifetime.

The very first lines of the *Tao Te Ching* display its profound and enigmatic nature:

The Tao that can be told of
    is not the eternal Tao;
The name that can be named
    is not the eternal name.

          (Chapter 1)

Echoes of such mystery are heard repeatedly:
Those who know do not speak;
Those who speak do not know.

          (Chapter 56)

Give up sainthood, renounce wisdom,
And it will be a hundred times better
    for everyone.

          (Chapter 19)

Such statements are paradoxes. Paradoxes are statements that seem illogical and contradictory on the surface, and yet contain deeper truths that are accessible more through intuition than through logical thinking. Paradoxes such as these are at the heart of mystical religious traditions. All the great religions include some elements of mysticism, but none are so thoroughly mystical as Taoism. And the *Tao Te Ching* is the mystical sacred text par excellence. As we will see, amid these paradoxes lie profound teachings on living in harmony with nature.

1
Paradoxes are found in many religious traditions, as well as in literature and poetry. Think of two or three paradoxes you have come across in religion or literature. If you cannot think of any, invent two or three based on the paradoxes quoted from the *Tao Te Ching.*

Above: Lao Tzu is seen in this portrait from the Ming Dynasty.
Left: Taoism emphasizes living in harmony with Tao, the Way of nature.

Chuang Tzu: Taoism's Second Founder and His Text

Chuang Tzu, Taoism's second founder, seems to have lived from about 369 to 286 B.C.E. The text attributed to him, simply called the *Chuang Tzu,* is not as famous as the *Tao Te Ching,* but it is equally important. It is also delightful, full of humorous yet profound lessons and stories. Though probably only parts of the text were authored by Chuang Tzu, the inspiration of his character is evident in all its pages.

A central theme of the *Chuang Tzu* is the relativity of things. Who is to say, it asks, exactly what is good, what ought to be done, or even who we are, when answers to such questions are so dependent on particular circumstances? In one famous passage, Chuang Tzu (here referred to by his family name, Chou) questions the nature of his existence:

Once Chuang Chou dreamt that he was a butterfly. He did not know that he had ever been anything but a butterfly and was content to hover from flower to flower. Suddenly he woke and found to his astonishment that he was Chuang Chou. But it was hard to be sure whether he really was Chou and had only dreamt that he was a butterfly, or was really a butterfly, and was only dreaming that he was Chou. (*Chuang Tzu,* chapter 2)

The Philosophy of Tao

The title *Tao Te Ching* literally means "the book of the Way and its power (or virtue)." The text explains the meaning of Tao and its accompanying concept, *te,* which is the power or virtue acquired by the individual through living in harmony with Tao. (The Latin root of virtue, *virtus,* means both "virtue" and "strength.") The *Chuang Tzu* continues this explanation, emphasizing the relative nature of all things. This relativity is based in the balance of yin and yang, twin polarities that can be likened to the opposite poles of a magnet. Let us consider each of these concepts in turn.

Tao: The Way of Nature

The word *tao* is generally translated as "way," in the sense of a path on which one travels. Taoism deepens this general meaning considerably. In the *Tao Te Ching,* which openly admits the impossibility of ever producing a full explanation, Tao is both the ultimate source and the principle of order in the universe. It is the Way of nature.

According to the *Tao Te Ching,* Tao is the ultimate source, the original, "unified something" from which all things arise. It is not a personal Creator God in the Western sense, but an unseen force that is the origin and the order of the universe. It is beyond the reach of intellectual knowledge. For lack of a better name, Lao Tzu calls it "Tao" and "Great":

There was something undifferentiated and
    yet complete,
Which existed before heaven and earth.
Soundless and formless, it depends
    on nothing and does not change.
It operates everywhere and is free
    from danger.
It may be considered the mother
    of the universe.
I do not know its name; I call it Tao.
If forced to give it a name,
    I shall call it Great.

(*Tao Te Ching,* chapter 25)

As the unseen, incomprehensible, ultimate source, Tao is thought to exist both before and beyond all else, transcendent of humanity and the rest of creation. But Tao is also the "mother of the universe," and so is immanent; it pervades the natural world, constantly ordering and nurturing it.

The Great Tao flows everywhere.
It may go left or right.
All things depend on it for life,
    and it does not turn away from them.
It accomplishes its task, but does not claim
    credit for it.
It clothes and feeds all things
    but does not claim to be master
    over them.

(*Tao Te Ching,* chapter 34)

2
Taoists are the first to admit that Tao can never be completely explained in words. After reading the textbook section "Tao: The Way of Nature," describe Tao as completely as you can in your own words.

The Art of Translation

Translating from a foreign language involves more than just converting sentences word by word into a different language. It also requires a general process of interpretation, determining the overall meaning of the text and expressing it accurately.

Chinese is considerably more open to varying interpretations than European languages such as Spanish, French, or German. And the mystical character of the *Tao Te Ching* makes it an especially challenging text for the translator. The word *tao,* for example, occurs seventy-six times. Each occurrence has its own unique meaning.

Let us again consider the first line of the *Tao Te Ching,* this time with a variety of translators' renditions. First, here is a literal translation by Frederic Spiegelberg, proceeding word by word:

Tao, insofar as it is termed tao is not the real tao.

In the translation of Wing-tsit Chan, this line reads:

The Tao that can be told of is not the eternal Tao.

And here are three more translations, by Arthur Waley, R. B. Blakney, and D. C. Lau, respectively. (These are just a few of the more than eighty English translations of the *Tao Te Ching.*)

The Way that can be told of is not an Unvarying Way.

There are ways but the Way is uncharted.

The way that can be spoken of
Is not the constant way.

To do justice to the wide variety of possible interpretations, we will draw from a variety of translations of the *Tao Te Ching* as we proceed with this chapter.

The Universe in Balance: Yin and Yang

Tao can be compared to magnetism. Magnetic force is invisible and does not seem to be significant, but it actually pervades the world, constantly affecting its order. Tao is thought to be similarly invisible, and yet pervasive and powerful. And just as magnetic force is accompanied by two polar opposites—negative and positive—so too is Tao. **Yin** is the negative, passive, feminine, earthly component, characterized by darkness and weakness. **Yang** is the positive, active, masculine, heavenly component, characterized by light and strength. Like the negative and positive poles of magnetism, yin and yang are not really opponents. Rather, they complement each other. Without one, the other would make no sense, just as we could not describe east if there were no west.

The balance of yin and yang is captured graphically by the famous symbol in which the dark yin and the light yang are perfectly balanced, and each contains an element of the other. Neither yin nor yang is essentially superior over the other. However, because Taoists perceive that humanity tends to overindulge in the yang aspects of life, Taoism emphasizes the need to embrace the yin—the weak, the passive, the feminine. The *Tao Te Ching* describes the embracing of yin by drawing on the image of a stream, which is naturally found low in the valley:

Know the strength of man,
But keep a woman's care!
Be the stream of the universe!
Being the stream of the universe,
Ever true and unswerving,
Become as a little child once more.

(Chapter 28)

The "feminine" and "masculine" characteristics of yin and yang (here personified as woman and man) do not correspond to differences in gender. All people are made up of both components. Many, however, manage to work themselves into a state of imbalance, usually tending toward too much yang. Taoism counters this problem by advocating virtues oriented toward yin, such as humility, noncompetition, and pacifism. These virtues are the marks of the perfectly balanced individual, which Taoism calls the sage. Due to the patriarchal nature of ancient Chinese society, the Taoist classics assume the sage to be male. To become a sage, though, is primarily a matter of embracing the feminine yin.

Relativity of Values

In keeping with its perspective of the universe as an ongoing balance of yin and yang, Taoism regards moral values as relative. For example, goodness is only meaningful because of its opposite, evil. For the Taoist, there is no such thing as absolute goodness. Just as in the symbol of yin and yang each quality contains a spot of the other, so too is goodness tinged by evil and evil by goodness. Taoism avoids absolute moral judgments, insisting instead on the relativity of

3
Magnetism provides a helpful analogy for understanding Tao. Think of another helpful comparison from nature, art, or technology, and explain how it is like Tao.

4
Draw the symbol of yin and yang. Explain its meaning.

values. The *Tao Te Ching* makes this point by demonstrating that no value could exist if it were not for its opposite:

When the people of the world all know
    beauty as beauty,
There arises the recognition of ugliness.
When they all know the good as good,
    There arises the recognition of evil.

                    (Chapter 2)

Chuang Tzu is the master of this aspect of Taoism. We have already seen that he questioned the very nature of his existence, not sure if he was really Chuang Tzu or a butterfly. The *Chuang Tzu* contains several such insights on the relativity of values. One famous story points out how easily humans (or in this case, monkeys) get overly distraught over value distinctions that seem important but are actually superficial:

In Sung there was a keeper of monkeys. Bad times came and he was obliged to tell them that he must reduce their ration of nuts. "It will be three in the morning and four in the evening," he said. The monkeys were furious. "Very well then," he said, "you shall have four in the morning and three in the evening." The monkeys accepted with delight. (Chapter 2)

Harmony of Life and Death

The problem of death and what happens afterward is central to most religions. Taoism has little to say on this issue. Like yin and yang, and moral values such as good and evil, life and death are thought to be merely two harmonious parts of the same whole.

The Taoist classics say nothing of an afterlife, or of the continued existence of a personal soul. The *Tao Te Ching* describes death as a return from life back into the original unity of the Tao. The *Chuang Tzu* depicts death merely as one among nature's many transformations from one state to another, as illustrated in this famous account:

Chuang Tzu's wife died. When Hui Tzu went to convey his condolences, he found Chuang Tzu sitting with his legs sprawled

5
Chuang Tzu points out the relativity of values in his story of the monkeys in Sung. For no apparent reason, the monkeys were furious with the first arrangement and delighted with the second. Think of an example in which you or someone you know has gotten overly distraught over a superficial distinction. What might have been the reason for this reaction?

In this print entitled *Huai River Moon*, a Chinese general encounters the Taoist sage Jiang Ziya, a man who fished with a straight hook: he was so virtuous that the fish impaled themselves voluntarily.

she had a spirit. In the midst of the jumble of wonder and mystery a change took place and she had a spirit. Another change and she had a body. Another change and she was born. Now there's been another change and she's dead. It's just like the progression of the four seasons, spring, summer, fall, winter.

"Now she's going to lie down peacefully in a vast room. If I were to follow after her bawling and sobbing, it would show that I don't understand anything about fate. So I stopped." (*Chuang Tzu,* chapter 18)

Living in Accord with Tao: The Way of the Sage

Taoism emphasizes that human beings are part of the grand harmony of nature. Tao, the Way of nature, is therefore relevant in human life, too. Indeed, living in accord with Tao is the only way for the individual to thrive. This is the manner of living perfected by the sage, who attains oneness with Tao through insight regarding its simplicity and natural unity. Such insight is radically different from common knowledge, which tends to confuse the issue by seeing in nature a multiplicity of things, while missing nature's basic unity. Instead the sage proceeds with an undistracted mind, so that the simple truth of Tao can be seen.

A four-footed friend can help clarify this point. When trying to understand Taoism, it helps to consider the cat, with which the sage has much in common. Like the sage, the cat avoids the mistake of thinking itself into a state of distraction. By not deviating from its own nature, its tao, the cat is fully attentive to the situation at hand. Responding spontaneously and with sufficient, but not excessive, effort, the cat simply does what needs to be done, and always lands on its feet.

Because Tao is thought to pervade everything, it is always present. It is *the* Way, and there is no other. Living in accord with Tao is therefore potentially a simple thing to do. But human beings, unlike cats, are burdened with the ability to think themselves into distrac-

out, pounding on a tub and singing. "You lived with her, she brought up your children and grew old," said Hui Tzu. "It should be enough simply not to weep at her death. But pounding on a tub and singing—this is going too far, isn't it?"

Chuang Tzu said, "You're wrong. When she first died, do you think I didn't grieve like anyone else? But I looked back to her beginning and the time before she was born. Not only the time before she was born, but the time before she had a body. Not only the time before she had a body, but the time before tion. They are able to deviate from the Way. Lao Tzu expressed it this way:

My doctrines are very easy to understand
    and very easy to practice,
But none in the world can understand
    or practice them.
(*Tao Te Ching,* chapter 70)

Doing Without Acting:
Wu-wei and Its Related Virtues

The primary virtue of Taoism, and the means by which the sage maintains harmony with *Tao,* is **wu-wei.** Some suitable English translations of *wu-wei* are "actionless activity," "pure effectiveness," "yielding to win," "creative quietude," to name but a few. *Wu-wei* literally means "nonaction." But Taoists do not advocate simply doing nothing. The practice of *wu-wei* ultimately accomplishes the task at hand. "No action is undertaken, and yet nothing is left undone" (*Tao Te Ching,* chapter 48). The person who practices *wu-wei* avoids the yang tendency to act, embraces the yin—the passive, the weak, the feminine—and is thereby more effective.

To practice *wu-wei* is to be so perfectly in harmony with nature that its energy infuses and empowers the individual. Unnatural action, a mistake rooted in deviation from Tao, is avoided. Instead the sage maintains an undistracted state, allowing the energy of Tao to accomplish the task at hand.

Act without action.
Do without ado.
Taste without tasting.
Whether it is big or small, many or few,
    repay hatred with virtue.
Prepare for the difficult while it is still easy.
Deal with the big while it is still small.
Difficult undertakings have always started
    with what is easy.
And great undertakings have always started
    with what is small.
Therefore the sage never strives for the great,
And thereby the great is achieved.
(*Tao Te Ching,* chapter 63)

Water is another helpful analogy for understanding Taoism. In its capacity to nourish and in its ordered yet constantly changing patterns, it represents Tao. In water's ability to achieve without acting, it illustrates *wu-wei.* A gently flowing stream can create a valley or canyon merely by staying its course. Of course this usually takes much time. But taking sufficient time—patience—is another aspect of embracing the yin.

There is nothing softer and weaker
    than water,
And yet there is nothing better
    for attacking hard and strong things.
For this reason there is no substitute for it.
All the world knows that the weak
    overcomes the strong and the soft
    overcomes the hard.
(*Tao Te Ching,* chapter 78)

Wu-wei is at the heart of all other Taoist virtues. The virtues to be discussed next—humility and noncompetition, naturalness and naturalism, nonaggression and passive rule—all demonstrate the basic virtue of *wu-wei.*

Humility and Noncompetition

Among Taoism's many paradoxes is the outward appearance of the sage as one who is unattractive and lacks ability. Humility is one of the chief virtues of the sage. And yet, just as *wu-wei* is "actionless activity" that ends up accomplishing the task at hand with utmost efficiency, so too the humility of the sage is not a sign of weakness but one of strength. To be in accord with Tao requires humility but at the same time yields optimal results. "Therefore the sage wears rough clothing and holds the jewel in his heart" (*Tao Te Ching,* chapter 70).

The same paradox applies for a similar virtue, noncompetition. The sage chooses not to compete, but this is not at all the same as giving up the fight. On the contrary, through the virtue of noncompetition the sage emerges victorious: "It is precisely because he does not compete that the world cannot compete with him" (*Tao Te Ching,* chapter 22).

6

Compare Chuang Tzu's perspective on the death of his wife with your own perspective regarding death. In what ways do you agree and disagree with Chuang Tzu?

7

Based on your own observations, expand on what the textbook has to say about the "sagely" ways of the cat. In addition, choose another type of pet; does it too have much in common with the Taoist sage?

8

Reflect on the following topic: How might the Taoist virtue of *wu-wei* be applied to the task of writing a one-page essay?

The Taoist Sage

The two most famous repositories of Taoist wisdom are its classic texts, the Tao Te Ching *and the* Chuang Tzu. *But in China, ever since ancient times a third source of teachings has been prominent: the Taoist sage.*

In this excerpt from a European's memoir of his life in China, Peter Goullart relates one of his first encounters with an old Taoist sage. The sage teaches through words, as well as by his actions and simple lifestyle.

Sitting one afternoon at the small temple at the base of the mountain, I saw how he came in having walked all the way from town. He was dressed in an old robe of faded blue with picturesque patches of a lighter material here and there, and wore a huge straw hat with a tip in the shape of a miniature pagoda, the usual head-covering of an itinerant Taoist. He carried a long and twisted wooden crook. We agreed to walk together to the monastery, and in spite of all my efforts I could not keep up with him. With a sly wink he continued the ascent, his immense sleeves billowing in the breeze like wings. He soon disappeared among the boulders while I sat down exhausted, my heart pounding, for a brief rest. I found him later in the afternoon at the back of the monastery where there was a tea plantation. Wearing only a short jacket and wide trousers, he was puttering around a tea bush loosening the soil. Wiping sweat from his rosy cheeks he sat down on a stone leaning his chin on a mattock. Now is the time to ask him something about Taoism, I decided, and I poured out my questions. He looked up at me with his innocent, childish eyes, his smile gentle but, I thought, slightly ironical.

"Take time, observe and learn," he said simply. "Words spoken in haste will not stick; a cup of water splashed into a parched field will do it no good. It is only a slow and gentle rain that will saturate the soil and produce life." He became silent ready to resume his work.

His rebuke abashed me. I saw what he meant. He probably thought I was an idle tourist, or worse, a young writer, who wanted to learn something about Taoism in an hour or so, and then write a smart article, boasting of the mysteries revealed to him. Seeing my obvious confusion, the old man relented. His face was all smiles now, but his eyes became thoughtful.

"If you want to learn about the Eternal Tao, do not be casual and in a hurry. Don't glean too much from too many books, for each book is full of opinions, prejudices and corruptions. Read only one book and only one—our Old Master's Tao Te Ching, and then try to understand it, not by juggling the words and meanings, but intuitively, through your heart and spirit. Don't ask too many questions, but patiently watch what we Taoists do, and perceive the hidden motives of our actions, and not that which is only for display. Do not be guided so much by your intellect as by faith, love and your heart, which is another name for understanding and compassion. What you need is wisdom, and not knowledge; for if one has wisdom, knowledge will come naturally. Always remember that the Eternal Tao is Infinite Wisdom, Infinite Love and Infinite Simplicity." And with this the old man took up his pickaxe and resumed his hoeing of the bush. (*The Monastery of Jade Mountain,* pages 30–31)

From a Western perspective, in which the competitive spirit is generally encouraged, Taoist teachings on noncompetition might appear paradoxical (as Lao Tzu intended for them to appear!):

To yield is to be preserved whole.
To be bent is to become straight.
To be empty is to be full.
To be worn out is to be renewed.
To have little is to possess.
To have plenty is to be perplexed.

(*Tao Te Ching*, chapter 22)

Upon careful reflection, however, these paradoxical teachings provide wisdom for living. For example, the skilled musician chooses not to compete with the tempo of the piece, waiting for the correct moment to play. The athlete who sidesteps the opponent is practicing the Taoist virtue of non-competition. The martial arts demonstrate how effective this can be. Popular images of the martial art known by the Japanese name judo often lead to the assumption that it is a competitive, aggressive technique of physical combat. The name judo, however, comes from the Chinese *rou-tao,* or the "yielding way," in which the practitioner prevails by giving way. Noncompetition is also highly relevant in social situations. If someone feels especially lonely, it rarely helps if he or she tries to compete for friendship. Simply being himself or herself yields the best results.

Naturalness and Naturalism

Taoism also teaches the virtue of naturalness—behaving as nature dictates, not as social pressure or personal pride demand. The Taoist sage, for example, would dress according to the weather, not according to the requirements of fashion. Always attentive to the Way of nature, the sage rejects showiness and pomposity:

He who stands on tiptoe is not steady.
He who strides cannot maintain the pace.
He who makes a show is not enlightened.
He who is self-righteous is not respected.
He who boasts achieves nothing.
He who brags will not endure.

(*Tao Te Ching*, chapter 24)

9

Imagine a stream of running water (if possible, go and observe a stream or river). The *Tao Te Ching* uses the stream as the ideal image of the yin—weak, passive, and feminine. Reflect on how the stream embodies the characteristics of yin.

10
State your response to the following situation. Then compare your personal response with the response of a Taoist: Because of bounties offered to hunters throughout the twentieth century, the wolf population was severely reduced. This resulted in a great growth in the deer population. Now many deer starve to death each winter due to lack of food and territory.

11
Consider carefully what chapter 17 of the *Tao Te Ching* says about good government. How does the government of your nation rate according to Lao Tzu's perspective? Do you think Lao Tzu's assertion that the best rulers are merely known to exist (and rule passively) is true in the case of your own nation?

The Taoist sage also practices naturalism, resisting the temptation to meddle with nature. This virtue is similar in many respects to modern environmentalism. Naturalism and environmentalism both involve caring for nature. But unlike some forms of environmentalism, which strive to fix things through human ideas and efforts, Taoist naturalism is always a hands-off approach. Leave nature well enough alone, and nature will thrive:

Do you think you can take over the
    universe and improve it?
I do not believe it can be done.

The universe is sacred.
You cannot improve it.
If you try to change it, you will
    ruin it.
If you try to hold it, you will lose it.

(*Tao Te Ching*, chapter 29)

Nonaggression and Passive Rule

The Taoist virtue of nonaggression is much like the virtue of *wu-wei*. Just as *wu-wei* produces efficient results, the sage who practices nonaggression ultimately prevails. Nonaggression is also applied in the case of warfare. Though Taoism admits that warfare is sometimes necessary, it encourages pacifism. But even in warfare, as in other realms of life, violence and aggression should be minimized:

A good soldier is not violent.
A good fighter is not angry.
A good winner is not vengeful.
A good employer is humble.

(*Tao Te Ching*, chapter 68)

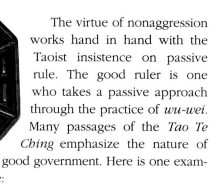

The virtue of nonaggression works hand in hand with the Taoist insistence on passive rule. The good ruler is one who takes a passive approach through the practice of *wu-wei*. Many passages of the *Tao Te Ching* emphasize the nature of good government. Here is one example:

The best (rulers) are those whose existence
    is (merely) known by the people.
The next best are those who are
    loved and praised.
The next are those who are feared.
And the next are those who are despised.
It is only when one does not have
    enough faith in others
    that others will have no faith in him.

(chapter 17)

Passive rule, like all Taoist teachings, functions by letting nature take its course. The best way to govern is simply not to interfere with the natural way of the people. Lao Tzu and Chuang Tzu insist that Tao will prevail if it is left well enough alone.

Taoism in East Asia and the World

For over two thousand years, Taoism has been a central part of the religious life of China and, as it spread through the centuries, all of East Asia. For one thing Taoism mixed with Buddhism to produce Zen, the subject of our next chapter. More important, though, Taoism has functioned alongside Confucianism, and the two together have basically determined the character of East Asia. Indeed it is commonly suggested

This pendant containing the symbol of yin and yang was made in China in the eighteenth century.

that Taoism provides the yin to balance Confucianism's yang. For whereas Confucianism encourages conforming to the social order through rigorous activity, Taoism promotes a passive existence free from Confucian demands, celebrating the individualistic life of harmony with the Way of nature.

Perhaps Western society needs a similar sort of balancing. From the Taoist perspective, the West is alarmingly yang-oriented, with its massive machines, towering skyscrapers, and bustling marketplaces. Technological advancement and economic drive often seem to outrun wisdom.

Apparently many Westerners are feeling a need for Taoist teachings. As evidence consider the numerous English translations of the *Tao Te Ching,* and that recent best-seller lists have included titles like *The Tao of Pooh* and *The Te of Piglet,* humorous yet instructive books that teach Taoism through Winnie-the-Pooh and his friends. (Pooh, according to author Benjamin Hoff, is a natural Taoist.)

From the Taoist perspective, it is not surprising that Taoism has gained a substantial number of admirers in the West. After all, in the grand harmony, the yin is bound to balance the yang. And even in those times and places where the insights of Taoism are neglected, perhaps it is Lao Tzu who has the last laugh:

> When the highest type of men hear Tao,
> They diligently practice it.
> When the average type of men hear Tao,
> They half believe in it.
> When the lowest type of men hear Tao,
> They laugh heartily at it.
> If they did not laugh at it,
> it would not be Tao.
>
> (*Tao Te Ching,* chapter 41)

Glossary

Chuang Tzu (jwahng dzuh). The second foundational text of Taoism (along with the *Tao Te Ching),* containing teachings and anecdotes traditionally thought to have come from the sage Chuang Tzu, who lived in the fourth century B.C.E.

Tao (dow; Chinese: "Way"). For Taoism, the Way of nature, the ultimate source and the principle of order in the universe. When the word *tao* is lowercased, it refers more generally to an individual tao, or "way."

Tao Te Ching (dow day jing; Chinese: "the book of the Way and its power [or virtue]"). Taoism's foundational text, traditionally thought to have been authored by Lao Tzu in the sixth or seventh century B.C.E.; sometimes called the *Lao Tzu.*

wu-wei (woo-way; Chinese: "nonaction"). The supreme Taoist virtue, rendered in English variously as actionless activity, pure effectiveness, yielding to win, creative quietude, and so on. To practice *wu-wei* is to be so perfectly in harmony with nature that its energy infuses and empowers the individual.

yang. The positive, active, masculine, heavenly component of the universe, characterized by light and strength; complements yin.

yin. The negative, passive, feminine, earthly component of the universe, characterized by darkness and weakness; complements yang.

RUSSIA

CHINA

NORTH
KOREA

Seoul

SOUTH
KOREA

Sapporo

Tokyo

Hiroshima   Osaka

9 Zen Buddhism

A monk told Joshu: "I have just entered the monastery. Please teach me."

Joshu asked: "Have you eaten your rice porridge?"
The monk replied: "I have eaten."
Joshu said: "Then you had better wash your bowl."
At that moment the monk was enlightened. (Reps, *Zen Flesh, Zen Bones,* page 96)

Zen: The Spirit of Buddhism

Zen Buddhism developed within Mahayana (The Great Vehicle) Buddhism, first in China and later in Japan. For centuries Zen has had a major influence on the religious and cultural life of the people of these lands. Zen has also received much attention in the West during the past century.

Zen is a unique form of Mahayana Buddhism that focuses on what it regards as the spirit of Buddhism: the experience of enlightenment. Fixing its attention fully on this experience, Zen tends to discard most other aspects of Mahayana Buddhism—devotion to Buddhas and *bodhisattvas,* speculations regarding the nature of reality, and philosophical elaboration on Buddhist scripture. And the insight born of Zen enlightenment is profoundly simple: If you have eaten from your bowl, wash it. But such attentiveness to the situation at hand, or mindfulness, tends to get lost in the thicket of thoughts and feelings that typically crowds the mind. Those who practice Zen seek to clear the mind in order to discover the simple truth that is at the heart of things. Such a discovery can only be made through direct experience, not through thoughtful analysis.

Transmission of the Teachings: Historical Development

Focused as it is on the experience of enlightenment, Zen does not concern itself much with the history of its own tradition. We can likewise be brief with our overview. Still, several facts about Zen's history help to shed light on its teachings.

Indian *Dhyana,* Chinese Ch'an, Japanese Zen

A brief overview of Zen is present in its very name. The word *zen,* which means "meditation," is the Japanese pronunciation of the Chinese word *ch'an.* This, in turn, comes from the Chinese attempt to pronounce the Sanskrit word *dhyana,* a term commonly used among early Buddhists in India. Zen also traces the origins of its tradition back to ancient India, and to the Buddha himself.

According to Zen legend, one day the Buddha was teaching on a mountain. He wished to teach a truth too subtle for words and so, rather than speaking, he held up a flower. All his followers were puzzled except for one,

Mahakasyapa, whose gentle smile indicated that he understood what the Buddha was teaching. Like much of what the Buddha taught, this subtle truth could be fully conveyed only through direct experience, not through words or analysis. The Buddha chose Mahakasyapa as his successor, thereby establishing a line of Zen patriarchs that would remain in India for several centuries.

According to legend, the twenty-eighth patriarch in this line, Bodhidharma, brought Zen to China about one thousand years after the Buddha's life, around the year 520. This legend clearly attempts to establish a direct connection back to the Buddha. Zen as it is known today, however, developed mainly in China. It can be described as a mixture of Indian Buddhism and Chinese Taoism.

In China a separate line of Zen patriarchs was established, and Zen began to flourish under the influence of Hui Neng (638 to 713), the sixth patriarch of Chinese Zen, or **Ch'an.** Hui Neng came to the monastery of the fifth patriarch when he was merely a poor boy selling firewood. But his mastery of Zen quickly showed through, and he was named successor. Hui Neng's impact on Ch'an was enormous, and remains imprinted on Zen Buddhism to this day. One of his many contributions was intentionally putting an end to the traditional position of patriarchs by refusing to name a successor. Ever since, authority in Zen has been distributed among those who are competent to teach others, commonly referred to as masters, or **roshis** in Japan. Hui Neng, like Bodhidharma, remains one of Zen's most revered figures.

Ch'an continued to be an important tradition in China until about three centuries ago, when it gradually began to decline. Today it is a minor tradition in China, but in Japan, Zen has flourished since the Middle Ages.

Rinzai and Soto: Two Sects of Japanese Zen

Zen was first brought to Japan with lasting impact by two masters who had spent some years living in China. The Zen master Eisai

(1141 to 1215) brought the **Rinzai** sect, which is known as the school of sudden awakening. In general, Rinzai emphasizes the experience of awakening, called *satori* in Japanese. (*Satori* will be discussed later in this chapter.) In fact, Rinzai contends that Zen training really begins only after one's first *satori*. Rinzai employs the spiritual exercise known as the *koan* as the primary means of bringing about *satori*. The *koan* is designed to frustrate the thinking process. (*Koans,* too, will be described in some detail later in this chapter.)

The other primary sect of Zen in Japan is **Soto,** the school of gradual awakening. It was brought by Dogen (1200 to 1253), a master revered by all Zen Buddhists, regardless of sect. Rather than focusing on the crowning achievement of *satori,* the Soto sect emphasizes the day-to-day practice of Zen, especially *zazen,* the method of seated meditation.

At some points in our study the differences between these sects will prove relevant, so it is important to be aware of them. But they are differences in emphasis only. The *koan,* for example, is not shunned completely by the Soto sect, and *zazen* is a basic method in Rinzai, too. Moreover, it is common for Zen Buddhists to be involved with both sects.

Zen Teachings

Zen in its essence is the art of seeing into the nature of one's own being, and it points the way from bondage to freedom. (Suzuki, *Essays in Zen Buddhism,* page 13)

What could be simpler than "seeing into the nature of one's own being"? After all, one's own being is always present, always there to be known. The problem, according to Zen, is that our true nature lies hidden behind a tangle of thoughts and feelings, and behind the personality, or ego, that we mistakenly think we are. The ego is the source of selfish desire. This whole tangled mass of logical concepts and mental descriptions, of fears and longings, of self-centeredness, constantly covers up the true being—the "Zen mind" or "Bud-

Egyoku Hata, a modern Zen master of the Soto sect

dha nature"—that we really are. Hence we are in bondage. Zen offers a path to freedom.

Direct Experience, Beyond Words and Logic

A student once asked [Zen master Joshu]: "If I haven't anything in my mind, what shall I do?"

Joshu replied: "Throw it out."

"But if I haven't anything, how can I throw it out?" continued the questioner.

"Well," said Joshu, "then carry it out." (Reps, *Zen Flesh, Zen Bones,* page 39)

1

Due to its experiential nature, Zen cannot adequately be described in words. Such a problem is not unique to Zen. Describe the experience of eating your favorite food. Now repeat your description, comparing it to your memory of the actual experience. In what ways does your verbal description fall short of adequately expressing the full experience?

2

Read the conversation between the emperor and Gudo about death. What kind of answer do you think the emperor expected from Gudo? What do the emperor's expectations reveal about his understanding of Zen? How do you suppose the emperor reacted to Gudo's reply? What might the emperor have said to encourage Gudo to elaborate?

[Zen master] Tokusan said:

"Even though you can say something about it,

I will give you thirty blows of the stick.

And if you can't say anything about it,

I will also give you thirty blows of the stick."

(Kapleau, *Three Pillars of Zen,* page 195)

To the outsider, Zen can appear comical, illogical, even infuriating. To the practicing Zen Buddhist, who has gained at least an initial insight into the truth that Zen teaches, it all makes perfect sense. What are we to make of this paradox, this seeming contradiction?

Zen is direct experience of truth, which is beyond the reach of thoughts and feelings about truth, and beyond the words that are used to express thoughts and feelings. The outsider who looks at Zen and fails to make sense of it is looking precisely with the mechanisms of thought and words. But the experience that is the focal point of Zen is beyond these mechanisms. In fact, a textbook explanation such as this one, constructed with words to communicate thoughts, is itself inadequate for imparting a full understanding

A nun meditates in a temple in Vietnam.

of Zen. But just as a finger can point to the moon (to borrow a teaching from Zen), so too a textbook can point to true understanding. The person who chooses the way of Zen must avoid the mistake of identifying the finger with the moon, or the verbal explanation with the real truth Zen reveals.

Let us see how far words can take us toward understanding Zen. To begin with we will further explore three characteristics of Zen: it is experiential; it is beyond words; and it is beyond logical thinking.

Zen Is Experiential

On another day the emperor asked [Zen master] Gudo: "Where does the enlightened man go when he dies?"

Gudo answered: "I know not."

"Why don't you know?" asked the emperor.

"Because I have not died yet," replied Gudo. (Reps, *Zen Flesh, Zen Bones,* page 55)

This simple conversation illustrates Zen's insistence on firsthand experience and its rejection of speculation regarding the nature of reality. The Buddha himself emphasized experience over speculation, most significantly the experience of enlightenment. And like the Buddha, Zen Buddhists regard meditation as the primary means of attaining enlightenment.

Zen Is Beyond Words

The insight of Zen cannot be expressed in words. That is why the Buddha, when attempting to teach this most subtle lesson, resorted to holding up a flower rather than speaking. Zen masters have always realized the futility of trying to teach their insights in conventional ways. According to D. T. Suzuki, the person most responsible for explaining Zen to the West, Zen teaches "nothing":

If I am asked, then, what Zen teaches, I would answer, Zen teaches nothing. Whatever teachings there are in Zen, they come out of one's own mind. We teach ourselves; Zen merely points the way. (*Introduction to Zen Buddhism,* page 38)

Zen depends on direct experience of the truth. Ultimately, then, it cannot be taught.

Zen is beyond logical thinking. To see a thing—a tree, a waterfall—as itself, in its most basic simplicity, that is Zen.

Still, Zen "points the way," and this leaves room for the usefulness of words. Like the finger pointing to the moon, words can point in the direction of the truth. For this reason Zen stops short of completely rejecting verbal teachings, including Buddhist texts. But it regards them as a ladder whose highest rung is still short of the goal. Words can assist, but they can never complete the task.

Zen Is Beyond Logical Thinking

Nan-in, a Japanese master during the Meiji era (1868 to 1912), received a university professor who came to inquire about Zen.

Nan-in served tea. He poured his visitor's cup full, and then kept on pouring.

The professor watched the overflow until he no longer could restrain himself. "It is overfull. No more will go in!"

"Like this cup," Nan-in said, "you are full of your own opinions and speculations. How can I show you Zen unless you first empty your cup?" (Reps, *Zen Flesh, Zen Bones,* page 5)

Most people—not only university professors—have their "cups" filled with opinions and speculations, views born of logical thinking and of affirmations and denials regarding the nature of things. According to Zen, such views clutter the mind and prevent pure insight into the truth. As long as the logical, reasoning process is at work interpreting reality, direct experience is impossible. To attain such experience, to "empty your cup," is to see things as if for the first time. Zen mind, it is often said, is "beginner's mind."

Let us approach this idea with an example. When most people look at a tree, their minds become full of affirmations and denials, of opinions and speculations: "It is an oak tree; its leaves are changing color; it is at least fifty years old. . . ." What is missed in all these observations, according to Zen, is the tree itself in its most basic simplicity. To see a tree simply as a tree, as if for the first time—that is Zen.

Zen Enlightenment: *Satori*

The enlightenment Zen seeks is known in Japanese as **satori.** It is especially emphasized in Rinzai Zen, the sect of sudden awakening. For this sect *satori* is essential; it is

3
Explore what you think D. T. Suzuki means when he writes that "Zen teaches nothing."

4
The next time you are outside with some free time, observe a tree. Try to see it simply for what it is, without categorizing, affirming, denying, or speculating.

both the beginning and the end of Zen practice. Until a person has had an initial experience of *satori*, the insight of Zen teachings cannot be fully understood. *Satori* is freedom from the bondage of thought, feeling, and self-centered ego; it is a pure experience in which the true nature of one's being is known directly. *Satori* is beyond the reach of verbal description and logical thinking, so it must be experienced to be known.

Most other forms of Buddhism refer to the highest spiritual experience as *nirvana*, which is thought to be a permanent state. *Satori*, however, is not permanent. The initial *satori*, which usually occurs within the first few years of Rinzai Zen training, is followed by other *satori* experiences, occurring with increasing frequency and intensity. With each *satori* the person is transformed. Gradually the person attains a new, enlightened perspective.

This Chinese statue depicts a monk at the moment of enlightenment.

Koans: Puzzles to Frustrate the Mind

"You can hear the sound of two hands when they clap together," said Mokurai. "Now show me the sound of one hand." (Reps, *Zen Flesh, Zen Bones*, page 25)

This is a famous example of a **koan**, a puzzle designed to short-circuit the workings of the rational, logical mind. Searching every nook and cranny of its intellect for an answer that conforms to logic, the mind finds none and is eventually completely frustrated. At this point the wall of rationality can finally be broken through so that direct insight into reality can be attained.

The *koan* is emphasized in the Rinzai, or sudden awakening, sect. The master presents the student with a *koan*, and, in the periods between their private meetings (called **dokusan**), the student grapples with it. At their meetings the student offers an answer, and the master determines whether it is acceptable. If the answer is rejected, the student continues grappling with the *koan* and attempting new answers until one is accepted. The *koan* is not to be discussed with anyone other than the master. There are about seventeen hundred *koans*, but usually only a few are needed during the course of Zen training. Some *koans*, like "the sound of one hand clapping," are particularly famous. Others are less famous but equally, or more, perplexing:

Master Gettan said to a monk: "Keichu made a cart whose wheels had a hundred spokes. Take both front and rear parts away and remove the axle: then what will it be?" (Shibayama, *Zen Comments on the Mumonkan,* page 74)

Goso said, "To give an example, it is like a buffalo passing through a window. Its head, horns, and four legs have all passed through. Why is it that its tail cannot?" (Page 272)

Master Kyogen said, "It is like a man up a tree who hangs from a branch by his mouth; his hands cannot grasp a bough, his feet cannot touch the tree. Another man comes under the tree and asks him the meaning of Bodhidharma's coming from the West. If he does not answer, he does not meet the questioner's need. If he answers, he will lose his life. At such a time, how should he answer?" (Page 54)

Is there such a thing as a "right" answer to a *koan?* Many answers could be deemed by the master to be right, and many could be deemed wrong. It all depends on the degree of insight exhibited by the student. One thing is certain: If an answer is dependent on logical thinking rather than direct insight into reality, it will be rejected.

The Fruits of Zen

Zen's severe contention with words and logic might lead the outside observer to dismiss it as a negative, world-denying religion. From the accounts of those who have adhered to Zen, however, nothing could be farther from the truth.

Zen Achieves a Healthy, Vigorous Mind

First of all it must be understood that Zen insight, even though it flies in the face of logical thinking, is not abnormal or unhealthy. In fact, from the Zen perspective, full mental health can be attained only when the mind breaks through the bondage of thought and feeling and sees things as they really are. *Satori* is not a withdrawal from sanity; on the contrary, it is perfected sanity and complete mental health.

Zen insight, according to its adherents, vastly enhances the mind's strength and vitality. When it is set free from the bondage of the mass of thoughts and feelings that ordinarily entangle it, the mind is no longer burdened by unnecessary mental activity. This newfound vigor allows for much greater clarity and alertness.

Zen Is Practical and Attentive to This World

Zen is practical, as we have observed in Joshu's remark that triggered the enlightenment of a novice monk: "If you have eaten from your bowl, wash it." Zen is also fully attentive to this world. It does not deny the world or see everyday reality as irrelevant. The world viewed through the perspective of Zen, though, is seen in a new light. To recall our earlier example, a tree is seen not as a bundle of observations and opinions, but fully and truly *as a tree*. The following advice of a Zen master, Gensha, also points out Zen's attention to being in this world:

A monk once went to Gensha, and wanted to learn where the entrance to the path of truth was. Gensha asked him, "Do you hear the murmuring of the brook?" "Yes, I hear it," answered the monk. "There is the entrance," the master instructed him. (Jung, foreword to *Introduction to Zen Buddhism,* by Suzuki, page 10)

Zen Focuses on the Here and Now

Finally, Zen neither affirms nor denies the existence of an afterlife. In this way it overcomes the duality of life and death. The focus of Zen is on the here and now. People who perceive life from the perspective of *satori* simply have no need for concern about the future, including what happens after death.

This approach is powerfully communicated in a Zen story of a man being chased by a tiger. Running away, the man came to a cliff. He grabbed the end of a wild vine and swung over the edge. Hanging off the cliff, he trembled as he looked up at the tiger waiting to devour him; below, a second tiger waited hungrily. The thin vine was all that kept the man from certain death. The story continues:

Two mice, one white and one black, little by little started to gnaw away the vine. The man saw a luscious strawberry near him. Grasping the vine with one hand, he plucked the strawberry with the other. How sweet it tasted! (Reps, *Zen Flesh, Zen Bones,* page 23)

The stories of Zen masters are full of accounts regarding their awareness of the approach of death. When this time is upon them, many have composed poems, leaving behind their "last words" to their followers. This one is from the hand of Zen master Shoun:

For fifty-six years I lived as best I could,
Making my way in this world.
Now the rain has ended, the clouds are
    clearing,
The blue sky has a full moon.
    (Reps, *Zen Flesh, Zen Bones,* pages 19–20)

5

Try to compose your own Zen *koan.* When you have done so, whether you think you have succeeded or failed, reflect on why you found the task difficult or easy.

6

Consider carefully the poem written by Master Shoun as he approached death. Based on his poem, how would you characterize his perspective on death? on life?

A Western Woman Masters Zen

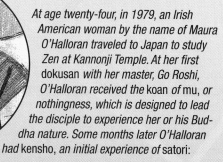

At age twenty-four, in 1979, an Irish American woman by the name of Maura O'Halloran traveled to Japan to study Zen at Kannonji Temple. At her first dokusan *with her master, Go Roshi, O'Halloran received the* koan *of mu, or nothingness, which is designed to lead the disciple to experience her or his Buddha nature. Some months later O'Halloran had* kensho, *an initial experience of* satori:

Dokusan. I did mu with all my heart and all my soul and all my being. Everything was squeezed out until my head touched the floor.

"Is it your mind or your heart or your body saying mu?"

"I don't know." Tears are flowing without reason; I laugh without reason.

"What is the difference between I don't know and mu?"

"No difference." Go Roshi whacks me.

"Ouch!"

"Who feels pain?"

"I do."

Then, when I'm not looking, he jumps up, embraces me. *"Bikkuri shita!" [You surprised me!].* I tumble backwards, laughing. He holds my hand tightly, my thumb.

"This is I don't know."

"I know."

"You must see mu in everything." I leave dokusan, crying and laughing, with Tachibana Sensei apologizing for his English translation. That's okay. He encourages me.

I go to dokusan with Kobai-san.

"Where does mu come from?"

"I don't know—how can it come from somewhere? It doesn't have a place."

Kobai-san is very fish-like, cold comfort.

"We've all struggled with the problem."

"It comes from me," I told her.

"If that's your answer, go to dokusan."

In we go again. Go Roshi says *"zenzen wakaranai" ["You don't understand at all."].*

I'm crushed, devastated. Roshi says, "Next time, come alone."

. . . I'm called to dokusan. I feel so dejected, empty-minded. It doesn't even occur to me to wonder why Go Roshi wants me to come alone.

"Mu—do? [How is your mu?]"

I mu for him with all my strength, raising myself high and squeezing every bit of breath into mu until my head touches the floor.

"Once more again," he says in English. (He doesn't speak English, but I don't register surprise.)

I do so.

Then "Once more again."

My first and only thought was "He may make me do this for ages." Then he jumped at me, grabbed me—"This body is *muji [the figure of mu],* this head, eyes, ears."

Suddenly I'm laughing and crying muji. I don't even realize "Now I am muji," but I simply was muji and everything around me.

And he hits different parts of my body. "This is muji." Count 20 in muji—20 parts of me, 20 muji in Kannonji, all around me. We're holding on to each other, laughing and laughing. "Heart muji," he says, thumping me. "And Go Roshi's heart muji," I say, belting him back. We're embracing.

"Kensho shita [You have realized your Buddha-nature]," says he.

I'm surprised. I was too self-conscious even to know that it was kensho. Only when I got outside and was looking at everything and really seeing mu did I finally know. Suddenly I understood why we must take care of things just because they exist; we are of no greater and of no lesser value.

At dinner the only words spoken aloud rang in my ears, *"Maura-san go kensho itashimashita [Maura has seen into her Buddha Nature]."*

At first I was so exhausted I felt neither joy nor sorrow, just relief. The next day I was ecstatic, couldn't stop smiling. Then all was as before—or at least, so it seems. Everyone tells me I look different. It's hard to be sure. I can't be bothered looking for big changes. (O'Halloran, *Pure Heart, Enlightened Mind,* pages 102–105)

After another year of study, O'Halloran revealed the outgoing nature of Zen when she wrote in her journal:

I'd be embarrassed to tell anyone, it sounds so wishy-washy, but now I have maybe 50 or 60 years (who knows?) of time, of a life, open, blank, ready to offer. I want to live it for other people. What else is there to do with it? Not that I expect to change the world or even a blade of grass, but it's as if to give myself is all I can do, as the flowers have no choice but to blossom. At the moment the best I can see to do is to give to people this freedom, this bliss, and how better than through zazen? So I must go deeper and deeper and work hard, no longer for me but for everyone I can help. And still I can't save anyone. They must work themselves, and not everyone will. Thus I should also work politically, work to make people's surroundings that much more tolerable, work for a society that fosters more spiritual, more human, values. A society for people, not profits. What better way to instill the Bodhisattvic spirit in people? (Page 233)

Maura O'Halloran was killed in a traffic accident in October of 1982. The inscription on a statue dedicated to her at Kannonji Temple declares that she is to be known by the name "Great Enlightened Lady, of the same heart and mind as the Great Teacher Buddha," and that she is "to be loved and respected forever" (page 301).

Zen Life

The teachings of Zen invariably aim at the spirit of Buddhism: the attainment of direct insight into truth. All other aspects of religion are considered secondary to this primary goal. Still, Zen is a religious tradition, and it has many of the trappings we normally associate with a religion. We have already considered Zen's historical development. Now let us turn to the formal training methods, the daily practices, and the cultural influences that together constitute Zen life.

The Monastic Lifestyle: Rigorous Training and Menial Tasks

Earlier we questioned whether practicing Zen is really difficult. After all, what could be simpler than "seeing into the nature of one's own being"? Probably our investigation of Zen's teachings—with their insistence on moving beyond logic, their puzzling *koans,* and their talk of a *satori* experience that is impossible to describe in words—have provided proof enough that practicing Zen is not so simple a task. Zen Buddhists themselves understand fully the deep difficulty of accomplishing it. And so Zen prescribes a monastic lifestyle that is designed in every way to move the disciple closer to enlightenment. (Though this discussion speaks of monks and the monastic life, women are not excluded from Zen monastic life. There are far fewer Zen nuns than monks, but the lifestyle described as monastic applies to women as well as men.) We begin by considering the most prominent method of training, *zazen.*

Zazen: "Seated Meditation"

Zazen, which literally means "seated meditation," consumes most of the monks' time. Seated in rows on a slightly raised platform within the meditation hall, the monks assume the lotus posture, their eyes half-closed. Here they sit for hours each day, day after day, year after year. If ever a monk becomes sleepy or lacks concentration, an appointed attendant delivers a blow to the back with an "encouragement stick." Not intended to harm the monk, this blow serves to refresh and to focus, and is received with a gesture of gratitude. (The blow of the encouragement stick is delivered with precision and strikes at points that are also important in the healing practice of acupuncture.)

Zazen is practiced with the intent of clearing the mind, and thereby attaining insight. But Zen does not stop with this. The insight attained through *zazen* must be taken along through the daily routines of life, and not merely confined to the meditation hall.

Life in the Monastery

Work is an essential part of Zen monastic life. The physical activity involved in work helps to prevent the mind from becoming dull. So the monks engage in a variety of tasks, especially menial ones: preparing food in the kitchen, tending the fields, gathering firewood, and begging in local villages.

Eating and sleeping, like *zazen,* take place on small rectangular mats in the meditation hall. Meals are simple, consisting mainly of rice and vegetables. They are also very structured affairs, eaten in silence and conducted with a series of hand gestures indicating if more food is desired. Each of the everyday routines is intimately correlated with Zen teachings, so that all the routines move the monks closer to enlightenment.

Zen Master, Zen Disciple

One of the most impressive facts of Zen life, and one which would prevent most Westerners from ever practicing Zen in its true Chinese or Japanese form, is the master-disciple relationship. The degree of confidence that the disciple must invest in the master is virtually unheard of in the West.

The Zen master, or *roshi,* has almost complete authority over the disciples. Accounts of physical discipline abound: slapped faces, twisted noses, disciples being pushed to the ground. The authority and physical discipline involved in the master-disciple relationship might appear strange to Western eyes. But

7
Imagine yourself practicing *zazen* in a meditation hall and getting hit in the back with an encouragement stick. Describe what it would take for you to feel actual gratitude, rather than resentment, toward the attendant who hit you.

8
Zen acknowledges the spiritual benefits of work, especially menial tasks. In your own experience, how does work relate to your spiritual well-being?

9

Based on what you have learned about Zen in this chapter, describe an aspect of your own society that might benefit from Zen teachings.

like all aspects of Zen, these practices are intended to help bring about enlightenment. What might appear from the outside (and perhaps even to the disciple at the time) as unkindness, Zen intends as a nurturing concern.

In less dramatic fashion, the master and disciple meet periodically in a session called a *dokusan*. The *dokusan* provides an opportunity for formal discussion regarding Zen teachings and training. It is also in *dokusan* that the disciple offers an answer to the assigned *koan*. Usually the answer is deemed inadequate, relying on logical thinking rather than direct insight, and the disciple is curtly dismissed to return to *zazen* practice and continued grappling with the *koan*.

Zen Beyond the Monastery

10

Compose your own haiku. In it try to capture something of the spirit of Zen.

The central importance of *zazen* has, to some extent, freed Zen from the confines of the monastery. After all, a person does not need to be in a formal meditation hall to meditate. Whether in the company of others at a Zen center or on a retreat, or alone at home, men and women can practice Zen without becoming monks or nuns.

Another aspect of Zen beyond the monastery is its relevance to issues in the world at large. In the monastery the insight attained through *zazen* is applied to the daily routines of life. This holds true for Zen practice outside the monastery as well. In Japan, companies commonly recommend *zazen* to their employees, sometimes offering meditation sessions as part of the normal work schedule. Zen centers also offer such sessions, along with a variety of other services for Zen laity, such as youth hostels that foster good character development in children.

Zen's concern for social justice lies at the heart of its teachings. Zen insight into reality overcomes the bondage of self-centeredness. The ego (the "I") and the rest of humanity are no longer distinct. The suffering of others, then, becomes one's own. In this way Zen fosters a natural impulse to alleviate suffering by working to correct social injustices.

Zen's Influence on the Cultural Arts

Our discussion of Zen life would not be complete without recognizing Zen's vast influence on East Asian cultural arts. This influence springs from Zen's emphasis on simplicity and its overwhelming love of nature, which it inherited from Chinese Taoism. By the time of Zen's arrival in Japan, such love of nature had long been nurtured through Shinto, the traditional religion of the Japanese. This aspect of Zen was therefore very much welcomed, and today Japan's culture breathes the spirit of Zen.

The most famous example of Zen influence in the visual arts is *sumie,* or black ink landscape painting. Aside from beautifully portraying the elements of nature, *sumie* places great significance on empty spaces, thereby conveying Zen's concern for simplicity. This is also evident in Japanese landscape gardening and in the pervasive art of flower arrangement, which until recently was expected to be learned by most every Japanese girl. In all these arts, empty space is as important as space that is filled.

Zen has also strongly influenced physical arts, such as swordsmanship and archery. For centuries these arts have been practiced primarily as means of gaining Zen insight, not as tools for warfare. If the simplicity that comes from Zen can be applied to these arts, brilliant results follow naturally. The same spirit animates the simple but elegant Zen tea ceremony, which proceeds so spontaneously that it always seems as if it is being done for the first time.

Zen's influence on literature is recognized throughout the world in the poetic form of haiku. Consisting of seventeen syllables (in Japanese; English translations may vary), these poems elegantly display Zen's celebration of simplicity. The following haiku was composed by Matsuo Basho (1644–1694), Zen's greatest poet:

The old pond;
A frog jumps in—
The sound of the water.

(Aitken, *A Zen Wave,* page 25)

In Conclusion . . .

Concluding a chapter on Zen is something of a contradiction in terms. But then, so is beginning such a chapter in the first place. Nothing, after all, can be written to explain Zen completely. Zen itself diligently strives to free the mind from the bondage brought about by words. Furthermore, Zen never concludes. *Satori,* unlike *nirvana,* is not a permanent state. The Buddha himself, according to Zen, is still engaged in Zen training, still deepening his insight.

Zen refuses to affirm or to deny, even with respect to some of life's most pressing questions, such as the following: What happens after we die? Does God exist? But Zen does fully affirm one thing—life itself, life lived to the fullest, in perfect awareness and direct insight into the simple truth of things. "If you have eaten from your bowl, wash it."

Like haiku, Zen is a kind of poetry, presenting images in the form of methods and messages that prompt the mind to seek truth for itself. Like the finger pointing to the moon, Zen points to truth, but never is so bold as to come right out and declare it. It is perhaps fitting, then, to close this chapter with a Zen poem. Written many centuries ago, Han-shan's *Cold Mountain Poems* seem to describe not so much a physical mountain as a spiritual ascent:

Clambering up the Cold Mountain path,
The Cold Mountain trail goes on and on:
The long gorge choked with scree and
  boulders,
The wide creek, the mist-blurred grass.
The moss is slippery, though there's been no
  rain
The pine sings, but there's no wind.
Who can leap the world's ties
And sit with me among the white clouds?

(Snyder,
RIPRAP and Cold Mountain Poems, page 44)

Glossary

Ch'an (chahn; Chinese: "meditation"). The Chinese sect of Buddhism emphasizing meditation as the primary means to enlightenment; it began to flourish under the direction of Hui Neng in the seventh century C.E.; Japanese equivalent is Zen.

dokusan (doh-koo-sahn). The periodic meeting with the master during which the disciple offers an answer to the assigned *koan.*

koan (koh'ahn). A verbal puzzle designed to short-circuit the workings of the rational, logical mind; used especially in Rinzai Zen as a means of triggering *satori.*

Rinzai (rin-zi). One of the two major sects of Zen (along with Soto), the school of "sudden awakening," which was brought to Japan in the twelfth century C.E. by Eisai.

roshis (roh-shees). Zen masters who are deemed competent to teach others.

satori (suh-tor'ee). The Zen experience of enlightenment, a flash of insight in which the true nature of one's being is known directly.

Soto (soh-toh). One of the two major sects of Zen (along with Rinzai), the school of "gradual awakening," which was brought to Japan in the thirteenth century C.E. by Dogen.

zazen (zah-zen; Japanese: "seated meditation"). The basic method of Zen meditation, traditionally practiced while seated in the lotus position in the meditation hall.

Sendai

MT. ASAMA

Hiroshima

Kyoto
MT. HIEI   MT. FUJI   Tokyo

Nagasaki   Osaka

Ise

10 Shinto

"Way of the *Kami*"

Shinto is Japan's native religious tradition. With roots that date back to prehistoric times, Shinto has probably existed for as long as the Japanese have inhabited their islands. But Shinto has also been shaped through the ages by foreign influences. In fact, the very term *shinto,* which means "way of the *kami,"* is from the Chinese words *shen* (divinities) and *tao* (way). It was first used by the Japanese in about the sixth century C.E. to distinguish their native religion from new traditions coming from China, especially Buddhism (which the Japanese call *Butsudo,* the "way of the Buddha").

Japanese religion, like East Asian religion in general, is a fabric of interwoven traditions. Shinto provides the native threads. But the foreign traditions of Buddhism, Confucianism, and Taoism, along with native Japanese folk tradition, have contributed immensely. The religion of most Japanese people is drawn from all these traditions. It is very common, for example, for Japanese marriages to be held in Shinto shrines, and for Japanese funerals to be held in Buddhist temples. It would be a mistake to think of Shinto as existing independently of other traditions.

Shinto contributes to Japanese religion in a variety of ways. In one of its aspects, it is a vehicle for patriotism, conveying a long-standing respect for Japan as a nation. In another aspect, Shinto attends to everyday concerns of communities and individuals, helping to secure such necessities as good crops and safe homes. Most of all, Shinto is veneration of nature. The profound love of nature, which has always been a hallmark of the Japanese, is embodied in the difficult but crucial concept that lies at the heart of Shinto, the *kami*.

Kami: Divine Ancestors, Sacred Inhabitants

Shinto emphasizes ritual over theological or ethical teachings. Participation in rituals means far more than holding the correct "belief" (a notion quite foreign to Shinto). Shinto therefore has not concerned itself too much with theological explanations of the *kami*. Even the great scholar Motoori Norinaga (1730 to 1801), one of Shinto's most revered and influential figures, admitted, "'I do not yet understand the meaning of the term, *kami*'" (quoted in Earhart, *Religion in the Japanese Experience,* page 10).

Basically the **kami** are any people or things that have evoked the wonder of the Japanese. As we will note in the Shinto myth, *kami* include deities and certain human beings, such as emperors. But *kami* appear in a large variety of forms, including natural objects like mountains and animals. The *kami* are numerous, and can appear anywhere. Many are also ancient, existing long before the Japanese people, and even before their island home. Indeed, as the Shinto myth sets forth, the *kami* are Japan's divine ancestors.

Divine Ancestors: The Shinto Myth of Japan's Origins

Shinto has no sacred scripture, no Bible. But it does have authoritative histories that were compiled in the eighth century C.E. by order of the imperial court. The histories contain a mythological account of the origin of Japan.

Known at least in outline form by virtually all Japanese people, the Shinto myth tells of the divine ancestry of Japan and its people, and illustrates that the *kami* are always present and always close to Japan's land and people. Though most Japanese today would not assert the historical truth of the account, the myth is highly significant, serving to celebrate the greatness of Japan. It can be summarized as follows:

At the beginning of heaven and earth, seven generations of deities (*kami*) came into existence, including Izanagi and Izanami, the primal male and female. Other deities commanded these two to create land. And so, churning the sea with Izanagi's spear, they created an island from the brine that dripped from the spear.

The pair descended, and Izanami gave birth to the eight islands of Japan. Izanami then gave birth to many deities, the last one being the heat god, who burned his mother to death as she was giving birth to him. Overcome by despair, Izanagi killed the heat god, and then pursued Izanami to the underworld. Here, in spite of his wife's warnings, Izanagi beheld her decaying body. Embarrassed and outraged, Izanami pursued Izanagi, who barely managed to escape before blocking the entrance to the underworld with a huge boulder.

Izanagi, polluted from this encounter with death, waded into the ocean to purify himself. From filth in his left eye he produced Amaterasu, the sun goddess; from filth in his right eye and his nostrils he produced the moon god and storm god.

Eventually Amaterasu, who reigned as the chief deity, sent her grandson, Ni-ni-gi, to rule Earth as its emperor, and Ni-ni-gi's grandson became the first human emperor. The imperial line was thereby established, descended directly from Amaterasu.

In the meantime, elsewhere amid the islands, the Japanese people were descending from other deities.

It is easy to understand why the Japanese people have revered the Shinto myth over the centuries. After all, because of the myth, the Japanese can claim divine ancestry and can take pride in the divine origin of their homeland.

Sacred Inhabitants: "Eight Hundred Myriads" of *Kami*

In the Shinto myth, we encountered some of the *kami*. Amaterasu, still regarded as the most important deity, and the other gods and goddesses are *kami*. Included among them is Ni-ni-gi, Amaterasu's grandson and Japan's first emperor. The Japanese have traditionally regarded their emperors as *kami,* even while they are still living. (After Japan's defeat in World War II, Emperor Hirohito was forced to announce publicly that he was not divine; many of the Japanese were likely shocked by this.)

Not only deities and emperors, however, are included among the *kami*. In a famous passage, the great scholar Motoori Norinaga writes that a wide variety of things can be considered *kami:*

"Speaking in general . . . it may be said that *kami* signifies, in the first place, the deities of heaven and earth that appear in the ancient records and also the spirits of the shrines where they are worshipped.

"It is hardly necessary to say that it includes human beings. It also includes such objects as birds, beasts, trees, plants, seas, mountains and so forth. In ancient usage, anything whatsoever which was outside the ordinary, which possessed superior power or which was awe-inspiring was called *kami.*" (Quoted in Earhart, *Religion in the Japanese Experience,* page 10)

1
Myths, like the Shinto account of Japan's origins, are rich in meaning. They provide answers to fundamental questions about human life and history. Often these answers are given in symbolic images and events that do not have obvious meanings. With this in mind, consider carefully the Shinto myth. What fundamental questions does it answer, and how?

Japan's Emperor Hirohito, seen here shortly after World War II, renounced his divine status and broke with tradition by meeting directly with the Japanese people.

2

The concept of *kami* is central to Shinto. After reading the descriptions and examples of *kami*, close your textbook and describe *kami* in your own words.

Motoori goes on to cite thunder, dragons, echoes, foxes, tigers, wolves, peaches, and a necklace as *kami*. The list is seemingly endless. The ancient histories, in fact, assert that the *kami* number "eight hundred myriads," or eight million. This is not to be regarded as a literal figure, but as a recognition that the islands of Japan abound with the sacred forces that the *kami* embody.

In general it is helpful to think of *kami* as that which is sacred, whatever the specific form it takes. The importance of *kami* clearly relates to the Japanese love of nature. Nature, in all its manifestations, is considered sacred. This sacredness is celebrated and worshiped in its embodied form of *kami*.

Shinto in the Religious Life of Japan

We have already seen that the Shinto tradition has various aspects, and exists in the company of other traditions to make up the fabric of Japanese religion. In this section we will examine more closely Shinto worship practices and the various types of Shinto.

Revering the *Kami:* Shinto Worship

3

For Shinto, purification is necessary to allow the light of one's inborn divine essence to shine through. Think of purification rituals of other religions you are familiar with (including those you have read about in this textbook). Share some of your ideas about the reasons for the practices of religious purification.

Shinto worship focuses on simple expression of respectful gratitude to the *kami*, and to the experience of unity with them. Worship can take place in the home, at shrines, or during large and joyous seasonal festivals in which entire communities join together to worship the *kami* amid colorful pageantry.

Worship at Home: The *Kamidana*

The focal point of Shinto worship in the home is a small altar called the **kamidana**, or "*kami* shelf." The *kamidana* can contain a wide variety of items, depending on the family's particular objects of worship. Usually it contains the names of deceased ancestors. Statues of favorite deities, and items brought back from shrines are also common. These objects tend to be regarded as symbols of the presence of *kami*, although for the more tra-

ditional Japanese, they are thought to actually contain *kami* within them.

Worship at the *kamidana* is simple and commonly occurs daily. Family members first purify themselves by washing their hands and face. Then they present offerings such as food or flowers, clap their hands to signify their presence to the *kami*, and say prayers. The *kamidana* can also serve as the focal point for more elaborate celebrations, such as weddings.

Ceremonial Worship at Shinto Shrines

Shinto shrines have a natural beauty and are found most everywhere. Originally *kami* were worshiped in natural places, such as groves, waterfalls, and mountains. Some such places, like Nachi Waterfall and Mount Miwa, still function as shrines. The wooden structures that are typical of the shrines today feature a naturalness that expresses Shinto's profound veneration for its surroundings. The wood, for instance, is often left unpainted.

A visit to a Shinto shrine removes the worshiper from ordinary, everyday surroundings. The entrance to the sacred confines of the shrine is marked by a *torii*, an archway formed by two upright pillars and a cross beam, usually fortified with horizontal supports. The *torii* is recognized worldwide as the symbol of Shinto.

The shrine is usually rectangular and surrounded by a fence. Often a grove of trees or a park can be found nearby. Having passed through the *torii*, the worshiper finds a basin with water for the rite of purification. In this rite, water is splashed on the hands and the face, symbolically preparing the worshiper to appear before the *kami*. Next, one enters the worship hall, the space reserved for worshipers during the ceremony. A second building, the chief sanctuary, can be entered only by priests. Within this building lies the *kami* body, usually a common object such as a mirror or a sword. The *kami* of the shrine is believed to descend into the *kami* body during the ceremony. The *kami* body is an extremely sacred object, and is rarely seen even by the priests. Once the priest has invoked the

presence of the *kami,* prayers are offered on behalf of the worshipers. A typical shrine ceremony culminates in an experience of unity with the *kami.*

Most of Shinto's shrines conform to this description, though the details vary. The most notable shrines are considerably more elaborate. The Grand Imperial Shrine at Ise, dedicated to the sun goddess Amaterasu, is the grandest and most famous of all. Rebuilt every twenty years to ensure its purity, the Grand Imperial Shrine houses the three sacred regalia of Japan's imperial line: a bronze mirror, a sword, and a string of jewels. According to the Shinto myth, these were sent to earth with Ni-ni-gi by his grandmother, the sun goddess Amaterasu.

Seasonal Festivals

Festivals abound in Japan. When local and regional festivals are included, they number well into the hundreds. Shinto, along with Buddhism, is a significant element of many of the festivals.

Shinto has always been closely tied to the agricultural life of Japan, and many of its festivals reflect this. For example, in October and November, festivals celebrate the new rice harvest. The first grains of rice are offered to Amaterasu. Festivals like these are especially important in rural areas.

Of Shinto's many seasonal festivals, the most notable are the Great Purification and the festival of the New Year.

A collage of Shinto images
Upper left: Shinto visitors leave wooden prayer shingles containing prayers and wishes on kiosks outside shrines.
Lower left: A *torii*
Lower right: An urban shrine in Kyoto

Bushido: "Way of the Warrior"

Westerners continue to be fascinated by the Japanese kamikaze (divine wind) pilots who willingly crashed their warplanes into enemy ships in World War II. The fearless attitude of the kamikaze attack stems from a deeply rooted Japanese tradition established in medieval times: **bushido,** "way of the warrior."

Bushido is Japanese through and through. It resulted from the combined teachings of three of Japan's prevalent religions: Shinto nationalism, Confucian respect for one's superiors, and Zen self-discipline and transcendence of the duality of life and death. These teachings formed the code of conduct for the **samurai,** Japan's medieval knights.

Bushido is similar to the medieval European knight's code of chivalry. Its primary virtues are these:
• loyalty to one's master
• courage to fight, and to die if necessary
• honor, preferring death to dishonor
• politeness toward those in higher social positions
• justice; as a doer of just and benevolent deeds, the samurai protected victims of injustice

Most striking among the ways of the samurai—and a glaring difference from the chivalry of Europe's knights—is the willingness to commit suicide. In fact, a samurai carried two weapons—a sword to use against the enemy, and a dagger to use against himself. The ritual suicide, known as **seppuku** in Japan (and commonly called *hara-kiri* in the West), was a painful death brought about by cutting open the abdomen.

Bushido is illustrated vividly in the famous tale from medieval Japan of "The Forty-seven *Ronin.*" A nobleman, angered by repeated abuse on the part of his superior, attempted to murder him. The nobleman was required by the courts to commit *seppuku,* which he did. His forty-seven samurai attendants thus became *ronin,* or samurai whose superior is dead but who are bound by the code of *bushido* to avenge his death. Eventually, through cunning and great courage, the forty-seven *ronin* captured their superior's enemy, the man who had caused the tragedy in the first place. With politeness and humility, the forty-seven explained their duty and told the man that he must now commit *seppuku.* The man hesitated, afraid to take his own life. And so one of the forty-seven attacked, cutting off the enemy's head with a dagger. They then carried the washed head to the grave of their deceased superior and offered it to his spirit. There they waited for several days, until the courts issued the order that they must now commit *seppuku* for having murdered this man. This they calmly did. Ever since, the forty-seven *ronin* have been revered for having perfectly embodied *bushido,* the way of the warrior.

The Great Purification. The Great Purification is performed in shrines throughout Japan in both June and December. For a month before the ceremony, the priests engage in a number of practices and disciplines intended to enhance their purity. During the ceremony itself, the priest waves a cleansing wand over the people. Participants rub paper dolls on their bodies in order to transfer impurities from themselves to the dolls. The dolls, in turn, are thrown away by the priests.

Such emphasis on purification pervades Shinto. We have seen it in the Shinto myth, in which Izanagi washes himself in the ocean after being polluted in the underworld. Worship of *kami,* whether at home before the *kamidana* or at a shrine, always begins with a rite of purification. The rebuilding every twenty years of the Grand Imperial Shrine at Ise also stems from this emphasis on purification. Given this great emphasis, it is interesting to note that Shinto does not regard humans as being naturally sinful or impure. On the contrary, as descendants of the original deities, humans are thought to be born with a divine essence. Purification is needed, though, to allow the light of this essence to shine through with its true luster. The Japanese reputation for cleanliness is directly related to this aspect of Shinto.

The festival of the New Year. The most spectacular annual festival celebrates the New Year. The December Great Purification ceremony helps to prepare the people for this festival. They also clean their house in order to begin the year with purified dwellings. The festival begins on 1 January and lasts for several days. During this time the people are on vacation, and are free to worship at Shinto shrines and Buddhist temples. On 7 January a great feast marks the beginning of the New Year and the return to an ordinary lifestyle.

Types of Shinto

Shinto has had a long and varied history, and has taken on different forms through the centuries. Today three main types of Shinto can be identified, though there tends to be some overlap between them. Shrine Shinto is an organized institution, with officially designated shrines and priests. Sect Shinto, too, is organized, but consists of a large variety of separate institutions, or "sects." Popular Shinto, while including many of the practices of the other types, lacks any formal organization.

Shrine Shinto

The Japanese government officially coined the term *shrine Shinto* during the nineteenth century. The roots of shrine Shinto, however, extend into the distant past, when foreign religions first became prominent in Japan.

Already in the seventh century C.E., Buddhism had become a significant tradition for the Japanese people. Through the ages Buddhism and Shinto became closely intertwined. From the Buddhist perspective, the *kami* were local Japanese manifestations of universal Buddhist truths. Followers of Shinto, in turn, came to regard the Buddhas and *bodhisattvas* as *kami*.

Buddhism, however, was not embraced by everyone. Shortly after Buddhism first appeared in Japan, the imperial government began to take measures to preserve Shinto as the national tradition. It recorded the mythology, organized the priesthood, and began caring for the shrines. In the eighteenth century, Motoori Norinaga established himself as Shinto's most revered figure by

Top: Shinto priests at Meiji Shrine in Tokyo prepare for a New Year ceremony.
Bottom: A samurai is seen in this nineteenth-century engraving.

Shinto   165

Priestess of the Shrine

A young woman named Mine, from Aino, Japan, is a priestess of the Suwa Shrine in Nagasaki. Although the Shinto priesthood is made up primarily of men, women have always played significant roles in shrine life. Mine discusses her experience as a contemporary Japanese woman who is also a member of the Shinto priesthood:

"I like the feeling of being able to walk down the street, looking just like any other woman my age, and to have this little secret that I'm a Shinto priestess. . . . I'm proud to be who I am, even though it is a bit unusual for a woman in this day and age.

"My family is a Shinto family and has been in charge of the village shrine at Aino for longer than anyone can remember. When I was in high school, I promised my grandfather to study Shinto when I got older, thinking at the time that it would be a good way to get to Tokyo from my little village down in Kyushu. I was like anyone else who watched TV and had their favorite singers and shows; I thought that Tokyo was where it was all happening. . . .

"At one point during my university days, we had to undergo a training period. You know, the kind that is supposed to make you tough and pure and bright. We had to get up at 4:30 in the morning and thoroughly clean the shrine and gardens surrounding it, then study hard all day, even doing some meditation, and weren't allowed to sleep until 11:00 at night. The worst part was having to perform the *misogi* purification in the ocean while reciting the Oharae prayer about all the impurities and evils that we were washing away. Miyagi Prefecture is north of Tokyo, so that when we did it first in winter I was absolutely frozen to the bone. I remember thinking, 'Ah, so this is what they really mean!' There were only a few other women in my class but we all participated alongside the men. Other than that intense training session, it was all pretty much routine study.

"When I got out of school, I kept my promise to my grandfather and returned to Aino, and through his connections to Suwa Shrine, it was agreed that I come and further my studies. Now that I'm out in society, meeting a variety of people all the time, when they ask me what I do and I answer that I'm a priestess, their reaction is usually the same. 'Incredible!' they say. But this is my career and it seems very normal to me. I'm sure I'll have a relationship with a shrine all my life, even after marriage. If you ask what my career goals are I'd have to say that they're not easy to pinpoint in the way other young people talk about becoming the head of the department or making lots of money or marrying some up-and-coming young executive or doctor. No, for me, what I'd like to do is to make whatever shrine I'm involved with a place where people can come and feel like they are 'home' and want to linger.

"Maybe it's because I'm from a rural area where the shrine is old and there is a feeling of intimacy between the community members and the shrine, but I don't get that feeling from Suwa Shrine. . . . People need to be able to come to the shrine and feel, 'Ah, I'm glad I came,' and I don't know whether this feeling is as strong as it used to be. . . .

"I guess the biggest problem I face now is the old attitudes about women and what their role is supposed to be at a modern shrine such as this one. I don't have hard training or anything like that, other than the juvenile tasks I'm expected to perform because of my rank, which I suppose are similar to pouring tea or making copies in an office. It just seems that other priests, the men, who are licensed the same as me and of my rank do much more than I do. Maybe it's because people might be put off when they come to the shrine and see a woman officiating. They might say, 'Hey, there are men priests here—what's a woman doing at the ritual I'm paying for?' This is discrimination of course, and in a place like Nagasaki, which is still conservative and old-fashioned and where men are believed to be superior to women, I can't escape it, even here at the shrine.

"But you know, women have always had an important role in Shinto, right from the very beginning, whenever that was. The first priests were not men but women. Have you heard of Himiko? She was very powerful, not only as a priestess but also as one of the first rulers of Japan. Even today, at Ise Shrine, there is a woman priestess higher in rank than the chief priest. . . .

"If I could change something about Shinto—whether it's the shrine at Aino or Nagasaki or wherever—I'd like to somehow restore the presence of the Kami to a more direct feeling or contact. It seems that people feel the Kami is something far away, that they have to go to a shrine or be at the family altar before they can share things with the deities. But for me, I think it's a fundamental part of Shinto to have a sense that the Kami is with you, so that if something happens or you need guidance, you can communicate with it immediately, wherever you are. This closeness to the Kami is something our modern civilization and society have completely lost.

"Though this might sound contradictory to you, I see myself as a thoroughly modern Japanese woman and not as some traditionalist. I mean, I like to go on shopping sprees, eat delicious food in fashionable restaurants, hope to get a driving license, or date the person I choose just like anyone else. That's normal, right? . . . I know deep down that this place I'm in now is where I really belong. Eventually I'll go back to Aino and assume my place in the community after my grandfather retires, but it's still exciting to me to be here in Nagasaki, walking down the street just like anyone else, and to wear my mask which hides my role as a priestess. No one can guess!" (Nelson, *A Year in the Life of a Shinto Shrine,* pages 125–129)

purifying the religion of all Buddhist and other foreign elements.

These tensions between Shinto and foreign influences reached a climax in the nineteenth century. Challenged by the United States and other nations to enter the modern age, Japan in 1868 commenced upon the Meiji Restoration, a crucial project that transformed Japan into a modern nation. Massive political, economic, and religious transformations occurred. The religious transformation can be summarized briefly: Buddhism lost state support while Shinto gained it. By 1882 shrine Shinto was officially recognized as the state religion.

The period from 1868, the beginning of the Meiji Restoration, to 1945, the end of World War II, was both prosperous and tragic for Shinto. Adopted by the state as a vehicle for patriotism, Shinto was purified of its Buddhist elements. The state acquired authority over most of the shrines and over the priests who served them. It became the duty of every Japanese citizen to attend the shrines as a means of expressing patriotism. The Shinto myth of Japan's divine origins became a required part of every child's education so that students might learn loyalty to the emperor and his nation.

With Japan's defeat in World War II, the state support of Shinto ended in disaster. Japan's ancient and splendid tradition had been misused as a tool to fan the flames of extreme nationalism and militarism. This is not to say that Shinto somehow caused Japanese aggression. For one thing, Buddhism, Confucianism, and even Christianity within Japan were just as supportive of the nation's policies. Moreover, it was the state's misuse of Shinto, not Shinto itself, that fueled Japanese aggression.

Shrine Shinto, and Shinto in general, suffered a severe setback. Japanese people tended to blame Shinto for the humiliating defeat of World War II. The shrines themselves still stand, though they are assisted today through the private funding of the nationwide Shrine Association rather than through government involvement. And despite the setback, interest in Shinto has been growing in recent years. Shrine Shinto, therefore, still plays a vital part in the religious landscape of Japan.

4

Until the end of World War II, shrine Shinto illustrated an extreme case of religion involved with nationalism. Such involvement, usually on a smaller scale, has been common throughout world history. Consider your own nation. What kind of involvement do you detect between the nation and religion? What forms does it take? In general what do you think the relationship should be between religion and a nation?

Sect Shinto

When the Japanese government recognized shrine Shinto in 1882, it categorized the left-over elements of organized Shinto as sect Shinto. Thirteen sects were officially included. The government designated these as religions, along with other faiths such as Buddhism and Christianity. The sects were then required to call their places of worship "churches," to distinguish them from the "shrines" that were under the control of the state.

Many of these sects were founded and led by women. This could be a reflection of ancient times, when women were likely to have had prominent roles in Japanese religion.

Popular Shinto

Popular, or folk, Shinto has hardly been affected by the government's categorizing of Shinto into shrine and sect. Indeed, popular Shinto defies classification, for it has never been organized.

Popular Shinto includes a wide array of traditional practices, and in many instances can be best understood as Japanese folk religion. Virtually all forms of Shinto worship that do not require a priest or a formal shrine are practiced in popular Shinto. Rituals of purification are emphasized. Personal blessings are sought for protection from harm and assistance in times of crisis. For example, students commonly seek assistance on examination days. People also seek blessings at major stages of life, such as birth and marriage. Certain rites help to secure the successful growing of crops, especially rice. Such agricultural concerns have been central to Shinto through the ages.

Traditional Shinto in Modern Japan

Shinto thrived for centuries in a Japan that was predominantly rural. Shinto's deep veneration of nature and close ties to the agricultural life of the islands were in harmony with the rural lifestyle. During the twentieth century, however, Japan rapidly became predominantly urban. Shinto would therefore seem to be threatened by the changed situation in modern Japan. Yet, remarkably, the Shinto tradition seems to be faring quite well. Small shrines stand on street corners amid the towering skyscrapers of ultramodern cities like Tokyo and Osaka. The Japanese people, however technologically sophisticated and economically productive they have become, seem to maintain the deep reverence for nature that is central to Shinto.

Considering Shinto's long history of holding on to the oldest ways while adapting to new influences, it is perhaps not surprising that traditional Shinto is surviving in modern Japan. As the entire world strives to balance spiritual and environmental concerns with ever growing technology, the fate of Shinto should prove a telling measure of human commitment to love of nature and traditional ways.

Glossary

bushido (boo-shee-doh; Japanese: "way of the warrior"). Code of conduct for the samurai based on Shinto nationalism, Confucian ethics, and Zen Buddhist self-discipline.

kami (kah-mee). Anything that the Japanese hold as sacred, including deities, certain human beings, natural objects, and animals; *kami* can be either singular or plural.

kamidana (kah-mee-dah-nah). The "*kami* shelf," the small altar in the home, patterned after Shinto shrines, that serves as the focal point of domestic worship.

samurai (sam'uh-ri). A Japanese medieval warrior knight; samurai can be either singular or plural.

seppuku (sep-poo-koo; Japanese: "cutting the abdomen"). Also called *hara-kiri* (hair-i-kihr'ee), ritual suicide prescribed by *bushido* for samurai who have committed crimes or acts of dishonor.

torii (tor-ree-ee). An archway marking the entrance to a Shinto shrine or other sacred site, formed by two upright pillars and a cross beam; Shinto's most recognized symbol.

PART 4
The Ancient West

11 Ancestors of the West

The "Cradle" of the West

The region surrounding the eastern part of the Mediterranean Sea is commonly referred to as the "cradle" of the West. Here were born the religious beliefs and practices from which Judaism, Christianity, and Islam would eventually emerge. This chapter presents some of the religious aspects of early Western civilization. We have to be selective, because the religious traditions of the ancient West were numerous, diverse, and endured for ages.

We will examine the traditions of Iran, Greece, and Rome for two reasons. First, they include a variety of the beliefs and practices typical in the ancient West, such as polytheism (belief in many gods) and rituals of animal sacrifice. Second, these traditions had a strong influence on the emergence of Judaism, Christianity, and Islam. We will note many familiar features of these traditions that have been carried to modern times. Still, it is important to remember that these religions are not of

171

value merely because of their influences on Judaism, Christianity, and Islam. They are significant subjects of study in their own right. In addition, the religion of Ancient Iran—Zoroastrianism—is still alive today.

Religion in Ancient Iran: Zoroastrianism

Zoroastrianism is one of the world's oldest living religions. It arose and flourished in ancient Iran, which was known as Persia. Its present followers are few, made up mainly of the Parsis (which means "Persians") of India, whom we will consider at the close of this section.

Zoroastrianism has undergone a number of major changes since the time of its founder, Zarathustra (called Zoroaster by the Greeks). This ongoing transformation amounts to an incredibly diverse tradition with different features at different times. Let us begin by looking at Zarathustra and the Zoroastrianism of ancient times, when the religion exerted the most profound influence on the formation of Judaism and Christianity. The religious innovations of Zarathustra and the early Zoroastrians comprise a list that is both impressive and familiar: judgment of the soul after death, followed by an afterlife of either heaven or hell; a universe pervaded by forces of both good and evil; and even monotheism itself.

The Origins and Early Development of Zoroastrianism

Zoroastrianism originated in ancient Iran, an area now occupied by the nations of Iran and Afghanistan. Although we do not know for certain when Zarathustra lived, it was most

likely during the sixth or fifth century B.C.E. According to Persian tradition, he was born in 660 B.C.E.

Zoroastrianism began to flourish throughout Iran during the Persian Empire, which was at the height of its power and influence in the fifth and fourth centuries B.C.E. The Jews who remained in Babylon after having been forced into exile there (from 587 to 538 B.C.E.) lived in direct contact with the Persians who had conquered the region. After Persia was conquered by the Greek general Alexander the Great in 328 B.C.E., aspects of Persian culture, including Zoroastrianism, spread far and wide.

The Life of Zarathustra

Zarathustra's life story is shrouded in mystery. He seems to have been a son of a priest in a rural area. The traditional religion of Iran at this time was polytheistic, and a close relative of Hinduism. Zarathustra eventually initiated a large-scale religious conversion from polytheism to monotheism.

Legend has it that when Zarathustra was about thirty years old, he had an astonishing religious experience. An angel called Good Thought appeared to him and brought him, as a disembodied soul, before **Ahura Mazda,** the "Wise Lord." Zarathustra recognized Ahura Mazda as the one true God. After this experience Zarathustra went around preaching the radical message of monotheism to his polytheistic society. With the help of a king who had converted to Zoroastrianism, Zarathustra overcame hostile opposition and firmly established his religion. He is said to have died at the age of seventy-seven.

Given the legendary nature of Zarathustra's life story, we are fortunate to know his actual teachings. His hymns, or **Gathas,** are part of the sacred text of Zoroastrianism, the **Avesta.** Altogether the Avesta is a diverse set of writings, spanning a period of perhaps one thousand years. The Gathas are the oldest material, and in them we can observe Zarathustra's innovative religious ideas.

Ahura Mazda, the One God of Zarathustra

Monotheism is a notion so familiar to the West that its uniqueness can pass unnoticed. But we must be mindful of the entirely polytheistic nature of ancient Iranian society. Zarathustra's innovation was truly radical and courageous. The same can be said of the monotheism of the Hebrews (the ancestors of the Jews). We do not know whether Zarathustra and the ancient Hebrews influenced each other's thinking on this issue. In any event, the monotheism of both religions was a vast departure from the norm of the ancient world.

For Zarathustra, the one true God was Ahura Mazda, the Wise Lord. Ahura Mazda is eternal and universal goodness, controlling the cosmos and the destiny of human beings. In the following passages from the Gathas, Zarathustra celebrates Ahura Mazda's role as creator:

Who is by generation the Father of Right, at the first? Who determined the path of sun and stars? Who is it by whom the moon waxes and wanes again? . . .

Who upheld the earth beneath and the firmament from falling? Who the water and the plants? Who yoked swiftness to winds and clouds? . . . What artist made light and darkness?

What artist made sleep and waking? Who made morning, noon, and night, that call the understanding man to his duty?

. . . I strive to recognise by these things thee, O Mazdah, creator of all things through the holy spirit. (44.3–7)

Choosing Between Good and Evil: Ethical Dualism

Ethical dualism, the belief in universal forces of good and evil, is Zoroastrianism's most distinctive feature. In Zarathustra's theology the one God, Ahura Mazda, who is universal goodness, is opposed by "the Lie," depicted by Zarathustra as an evil, cosmic force.

With this approach, Zarathustra offered a straightforward solution to the problem

1
Review the passage from the Gathas on Ahura Mazda. To what extent does this strike you as a familiar description of God?

Far left: A portrait of Zarathustra
Left: A relief sculpture of Ahura Mazda stands among the ruins of Persepolis in Iran.

of evil: evil really exists, and manifests itself in the world. On the other hand, the belief in a cosmic force of evil poses a challenge to monotheism. For if evil really exists, is Ahura Mazda, who is perfect goodness, truly the only God? Such a question always challenges monotheistic theology, whatever the religion. Let us further consider Zarathustra's response, expressed in his theology of good and evil.

According to Zarathustra, Ahura Mazda had twin children, a beneficent spirit and a hostile spirit. (The hostile spirit later came to be known as Shaitan, which is related to the Hebrew name Satan.) Because both were born of Ahura Mazda, neither spirit was essentially evil. But they both were free to choose between the forces of good and evil. The beneficent spirit chose truth, but the hostile spirit chose the Lie, the evil force.

For Zarathustra, the universe was a cosmic battleground of good and evil forces, depicted as angels and demons (the demons were identified as the many gods of Iranian polytheism). This belief had a major influence on Judaism, Christianity, and Islam. Zarathustra believed that this cosmic battle would eventually be won by the good, angelic forces. He hinted at the doctrine of a future savior who would come to help restore goodness to the world. This doctrine was richly elaborated by later Zoroastrians, and it also seems to have influenced Judaism and its belief in the coming of a messiah.

This cosmic scheme of good and evil is crucial for human beings. For while the world awaits the ultimate triumph of goodness, humans must choose between truth and the Lie, between the beneficent spirit and the hostile spirit. Each person's choice has eternal consequences. In the Gathas, Zarathustra states the matter this way:

2
Consider carefully the Zoroastrian explanation for the existence of evil in the world. Based on your own experiences and observations, does this explanation account for evil? Why or why not?

Hear with your ears the best things. Reflect with clear purpose, each man for himself, on the two choices for decision, being alert indeed to declare yourselves for Him before the great requital. Truly there are two primal Spirits, twins renowned to be in conflict. In thought and word, in act they are two: the better and the bad. And those who act well have chosen rightly between these two, not so the evildoers. And when these two Spirits first came together they created life and not-life, and how at the end Worst Existence shall be for the wicked, but (the House of) Best Purpose for the just man. (30.2–4)

This passage shows how the dualism of Zoroastrianism unites ethics with human des-

tiny. At the "great requital," or day of judgment, the wicked will suffer the pains of "Worst Existence" (hell), while the just will enjoy the "House of Best Purpose" (heaven). Humans determine their own destiny by choosing either truth, goodness, and life, or falsehood, evil, and "not-life." This ethical dualism is the basis of Zoroastrianism.

Human Destiny

Zoroastrianism's doctrines regarding human destiny—resurrection and judgment of the dead, and vivid portrayals of heaven and hell

—are among its most famous and influential features. Zarathustra's own understanding of human destiny seems to have been as follows.

Shortly after death, each individual undergoes judgment. This requires crossing the "Bridge of the Separator," which goes over an abyss of horrible torment but leads to paradise. The ethical record of the individual is read and judged. The good are allowed to enter paradise, while the evil are cast down to the abyss. In the Gathas, Zarathustra emphasizes the individual responsibility for failing to pass the judgment:

Their own soul and their own self shall torment them when they come where the Bridge of the Separator is, to all time dwellers in the House of the Lie. (46.11)

Zoroastrians also believe in a final bodily resurrection of everyone, good and evil alike. Once resurrected, all will undergo a test by fire and molten metal; the evil will burn, while the good will pass through unharmed. It is not clear whether Zarathustra himself believed in resurrection, or if this belief developed later. We therefore do not know if Zoroastrianism influenced Judaism regarding the doctrine of resurrection or vice versa.

In any event, many aspects of the early Zoroastrian perspective on human destiny, such as descriptions of heaven and hell, were adopted by other religions. Heaven, or the House of Best Purpose, is said to be forever in sunshine, and its inhabitants enjoy the company of the saved. Hell, the Worst Existence, is a foul-smelling, dark place where the tormented are forced to remain completely alone.

Zoroastrian Life: Ethics and Worship

The traditional life of Zoroastrianism is centered on agriculture. Its ethical demands include such principles as caring for livestock and fields. Generally one is to lead a simple life, always telling the truth and doing what is right. Great care should be taken to avoid those on the side of evil, the followers of the demons for whom the Lie prevails.

Worship practices include prayer, which is to be done five times per day. (This seems to have influenced Islam, which sets forth a similar requirement.) The most famous form of Zoroastrian worship is the fire ritual. Fire is a symbol of the purity of Ahura Mazda. In the fire ritual, Zoroastrians do not worship fire itself, but rather Ahura Mazda's perfect purity. The fire ritual has always been central to Zoroastrian worship. According to tradition Zarathustra himself was killed while tending the sacred fire.

Modern Zoroastrians continue to emphasize the fire ritual. The fire burns continually within the inner sanctuary of a temple. The priests who tend the fire are extremely careful to maintain ritual purity, covering their mouth with a special cloth to avoid contaminating the fire. Worshipers wash themselves before approaching the fire, and bring offerings of sandalwood and money. In turn they receive ashes, which they rub on their face.

3
Fire is often used as a symbol. Recall several ways you have seen fire used as a symbol. Then think about what fire symbolizes for you personally.

Zoroastrianism Today: The Parsis

Once Islam had gained control of Iran in the tenth century, Zoroastrians began leaving. Very few remain in Iran today. Most of the world's Zoroastrians now live in India, where they are known as the Parsis.

The Parsis combine a wide variety of features from the Zoroastrian tradition. Basically, though, they maintain the monotheism of its founder, and continue to revere the Avesta as their sacred text.

Perhaps the most famous feature of Parsi religious practice is their manner of disposing of the dead. To avoid polluting the sacred elements of soil and fire, the Parsis neither bury nor cremate their dead. Rather, the corpse is placed on a "Tower of Silence," which is situated on a hilltop, out of view. Within hours vultures pick the bones clean. After several days the bones are gathered and thrown into a central well.

The Parsis are a rather closed society. Conversion to Zoroastrianism is generally not allowed, and marriages outside the faith are denounced. The Parsis are highly respected in Indian society because of their prosperous economic involvement and great emphasis on education. They also have a reputation for being philanthropic, devoting a good share of their wealth to societal needs.

Ancient Greek Religion

Western culture in general owes an enormous debt to ancient Greece. Democracy, drama, philosophy, and many forms of science and medicine—all were first developed by the ancient Greeks. In this respect ancient Greek culture is familiar to us. In the religious sphere, we will note both the exotic and the familiar, for both Judaism and Christianity developed within a cultural environment that was heavily influenced by Greek ideas.

The greatest cultural advancements were made during the classical period. This period began about 750 B.C.E. with the epic poet Homer, and ended with the death of Alexander the Great in 323 B.C.E. Alexander, who conquered a vast territory stretching from Egypt in the West to India in the East, imported classical Greek culture to the entire region. This is one of the main reasons Judaism and Christianity were so strongly influenced by the Greeks.

The Religious World of Homer

Sometime in the eighth century B.C.E., Homer composed the *Iliad* and the *Odyssey,* epic poems concerning the affairs of gods and humans in the Trojan War and its aftermath. For the next thousand years, Homer's influence was so great that he was known simply as "the poet." The *Iliad* and the *Odyssey* are commonly regarded as having been the "Bible" of the Greeks.

The nature of the religious teachings contained in the work of Homer differs greatly from those of the Jewish and Christian Bibles. The *Iliad* and the *Odyssey* do, nevertheless, contain an abundance of significant religious teachings.

The Olympian Pantheon

The most important of Homer's religious contributions is his portrayal of the Greek **pantheon,** or group of gods. The gods and goddesses inhabit the heavenly realm of Olympus (and so are called the Olympian pantheon), and form a loose-knit family. Zeus, the gatherer of clouds and bringer of storms, reigns as the father of the gods. When angered by the wrongful doings of mortals on earth, he is known to strike with thunderbolts. His wife is Hera, although he has other consorts as well. Hera is the goddess of marriage and of women. Homer often depicted quarrels between Zeus and Hera, but their marriage came to be revered by Greeks as ideal. They are the parents of Hephaestus, the god of fire, and of Ares, the god of war.

One major aspect of Homeric religion is already clear: it is polytheistic (which is a Greek word meaning "of many gods"). Other important deities of the Olympian pantheon include

Some members of
the Greek pantheon
Upper left:
Aphrodite
Above: Hermes
Center: Hera and
Athena
Lower left: Zeus

4
Religions of ancient cultures were primarily polytheistic. Think about the gods and goddesses of the Olympian pantheon, and speculate as to why polytheism appealed to people of ancient cultures.

Poseidon, god of the ocean, and Hades, god of the underworld. Both are brothers of Zeus. Offspring of Zeus by goddesses other than Hera include Hermes, messenger god; Aphrodite, goddess of love; Apollo, god of the lyre and of the bow (among other things); and Athena, goddess of wisdom.

Along with being polytheistic, the Olympian pantheon is notably **anthropomorphic** (another Greek word, meaning "of human form"). The gods have human attributes. No deity, not even Zeus, is all-powerful or all-knowing. Rather, they each have their specific talents, functions, and limitations. Morally speaking, too, they behave much more like humans than like gods (as we are accustomed to thinking of godlike behavior, that is). Examples of this abound. Zeus and Hera quarrel frequently. Ares and Aphrodite commit adultery. In general the Greek gods fail to maintain consistent principles of justice, both toward one another and toward human beings.

How could gods be plagued by such human shortcomings? This problem was addressed by many innovative Greek thinkers of the classical period.

Religious Innovations by the Greek Dramatists

Among the people who contributed new ideas to Homeric religion were the dramatists of fifth-century Athens. Aeschylus (525 to 456 B.C.E.) was especially concerned with the ideal of divine justice. Rather than focus on the anthropomorphic characteristics of Zeus, Aeschylus celebrated Zeus's great power and wisdom. Zeus is portrayed as ruling with perfect order and justice. For example, the *Agamemnon* explains human suffering as being a necessary part of the divine plan of Zeus:

Now Zeus is lord; and he
Who loyally acclaims his victory
Shall by heart's instinct find the universal key:

Zeus, whose will has marked for man
The sole way where wisdom lies;
Ordered one eternal plan:
Man must suffer to be wise.

(*The Oresteian Trilogy,* page 48)

This kind of direct and lofty theology is not found in Homer. The Olympian pantheon, and Zeus especially, takes on a new dignity.

Zeus is no longer merely a god of tremendous power; he is now the source and the enforcer of universal moral principles. Sophocles (496 to 406 B.C.E.), another of the great Athenian dramatists, followed Aeschylus in celebrating the justice of Zeus, and also emphasized the god's mercy.

Piety and Worship

The anthropomorphism of the Homeric deities is reflected in the way they are worshiped. Like parents demanding respect from their children, so do the gods and goddesses demand piety and proper worship. The mortals in Homer's poems are diligent in their prayers and words of praise, to which the deities respond favorably. On the other hand, the gods are quick and steadfast in punishing the impious. Throughout the *Odyssey*, for example, Odysseus (who is also known by his Latin name, Ulysses) is tormented by the wrath of Poseidon. The god is outraged because Odysseus blinded the cyclops (a one-eyed giant), Poseidon's son.

The Greek deities, much like human beings, relish receiving gifts, especially the gift of sacrifice. Sheep, calves, and other animals are ritually slaughtered, and the meat is cooked and offered to the gods (it is then eaten by the worshipers). Wine is poured out as libations, or sacrifices. Armor and other precious items are placed in temples as gifts. All such forms of sacrificial giving are pleasing to the gods, who in turn are believed to look out for the welfare of the worshipers.

Festivals

Along with daily worship practices, the Greeks throughout the classical period and beyond worshiped their gods in lavish festivals. Usually they were local events, specific to each city-state. Athens, for example, worshiped its patron goddess Athena in an annual celebration of her birthday.

Other festivals were not limited to specific city-states, but involved Greeks from across the land. One such festival developed in Olympia (a small village in southwestern Greece, not to be confused with the heavenly realm of Mount Olympus). Founded in 776 B.C.E., the Olympian Games were held every four years and endured for over one thousand years, until the Roman Emperor Theodosius I abolished them in 393 C.E. They were revived in a different form late in the nineteenth century, and continue to this day.

Theodosius, a Christian, did not tolerate the games due to their religious nature. Like our modern version, the Olympian Games featured athletic contests such as running, wrestling, boxing, and horse and chariot racing. They attracted the best athletes from the ancient Mediterranean world. But the Olympian Games were primarily a religious festival in honor of Zeus. The athletic prowess of the participants was itself a form of sacrificial gift, offered to Zeus through the performance of the various contests. A victorious performance was deemed an especially worthy gift. The first and final days of the five-day festival were devoted to sacrifices and ceremony. Olympia, situated in a beautiful valley amid wooded hillsides, was the main sanctuary of Zeus. Temples of both Zeus and Hera occupied the area adjacent to the stadium and other sites of athletic contests.

Oracles

The Greeks believed that the gods communicated their desires and intentions to mortals. In Homer's poems the gods frequently converse directly with heroes such as Achilles and Odysseus. The gods also reveal their will through dreams and ominous signs, such as the clap of thunder or the flight of birds. And the gods communicate through oracles.

An **oracle** was a sanctuary favored by a particular god, who communicated in some manner to those who visited the site. At one oracle, for example, the will of Zeus could be heard through the whispering leaves of its sacred oak grove. The most famous oracle was at Delphi, where the Greeks sought the wisdom of the god Apollo. Situated on the slopes of Mount Parnassus, high above the Gulf of Corinth, Delphi had been considered a sacred site from very early times and was thought to be the center of the earth.

The temple of Apollo stood amid an elaborate complex of structures, including a theater, a stadium, and a number of treasury buildings owned by the various city-states

throughout Greece. The god communicated through the Pythia, a woman who sat upon a tripod within the temple. The Pythia probably ingested some substance that brought on an ecstatic state—perhaps bay leaves, the sacred plant of Apollo. In her state of ecstasy, she uttered the will of Apollo in speech that was intelligible only to the oracle's priests. They, in turn, translated her utterances into Greek.

The oracle at Delphi was consulted for reasons ranging from private matters to public issues of far-reaching concern. Major political and military decisions were sometimes based on the oracle's revelation of the god's will. Apollo was considered to have favored philosophy, and he was credited with having pronounced at Delphi the famous Greek sayings, "Know thyself" and "Nothing to excess"; both were engraved on the temple. The oracle also proclaimed that the philosopher Socrates was the wisest of all people.

Like the Olympian Games, the oracle at Delphi endured for centuries. It too was abolished by Emperor Theodosius I in 390 C.E. But by this time the voice of Apollo had almost been silenced. The oracle itself had announced its own decline a short time before.

Homer's Perspective on Death and the Afterlife

Homer also set forth a view of death and the afterlife. When a person dies in the *Iliad* and the *Odyssey,* the soul departs from the body, entering the dark and dreary underworld ruled by the god Hades and his queen, Persephone. The House of Hades, through which flows the River Styx, offers little hope for happiness. The souls, or "shades," lack physical substance and strength, and yet remember their earthly lives with regret and longing.

In the *Odyssey* Odysseus journeys to the entrance of the realm of Hades to consult a famous seer, now dead. While there he encounters the shades of his fallen comrades. His conversation with Achilles, the greatest of all Greek warriors, leaves no doubt as to the gloominess of the afterlife envisioned by Homer. Odysseus talks with his friend:

"But you, Achilles, are the most fortunate man that ever was or will be! For in the old days when you were on Earth, we Argives honoured you as though you were a god; and now, down here, you have great power among the dead. Do not grieve at your death, Achilles."

"And do not you make light of death, illustrious Odysseus," he replied. "I would rather work the soil as a serf on hire to some landless impoverished peasant than be King of all these lifeless dead." (*The Odyssey,* book 2)

The Homeric conception of the afterlife left little room for optimism in the face of death. Homer makes brief mention of a paradise, the Elysian fields, but he identifies only one mortal, King Menelaus, who is destined to go there after death. For the Greeks of Homer's time, the emphasis was clearly on living a good and honorable life, not on the prospects of a happy afterlife.

Alternatives to Homer: The Mystery Religions

Homer's influence on Greek religion was vast, but he did not tell the entire story. Other forms of religion, some already firmly in place by Homer's time, flourished alongside the worship of the Olympian gods. Deities such as Demeter and Dionysus, who are barely mentioned in Homer's poems, rivaled the popularity of the Olympians. Such deities were worshiped in a diverse group of beliefs and practices that are now referred to as the **mystery religions.**

The word *mystery* is derived from a Greek term meaning "to cover," and the initiates of these religions did an extraordinary job of keeping their secrets covered. As a result we know very little about the actual rites. It is clear, however, that the mysteries included three basic aspects:

1. Individuals had to make the choice to become adherents, and they went through some form of initiation ritual.
2. The initiate experienced a personal encounter with the deity.

3. The initiate could hope for a better afterlife, along with the spiritual renewal attained through participation.

The mystery religions therefore offered important alternatives to the Homeric religion, especially to its dreary prospects for the afterlife in the dark realm of Hades.

The great and long-lived popularity of the mystery religions, together with the joyous pageantry of the days surrounding the actual initiation rites, bear witness to their power for enhancing the lives of those who adhered to them. As we will see, various mystery religions continued to play a central role in the religious life of Rome. Indeed, for people of the ancient Roman world, Christianity itself appeared to be a mystery religion, offering familiar and attractive prospects: a community of fellow initiates, a deeply personal relationship with Christ, and hopes for spiritual renewal and a blessed afterlife.

The Eleusinian Mysteries

The mystery religion par excellence, celebrated at Eleusis, near Athens, honored the grain goddess Demeter and her daughter, Persephone. Along with being very popular for centuries, the Eleusinian mysteries set forth a basic form that influenced the development of later mystery religions in the Roman world.

Mystery religions were typically based on a myth celebrating the theme of new life arising from death. The myth of Demeter and Persephone goes as follows: One day Persephone

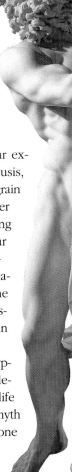

Hades kidnaps Persephone in this seventeenth-century sculpture by Italian artist Gian Lorenzo Bernini.

7

The theme of life arising from death, celebrated in classic fashion by the Eleusinian myth of Demeter and Persephone, is a universal theme. It is being expressed all around us, sometimes in myth and other literary and artistic forms, sometimes in nature, and sometimes even within our own personal and social worlds. Think of at least three ways you have seen this theme expressed. Briefly describe each.

was gathering flowers in a meadow. Hades sprang from beneath the earth and took her away with him to his dark, subterranean realm. Demeter searched everywhere but could not find her beloved daughter. In her grief and anger, Demeter prevented crops from growing on the land. The famine grew so quickly that humanity was threatened. Zeus was alarmed that his worshipers might all perish, so he sent Hermes to the underworld to order Hades to let Persephone leave. Hades did as he was told, but as Persephone was leaving, he gave her a taste of pomegranate, a fruit symbolic of marriage. Persephone and her mother were joyfully reunited, and the goddess made the crops grow abundantly. But because Persephone had eaten of the pomegranate, Zeus forced her to spend one-third of every year in the underworld as Hades's wife; the rest of the year she could be with her mother.

This myth clearly correlates with the agricultural cycle. For the four months that Persephone is in the underworld, the fields lie dormant. When she returns to Earth, new life is born and flourishes for the duration of her eight-month stay. The initiates of the Eleusinian mysteries experienced a similar sort of new life.

Through their initiation rites, they enjoyed spiritual renewal, along with the hope of a blessed afterlife, because they had gained the favor of Persephone, queen of the underworld.

The Cult of Dionysus

Another popular mystery religion, especially among women, was devoted to the god Dionysus. He was a god of fertility and vegetation, and specifically of the vine (and hence of wine). Dionysus is often depicted in Greek art with vines and grapes, and there are accounts of him miraculously turning water into wine.

Worship of Dionysus usually occurred in the remote countryside, among the wild vegetation of the hills and mountains, and involved frenzied, ecstatic behavior on the part of the worshiper. In a manner typical of the mystery religions, the worship aimed at

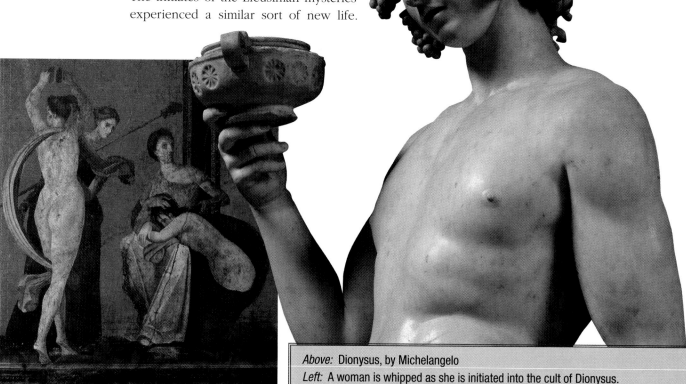

Above: Dionysus, by Michelangelo

Left: A woman is whipped as she is initiated into the cult of Dionysus.

attaining union with the deity. This was primarily accomplished through ritual drinking of wine and eating of animal flesh, in which the god was believed to reside.

Worship of Dionysus was often untamed and, at its most extreme, frenzied. Greeks likely regarded the more extreme forms of Dionysian worship with disgust. Orphism offered quite a different approach to the worship of Dionysus.

Orphism: Freeing the Soul from the Body

Orphism is named for the legendary Orpheus, famous in Greek mythology as a gifted musician and singer. According to the Orphics, Dionysus, the son of Zeus, was eaten by the evil Titans. In anger Zeus struck the Titans with his thunderbolts, burning them to death. From their ashes the first human beings were born.

For the Orphics, this myth established that humans possess a dual nature: the evil, bodily, Titanic aspect, and the good, spiritual, Dionysian aspect. The body, the Orphics believed, is the tomb of the soul (expressed in Greek as *soma sema,* "body [is] tomb"). The religious task of Orphism was to lead a pure life, through vegetarianism and other ascetic practices, so that the soul might eventually escape from the body and realize fully its divine, Dionysian nature. This task was thought to take many lifetimes; the Orphics believed in reincarnation of the soul. (We do not know whether these ancient Greeks were influenced by the Hindu doctrine of reincarnation.)

Orphic Influence on Plato

Orphism remained an important part of Greek religion for centuries. Its influence on the intellectual history of Western civilization is still being felt, for the great philosopher Plato adopted some of its primary beliefs.

Though reincarnation, or the transmigration of souls, has never become a widely popular belief in the West, it was an important part of Plato's philosophy, closely related to his theory of knowledge. Plato believed that we know things in this life partly because we have experienced them in previous lives. Knowledge, therefore, is *recollection.*

Plato also embraced the Orphic notion of the dual makeup of human nature: body and soul (or mind). According to Plato, truth exists independently of any bodily, or material, existence. Instead, truth consists of Forms (or Ideas), which are purely intellectual constructs. Wisdom lies in identifying oneself with the truth of the Forms, rather than with the material world. The influence of this **Platonic dualism,** even to the present day, cannot be overestimated. Most early Christian theologians, for example, were well educated in the philosophy of Plato. They incorporated this dualism of mind and body into their understanding of Christianity. One of the greatest theologians of all time, Saint Augustine of Hippo, was first attracted to Christianity largely because of its similarities with Plato's philosophy.

The Healing Cult of Asclepius

The ancient Greeks commonly turned to religion for the earthly reward of healing from sickness or injury. This was the special domain of Asclepius. Homer described Asclepius as a very able, yet mortal, physician, but Asclepius came to be regarded by the Greeks as a god. He was thought to be the son of the god Apollo, who was also revered for his

Left: Plato embraced the Orphic notion of the dual makeup of human nature.

8
The influence of Plato, especially of his dualism of body and soul (or mind), is deeply ingrained in Christian thought, and in Western culture generally. Reflect on Plato's notion of the body as being distinct from the mind. Do you tend to look at yourself this way? Do you think this is necessarily the correct perspective? Why or why not?

healing powers. Hygeia, the daughter of Asclepius, was closely associated with him. Her name means "health," and it is the root of the word *hygiene.*

The cult of Asclepius was very popular. In fact, for a time, Asclepius was probably the most popular of all Greek deities. Unlike the gods of the Olympian pantheon, Asclepius offered the joy of a close relationship between worshiper and god. Like any good doctor, Asclepius cared dearly for every individual who sought his aid.

Asclepius was believed to have tremendous powers of healing, and even the ability to bring the dead back to life. The great sanctuaries in which he was worshiped were really ancient health spas, where strict diets were enforced, and baths, gyms, and theaters were available for physical and recreational activities. Most of the actual healing occurred while the patient lay in a sacred chamber sleeping, when Asclepius was thought to visit and administer a cure. Patients commonly left offerings to the god, sometimes in the form of replicas of the ailing body part.

The healing cult of Asclepius influenced the development of Christianity. When people of the ancient Mediterranean world first heard about Christianity, Jesus seemed to have much in common with the ancient healer Asclepius. Both were called Savior, and the intimacy of the worshipers' relationship with Asclepius bore a strong resemblance to the relationship with Christ celebrated, then as now, by Christians.

Religion in the Roman World

Our word *religion* is derived from the Latin *religio.* The two terms do not mean the same thing, however. *Religio* is a bond or restraint; Roman religion was based on the notion that life is restrained by the numerous divine powers inhabiting the world. The Roman people strove to improve their lot in life through *pietas* (from which we get *piety*), the attitude of reverence toward the divine powers. Like

the Greeks of Homer's time, the early Romans did not have reason to hope for a blessed afterlife. Their religion was oriented toward achieving things in this world. The Romans, who were heavily influenced by Greek culture, eventually sought more from religion. Such alternatives as the mystery religions became popular throughout the Roman Empire.

Numina: Supernatural Powers

The Roman gods and goddesses eventually took on many characteristics of their counterparts in the Olympian pantheon, but in early times the deities of Rome differed significantly from those of the Greeks. The Romans did not think of their gods in human terms, as Homer had done. Rather, the gods tended to be vaguely defined. Sometimes they were not even assigned a gender. Venus, for example, who later became famous as the goddess of love (and was identified with the Greek goddess Aphrodite), was not originally seen as having a specific gender.

The deities belonged to a larger category known as **numina.** The *numina* were supernatural powers, each in charge of a very specific function. Roman homes, towns, and the countryside were thought to be populated by *numina.* They inhabited a wide variety of spaces, such as fields, streams, trees, doorways, altars, and shrines. The gods possessed **numen** in great abundance. Even human beings possessed *numen.* So too did the objects they used, such as tools or weapons. *Numen* could be transferred from one thing to another. This is crucial to understanding early Roman religion, for *numen* could be attained from the gods through *pietas.*

The Roman Pantheon

The most powerful of all Roman deities, because he possessed the most *numen,* was Jupiter, the sky god. Jupiter was one of a triad of deities that also included Juno, the goddess who looked after women, and Minerva, goddess of handicrafts. Vesta, goddess of the hearth, and Janus, god of doorways, were especially revered within the home. Because he

Songs for the Gods

Aelius Aristides was an accomplished public speaker and writer of Greek literature who lived in the second century c.e. He was frequently ill, and so spent many of his days at the Asclepium—the healing sanctuary of the god Asclepius—at Pergamum, a city in Asia Minor (modern-day Turkey). His Sacred Tales *record the events surrounding his many bouts with illness, especially the constant care he received from Asclepius, the god of healing. According to the* Sacred Tales, *Asclepius appeared often to Aristides, usually in dreams. In these dream revelations, the god would prescribe methods of curing whatever ailed Aristides.*

Along with providing important evidence regarding medical practices in antiquity, the Sacred Tales *offer some of the most elaborate and personal accounts of religious experience to have survived from ancient Greece and Rome. In this passage Aristides provides something of an introduction to his* Sacred Tales, *which he wrote as an expression of gratitude to "the God,"* Asclepius:

To narrate what came next is not within the power of man. Still I must try, as I have undertaken to recount some of these things in a cursory way. But if someone wishes to know with the utmost precision what has befallen us from the God, it is time for him to seek out the parchment books and the dreams themselves. For he will find cures of all kinds and some discourses and full scale orations and various visions, and all of the prophecies and oracles about every kind of matter, some in prose, some in verse, and all expressive of my gratitude to the God, greater than one might expect. (Quoted in Behr, *Aelius Aristides and the Sacred Tales,* page 224)

Aristides asserts that Asclepius himself approved the project by naming the writings the Sacred Tales, *and then goes on to recall what he refers to as "strange events"—his dream visions of Asclepius and miraculous healings of various types. Aristides also credits Asclepius, along with other gods, for having inspired him to produce hymns. The following passage makes clear the polytheistic nature of Aristides's religion, which was typical of the ancient West.*

Tale follows tale, and let us say again that along with other things, Asclepius, the Savior, also commanded us to spend time on songs and lyric verse, and to relax and maintain a chorus of boys. . . . The children sang my songs; and whenever I happened to choke, if my throat were suddenly constricted, or my stomach became disordered, or whenever I had some other troublesome attack, the doctor Theodotus, being in attendance and remembering my dreams, would order the boys to sing some of my lyric verse. And while they were singing, there arose unnoticed a feeling of comfort, and sometimes everything which pained me went completely away.

And this was a very great gain, and the honor was still greater than this, for my lyric verse also found favor with the God. He ordered me to compose not only for him, but also indicated others, as Pan, Hecate, Achelous, and whatever else it might be. There also came a dream from Athena, which contained a hymn to the Goddess.

. . .

And another dream came from Zeus, but I cannot remember which of these was first or second, and another again from Dionysus, which said to address the God, as "curly haired."

And Hermes was also seen with his dog skin cap, and he was marvellously beautiful and extraordinarily mobile. And while I was singing of him and feeling pleased that I had easily said the proper things, I awoke. . . .

But most things were written for Apollo and Asclepius through the inspiration of my dreams, and many of these nearly from memory, as whenever I was riding in a carriage, or even was walking. (Pages 261–262)

presided over the crossing of the threshold, Janus came to be associated in general with beginnings. That is why our first month of the year is named January.

Once the Romans had come under the influence of Greek culture (about the fifth century B.C.E.), their pantheon quickly took on the characteristics Homer had conveyed about the Olympians. Most of Rome's important deities became identified with Greek counterparts: Jupiter with Zeus, Juno with Hera, Minerva with Athena, Venus with Aphrodite, and so on.

In many ways the Roman pantheon is more familiar to the modern world than the Greek is. The names of seven of the nine planets in our solar system, for example, are derived from Roman deities. In addition to Jupiter and Venus, there is Mars, god of war (identified with the Greek Ares); Neptune, god of the sea (identified with Poseidon);

Pluto, god of the underworld (identified with Hades); Mercury, the god of traders (identified with Hermes, the Greek messenger god); and Saturn, the god of sowing (identified with the Greek Kronos, father of Zeus).

Greek influence was so great that some Greek gods, such as Apollo and Asclepius, were simply adopted by the Romans. The first Greek religious figure to be worshiped by the Romans was Heracles, the great hero known to the Romans as Hercules. He was especially popular among merchants because of his success at making long journeys through perilous lands.

Proper worship of the gods was thought to bestow *numen* on the worshiper, so the Roman state considered it essential to maintain official worship practices. Through official worship the state itself would prosper from the gods' favor. The state assigned a priest for each of the major deities. The priests were highly respected and deeply devoted. They were kept very busy attending to their tasks, because the gods were worshiped regularly and with utmost precision. Altogether, 104 official ceremonies occurred each year, sometimes accompanied by large public festivals, other times carried out by the assigned priest in solitude.

Roman goddesses: *Left:* Venus, with Ceres and Juno, from a painting by Raphael; *Right:* Juno, by sculptor Lorenzo Bartolini

A temple in Rome. Proper worship of the gods was thought to bestow *numen* on the worshiper.

A Multicultural World: Mystery Religions of Rome

By the end of the first century B.C.E., Rome had conquered most of the regions surrounding the Mediterranean Sea, along with vast stretches of western Asia. As a result many cultures were imported, each with its own religious forms. Most people freely adopted foreign ideas and practices. Mystery religions became especially popular. Along with the Greek mysteries, important new religions from Egypt, Syria, and Asia Minor gained widespread popularity. By the middle of the first century C.E., another new religion, this one from Palestine, had begun to attract adherents. For the next three centuries, Christianity would vie with these other mystery religions for the religious allegiance of the Roman populace.

The mystery religions had a universal appeal. Though the Eleusinian mysteries were located in a specific place, most mystery religions could be celebrated anywhere. It was also perfectly common to be an initiate of more than one mystery religion (except for Christians, who, like the Jews, maintained devotion to only one religion). And most mystery religions welcomed members of any social class, ethnic background, or gender. One important exception to this inclusiveness was Mithraism, the favored cult of the Roman army, which allowed only men. In spite of this restriction, Mithraism had an enormous following and was one of the two main rivals to Christianity in the later Roman Empire. The other rival was the mystery religion celebrating the goddess Isis.

Goddess of Many Names: The Cult of Isis

The cult of Isis drew from an ancient Egyptian tradition about the goddess Isis and her husband, Osiris. According to the myth, Osiris was killed and hacked into pieces by his evil brother. Isis searched far and wide, finally finding Osiris's body parts. She mummified him, which brought him back to life. Osiris became god of the underworld.

This theme—of life overcoming death through the power of Isis—was central to her cult. Osiris's powerful position as god of the underworld likewise contributed. A blessed afterlife was one of the rewards the worshipers of Isis and Osiris anticipated.

Many aspects of the cult of Isis were preserved in a delightful novel from the second century C.E. called *The Metamorphoses* (also known as *The Golden Ass*), by Apuleius. The hero of the story, Lucius, is magically transformed into an ass, only to be changed back into human form through his devotion to Isis. The novel contains a long and detailed description of the ceremony associated with initiation. Most crucially, Apuleius describes the

10

The initiates of the mystery religions were forbidden to reveal the secrets of their rites. Apuleius's description of the moments within the inner sanctuary is therefore especially intriguing to specialists attempting to discover the secrets of the cult of Isis. You have read about the Greek and Roman mysteries, as well as Apuleius's brief—and intentionally sketchy—account of the rites of the inner sanctuary. Now come up with your own description of the rites. Include the elements described by Apuleius, but add details you think Apuleius may have left out. Use your imagination!

11

Roman worship of the genius of the emperor was really a means of expressing one's devotion to the state. In other words it was a form of patriotism. What forms of "emperor worship" do we practice today? Would you label such forms of devotion "religious"?

moments within the inner sanctuary of the temple of Isis:

> I approached the confines of death. I trod the threshold of [Persephone]; and borne through the elements I returned. At midnight I saw the Sun shining in all his glory. I approached the gods below and the gods above, and I stood beside them, and I worshiped them. (Quoted in *The Ancient Mysteries,* page 158)

Whatever we are to make of Lucius being "borne through the elements," it is clear that through the initiation rite he was "reborn" (as it is described later in the novel) after passing through a ritual death. Life is renewed and enhanced through symbolically overcoming death. This theme is common to all the mystery religions of ancient Greece and Rome.

The cult of Isis seems to have influenced early Christian veneration of the Virgin Mary. The ancient Romans recognized important similarities between these two. Like Mary, Isis was regarded by her followers as "queen of heaven." Artistic representations of Isis holding her son are stunningly similar to those of Mary with the infant Jesus.

Emperor Worship

The mystery religions influenced the development of Christianity because of the characteristics they had in common. Emperor worship was influential for quite a different reason, for it was the Christians' insistence on *not* worshiping the emperor that sometimes resulted in their being violently persecuted.

Like so many facets of Roman religion, emperor worship had its roots in Greece and other nations in the ancient Mediterranean world. Alexander the Great, for example, when he conquered the lands of Egypt and Persia, was worshiped as a god by their inhabitants.

Among the Romans, leaders such as Julius Caesar flirted with the idea of being worshiped; some, such as Caligula, Nero, and

Domitian, openly declared their divinity. Emperor Augustus (who was in power at the time Jesus was born), though, established a pattern that most of the later emperors were to follow. He encouraged the worship not of himself personally, but of his genius, or guardian spirit. This actually focused worship on Rome itself, because the emperor's genius was thought to guard the welfare of the entire state.

This notion of worshiping the Roman state was precisely the issue addressed in a fascinating letter from the early second century C.E. It was written by Pliny the Younger, who served as a governor under the emperor Trajan. To settle a local dispute, Pliny needed to know who among the populace was Christian. Whoever consented to worshiping the emperor in the proper manner, Pliny writes, could not have been Christian:

> Those who denied they were, or had ever been, Christians, who repeated after me an invocation to the gods, and offered adoration, with wine and frankincense, to your image, which I had ordered to be brought for that purpose, together with those of the gods, and who finally cursed Christ—none of which acts, it is said, those who are really Christians can be forced into performing—these I

thought it proper to discharge. . . . They all worshipped your statue and the images of the gods, and cursed Christ. (Kee, *The New Testament in Context,* page 44)

The Christians had obvious reasons for refusing to worship the emperor, just as they refused to worship any of the other Roman gods; to have done so would have contradicted their belief in only one God. The Romans, on the other hand, grew suspicious of the Christians for their very refusal to worship the emperor, for this appeared to imply that they did not support the state. Under such circumstances it was inevitable that conflicts would arise.

Legacies from Ancient Times

In this chapter we have glimpsed many beliefs and ideas that appear strange, and many others that appear familiar. In the religions of Greece and Rome, especially, the strangeness is striking. Belief in many gods, many of them of questionable moral fiber; a tendency to regard religion as a means to attaining things in this world; and the likelihood that an individual would embrace more than one religion—all these features probably strike the modern Westerner as being rather strange. And yet the similarities between these traditions, born of influences passed from one to another, are equally striking. Herein lies the essence of history: It is a vast flow, carrying bits and pieces from the past to the present, sometimes from ancient times to the modern age.

We do not need to limit ourselves to consideration of Western religions, however, when pondering the extent of influence exercised by the religions of ancient Iran, Greece, and Rome. Zoroastrian doctrines concerning saviors, for example, helped shape the Mahayana Buddhist pantheon of *bodhisattvas*. Nor do we need to limit ourselves only to a consideration of influences to make a study of the ancient world meaningful. Indeed the strange can be as meaningful as the familiar, for these strange ways were the innovations of the minds and hearts of human beings, our worthy ancestors.

Left: Priests of Isis perform a ceremony in this ancient wall painting.
Above: Emperor Augustus

Glossary

Ahura Mazda (ah'hoo-reh maz'dah). The "Wise Lord," the one true God worshiped by Zarathustra and later by Zoroastrians.

anthropomorphic. Of human form, characteristic of the deities of ancient Greek and later Roman religion.

Avesta (a-ves'tuh). The sacred text of Zoroastrianism, which includes the very old hymns known as the Gathas, along with more recent material.

ethical dualism. The belief in universal forces of good and evil; Zoroastrianism's most distinctive feature.

Gathas (gah'thuhs). Seventeen hymns attributed to Zarathustra that comprise the oldest and most important portion of the Avesta.

mystery religions. A diverse group of beliefs and practices of ancient Greek and Roman civilization that included initiation into a specific group, a personal encounter with the deity, and hope for spiritual renewal and a better afterlife.

numen (noo'men). The ancient Roman concept of supernatural power, possessed in abundance by the gods; also believed to inhabit a wide variety of things and places, as well as human beings.

numina (noo'men uh). Plural of *numen.*

oracle. A shrine or sanctuary at which the revelations of a god are received, often through a human medium; also, the medium or the revelation itself.

Orphism. An ancient Greek religion named for the legendary musician and singer Orpheus, which incorporated a myth of Dionysus, emphasized an ascetic lifestyle, and included belief in reincarnation, or the transmigration of the soul.

pantheon. A group of deities recognized by a society, such as the Olympian pantheon of the ancient Greeks.

Platonic dualism. Plato's highly influential perspective that true reality consists of intellectual constructs known as Forms, or Ideas, and that the material, bodily world is an imperfect reflection of the world of Forms, dependent on them for all its qualities.

The Ancient Near East

SYRIA

Damascus

Sea of Galilee

ISRAEL

Jerusalem

JUDAH

Dead Sea

Mediterranean Sea

Nile

SINAI

EGYPT

12

12 Judaism

The People of the Covenant

Judaism is not only the adherence to particular doctrines and observances, but primarily living in the spiritual order of the Jewish people, the living *in* the Jews of the past and *with* the Jews of the present. . . . It is not a doctrine, an idea, a faith, but the covenant between God and the people. (Heschel, *Man's Quest for God,* page 45)

The religion of Judaism can be summarized in several ways. Abraham Joshua Heschel, a renowned Jewish holy man of the twentieth century, refers to Judaism as "the covenant between God and the people." Heschel emphasizes the role of the Jewish people, both past and present. This summary will serve as our point of departure for exploring Judaism.

   We begin with the **Covenant.** This is an agreement established long ago between God and the ancient Israelites, first through Abraham and later through Moses. God spoke to Moses on Mount Sinai, promising that if the Israelites would keep the

Covenant by obeying the Law (or Torah), they would be God's "treasured possession," and "a kingdom of priests and a holy nation" (Exodus 19:5–6, Tanakh).

Because of the Covenant, the Jews are understood to be God's Chosen People, a status that carries serious responsibilities. The Jewish people are forever challenged to live as befits a "holy nation." Moreover, the Jews are challenged to live as a "nation," or people. The Covenant is between God and the people; thus Judaism places great emphasis on group identity. In modern times this emphasis has given rise to new challenges, for not all Jews are adherents of the religion of Judaism. It is therefore necessary to distinguish between "religious" (or "observant") Jews, and "cultural" (or "nonobservant") Jews.

Heschel remarks that Judaism is "the living *in* the Jews of the past and *with* the Jews of the present." These two notions refer to other, related ways of summarizing Judaism. First, Judaism is the interpretation of the history of the Jewish people, "the Jews of the past." Second, Judaism is the sanctification of life, the means through which Jews live with "the Jews of the present." We will devote a main section of this chapter to each of these summary statements. But in the first section, let us consider the central teachings of Judaism on God and the divine revelation.

A modern-day scribe explains the Torah to young children at New York's Temple Emanu-El.

Judaism's Central Teachings: On God and Torah

The first step in elaborating on our summary of Judaism is to consider God and the revelation of the divine will to the Chosen People. This revelation, or Torah, is recorded in the Hebrew Bible and in writings of the **rabbis** of the early centuries of the Common Era. We will investigate each of these in turn. We begin, though, by considering Jewish teachings regarding God.

Master of the Universe: Judaism's God

The deep and constant reverence that observant Jews show toward their God is evident in their avoidance of pronouncing the divine name—it is considered too holy to be spoken by human beings. The name is written, however, and appears in the Hebrew equivalents of the letters *YHWH*. (Hebrew had no vowels, so the name of God consists only of these consonants.) This name is pronounced (though not by observant Jews) as Yahweh (ya-way). When Jews come across the name while reading the Bible, they say "the Lord" instead of pronouncing the actual name. Often God is referred to by other phrases, too, the most common being Master of the Universe.

God has a personal name, and God is

thought to be a personal being, intimately involved in the welfare of humans and the rest of the created world. But God is also transcendent of creation, and is infinitely powerful, all-knowing, and beyond the limits of space and time. And God is believed to be the one and only God. In Judaism's basic theological statement, called the **Shema** (Hebrew for "hear"), the uniqueness of God is set forth: "Hear, O Israel! The LORD is our God, the LORD alone" (Deuteronomy 6:4, Tanakh). The Shema is recited at least twice daily, in morning and evening prayers.

This basic declaration of monotheism may sound obvious or commonplace today. But when it was first formulated, Israel's neighbors were all polytheists. It was a radical statement in that day. Monotheism itself was a radical religious development, and it marks one of Judaism's major contributions to Western civilization.

Torah: Revelation of God's Will

Torah is among the most important terms in Judaism. It literally means "instruction" and refers to the will of God as it is revealed to humankind. It is also loosely translated as "law"; on a practical level, the revelation of God's will sets forth the Law that guides proper human conduct. Finally, in a more specific—and more common—usage, Torah refers to the first five books of the Bible, which are traditionally believed to have been revealed directly by God to Moses. The five books of the Torah are the central statement of the religious laws of Judaism.

In its more general sense, as revelation, Torah is set forth in several ways, each one the extension of another. With God in the center, the divine will is revealed outward in a series of concentric circles, like the rings of a tree trunk. The first ring consists of the "written Torah," the word of God contained in the Hebrew Bible.

Written Torah: The Hebrew Bible

The Hebrew Bible contains three major parts: the Torah, the Prophets, and the Writings. In Hebrew the words *Torah, Prophets,* and *Writings* begin with *T, N,* and *K,* respectively. The Bible itself is conveniently referred to as the **Tanakh** (from *T-N-K*).

The contents of the Hebrew Bible are also found in the Christian Old Testament, but the books are named and ordered somewhat differently. Of course for Judaism the Tanakh is in no sense an "Old Testament." Nothing new has ever superseded it, and it remains the vital center of Jewish understanding.

The Torah. The Torah contains the first five books of the Bible. It is also called the *Pentateuch,* a Greek term meaning "five books." The Torah holds a position of prominence that sets it apart from the rest of the Tanakh. According to tradition, God revealed its contents once and for all time at Mount Sinai to Moses, who is regarded as the Torah's author. The Torah, the Law, stands forever as Judaism's central code of holiness. It is thought to contain 613 specific laws, the most famous being the Ten Commandments, which are set forth in Exodus, chapter 20.

1

The term *Torah* has three slightly different meanings: God's revelation (instruction), Law, and the first five books of the Bible. One of the books of the Torah is Leviticus. Read chapter 19 of Leviticus. List several of the specific laws given. Then discuss how these laws of Torah might also convey God's revelation.

In Marc Chagall's painting *Moses Receives the Tablets from the Lord,* the Ten Commandments are given to the Hebrew people.

Contents of the Hebrew Bible, or Tanakh

The Torah, or Law

Genesis, Exodus, Leviticus, Numbers, Deuteronomy

The Prophets

Joshua, Judges, 1 Samuel, 2 Samuel, 1 Kings, 2 Kings, Isaiah, Jeremiah, Ezekiel; and the twelve minor prophets: Hosea, Joel, Amos, Obadiah, Jonah, Micah, Nahum, Habbakuk, Zephaniah, Haggai, Zechariah, Malachi

The Writings

Psalms, Proverbs, Job, Song of Solomon, Ruth, Lamentations, Ecclesiastes, Esther, Daniel, Ezra-Nehemiah, 1 Chronicles, 2 Chronicles

---

2
Read at least the entire first chapter of the Book of Jeremiah. Illustrate how the prophet Jeremiah is one who speaks for God. What sorts of messages does Jeremiah deliver?

Every synagogue (building of Jewish worship) contains a scroll of the entire Torah, kept in a vessel called an ark.

The Prophets. The Prophets is composed of books that include both historical accounts of ancient Israel and proclamations of the will of God spoken by those called to serve as God's mouthpieces. The Greek term *prophet* literally means "one who speaks for."

The Hebrew prophets who spoke for God are among the world's most striking religious figures. With charisma and courage, they attempted to keep Israel on its religious course through times of severe difficulty.

The prophet is called to speak for God, a role that is illustrated clearly at the beginning of the Book of Jeremiah. Jeremiah was one of the most important prophets:

The word of the LORD came to me:
    Before I created you in the womb,
        I selected you;

Before you were born, I consecrated you;
    I appointed you a prophet concerning
        the nations.

(Jeremiah 1:4–5, Tanakh)

Jeremiah protests, insisting that he, a mere boy, is not capable of speaking for God. But God assures Jeremiah that he will succeed, promising to be with him. Then comes the central moment:

The LORD put out His hand and touched my mouth, and the LORD said to me: Herewith I put My words into your mouth. (Jeremiah 1:9, Tanakh)

The Writings. The books that comprise the Writings are highly diverse in both content and literary form. With the poetry of the Psalms, the wisdom literature of Proverbs and Ecclesiastes, the short stories such as Esther and Ruth, and the historical accounts like Chronicles, just to name some examples, the Writings contribute much to the overall richness of the Bible. For the most part, the Writings were composed later than the rest of the Tanakh.

Mishnah and Talmud: Teachings of the Rabbis

The Bible, or written Torah, is complemented by the vast and ingenious wealth of religious teachings of the "oral Torah." This is the material taught and transmitted by Judaism's great rabbis of antiquity. Their teachings were eventually written down, most notably in the Mishnah and later in the Talmud, among other texts.

The written revelation of God's will would always remain the central teaching, but the varying circumstances of life demanded that the religious laws be elaborated on. The written Torah did not always say enough; it also could not directly address the continually changing situations of the Jews in a world that was always changing. The oral Torah continues the task begun by the written Torah.

Moving outward from the Bible, the next ring of interpretation is the **Mishnah**. It was written down in about 200 C.E., but it contains teachings that were formulated and transmitted orally by the rabbis of the previous four centuries. Soon after it was written, the Mishnah came to be regarded as a sacred text, like the Bible. It remains the starting point for rabbinic study of the oral Torah.

The **Talmud** forms the next ring of interpretation, and it is highly significant. A great modern scholar of Judaism has stated: "If the Bible is the cornerstone of Judaism, then the Talmud is the central pillar, soaring up from the foundations and supporting the entire spiritual and intellectual edifice" (Steinsaltz, *The Essential Talmud,* page 3).

The Talmud is based directly on the Mishnah. Small portions of the Mishnah are cited, followed by intricate commentary, usually page after page of it. The rabbis support their arguments by citing biblical passages. The Talmud presents a grand scheme of interpretation of God's will, blending together the oral and written forms of Torah. It is a massive work, spanning thousands of pages. Amazing though it may seem, great rabbis through the centuries are thought to have committed the entire Talmud to memory.

The Talmud itself continued to be interpreted for centuries. The most important commentary, by rabbis who lived as late as the Middle Ages, is included in modern

Left: Boys study the Talmud in Jerusalem. *Below:* Scholars discuss a passage from the Talmud.

3

Choose a discipline or subject area that interests you, such as religion, science, mathematics, or literature. Then choose a specific activity from that discipline and describe the concentric rings of creation and interpretation that surround it. For example, a certain scientific theory is formulated by one person, studied and commented on by another, revised by yet another, applied in a practical way by someone else, and so on. Be very specific in your choice of an activity from the discipline.

editions. And in a real sense, the Talmud is still being interpreted; the concentric rings of the tree trunk are still growing outward. Modern Jews, like those of ancient times, strive for deeper understanding of God's will. This process of interpretation is itself a meaningful act of worship, occupying a significant place in the ongoing sanctification of life.

Blessings and Tribulations: The History of the Chosen People

Earlier we noted that Judaism can be summarized as the interpretation of the history of the Jewish people. Who are the Jewish people, and why is their history of such vital importance?

Originally the Jews were the descendants of the ancient Israelites (who are also known as Hebrews). Around the time of the Exile and following, they became known as Jews, and their religion became known as Judaism, because their country was Judah. Conversion to Judaism was quite common in ancient times, and continues in the present day. No single Jewish "race" of genetically related people exists. It is more accurate to think of the Jews as an ethnic group that shares a common history and religion (though recently, as we have noted, some Jews do not practice Judaism).

History has great significance for Judaism. This is due to a basic religious premise: God is believed to be providential, or directly involved in history. God knows what is happening and provides for the Chosen People. History for the Jews is therefore a record of God's will as manifested in the events of the world.

This explains why Judaism itself can be thought of as the interpretation of Jewish history. God is loving, all-knowing, all-powerful, and providential. The Jews are the Chosen People of God. But as the Chosen People, the Jews must live up to their end of the covenantal agreement. History provides a means of measuring how adequately the Jews

have done this. To the extent that they honor the Covenant, God will reward them as a "treasured possession" (Exodus 19:6). Through the centuries the difficulties encountered by the Jews have challenged them to question over and over again just how adequately they have upheld their covenantal responsibilities.

Classical Judaism

Roman armies destroyed the Second Jerusalem Temple in 70 C.E. This was both an unprecedented catastrophe and a new opportunity for Judaism. The Pharisees, who focused on the study of Torah rather than on the rituals observed at the Temple, emerged from this event with their religious ways intact. With the impetus provided by Pharisaic Judaism, and with the compilation of the Mishnah and the Talmud over the next few centuries, classical Judaism was established. It remains the standard for Jews down to modern times.

The classical period itself stretches from the end of the first century C.E. through the seventh century, when Muslim forces conquered Palestine and the surrounding area. The Jews of the classical period were forced to live under the threat of Roman political oppression, which sometimes had violent consequences. Several decades after the Jewish War and the destruction of the Temple in 70 C.E., the Jews waged a second large-scale revolt against the Romans. This ended in 135 C.E., when the victorious Romans leveled the city of Jerusalem and set forth a decree forbidding Jews to inhabit the region of Palestine. The Jews were now technically in exile from their homeland.

However, neither exile nor oppression was new to the Jewish people. Through the centuries their ancestors had endured oppression by foreign rulers: Egyptians, Assyrians, Babylonians, Persians, Greeks, and Romans. In the classical period and beyond, Jews encountered new threats: Christianity arose in the fourth century to become the official religion of the Roman Empire. A few centuries later, many Jews found themselves living under Muslim rule.

Far left: Young people gather for a celebration at Jerusalem's Western Wall. *Center and above:* Worshipers pray at the Western Wall.

From the Ancient Israelites to Classical Judaism

Judaism emerged over a number of centuries, not taking on its present form until after the biblical period. The events of the Israelites, however, are of central significance to Judaism. To begin with, the Jews themselves were descended from Abraham and the rest of the biblical patriarchs.

The Patriarchs (2000 to 1500 B.C.E.)

According to the Book of Genesis, God called forth Abraham to be the father of a great nation, leading him from his home in Mesopotamia to the Promised Land of Canaan. The males among Abraham's people were thereafter marked by circumcision (removal of the foreskin of the penis), distinguishing the Israelites from people of the other nations. The stories of Abraham and his wife Sarah, their son Isaac, and his son Jacob (who is also known as Israel) are integral to the Jewish sense of history and identity as a people.

Exodus and Revelation (1280 B.C.E.)

During the centuries after the patriarchs, the Israelites moved from the land of Canaan to nearby Egypt, where food was easier to come by. Eventually they were forced into slavery by the Egyptians. This set the stage for the most important events in Israelite history: the Exodus from Egypt and the revelation on Mount Sinai. These events likely occurred in about 1280 B.C.E.

The central figure in both of these events, and the greatest prophet and most revered person in Judaism, is Moses. God called Moses to go forth to Egypt and free the Israelites from slavery. Through God's miraculous acts, including the ten devastating plagues on Egypt, and the parting of the Red Sea, Moses succeeded. In the months that followed, Moses led the people to Mount Sinai, where they agreed to enter into the Covenant with God. The Torah, with its 613 laws, was revealed at that time to Moses.

Monarchy of David and Solomon (1004 to 928 B.C.E.)

King David led the Israelite monarchy to its height of power. He managed to conquer many neighboring lands, along with the city of Jerusalem, which he made the capital. David's son, Solomon, built the Temple in Jerusalem, a structure of unsurpassed splendor that became the center of Israelite worship.

The kingship of David continues to hold special significance for Judaism. David has always been regarded as a prototype, or model, of the Messiah, a savior whom Jews believe will be sent by God to restore peace and justice to the world.

Babylonian Exile (587 to 538 B.C.E.)

At the end of Solomon's reign, the united monarchy was divided. The northern kingdom of Israel endured only until 722 B.C.E., when it fell to the Assyrians. The southern kingdom of Judah endured until about 587 B.C.E., when the Babylonians, led by their king, Nebuchadnezzar, conquered the land, destroyed the Temple, and carried off many of its leading citizens to exile in Babylon. The Exile lasted until 538 B.C.E., when the Persians conquered Babylon. Many Jews returned to Judea (as Judah came to be known) where, in about 516 B.C.E., they rebuilt the Temple. Judaism underwent further changes and revitalization about a century later, when Ezra and Nehemiah led a period of great religious reform.

Greek Conquest of Palestine (332 B.C.E.)

Under the leadership of Alexander the Great, the Greeks conquered Palestine in 332 B.C.E., profoundly challenging the Jewish way of life. Greek language and culture quickly became established among the elite. Some Jews embraced this Greek influence and gradually lost hold of their traditional religious identity. Different forms of Judaism arose during this time. The Sadducees, members of the priestly class who enjoyed the wealth provided by Temple revenues, were generally friendly toward the Greek rulers, though the Sadducees were highly conservative about their Jewish religious ways. The Essenes actively rejected all the Greek ways and chose to live on their own in desert communities. The Pharisees adopted some facets of Greek culture, but ignored its religious aspects. Put off by the Sadducees' control of the Temple, the Pharisees focused on Torah, in both its written and oral forms.

Destruction of the Second Temple (70 C.E.)

In 63 B.C.E. the Romans conquered Palestine. Their rule lasted for centuries and was often harsh. The crucifixion of Jesus of Nazareth in 30 C.E. was one among many executions of Jews that the Romans carried out to ensure control of the area. In 66 C.E. the Jews initiated a large-scale revolt, known as the Jewish War. This was eventually won by the Romans, who, in 70 C.E., destroyed the Jerusalem Temple for the second time. This event remains one of the greatest moments of tribulation in the history of Judaism. It was an enormous loss, removing from the Jews the physical center of their religious and cultural life. The Pharisees, however, had for centuries focused on Torah rather than the Temple, so they managed to emerge from this defeat with their form of Judaism intact. It is this form that produced classical, or rabbinic, Judaism.

As for exile, the Jews of the classical period could look to the Babylonian Exile (587 to 538 B.C.E.) as a precedent. Those exiles were eventually allowed to return to their homeland. This event was highly significant, instilling among all Jews hope for a return from exile to a situation of peace and prosperity. However, the Babylonian Exile also taught the Jews how to survive without returning home. Following the Exile many remained in Babylon or elsewhere in Persia, and in Egypt. For the first time, there were Jews living away from their homeland who maintained their religious identity. This situation, known as the **Diaspora** (or Dispersion), continued throughout Jewish history. Indeed the vast majority of Jews have lived in the Diaspora, from the classical period to the twentieth century.

Medieval Judaism

The medieval period of Judaism spans from the eighth to the middle of the eighteenth centuries. Scattered throughout a large Diaspora, Jews lived under various political and social conditions. In some places Jewish culture thrived. Medieval Spain, for example, produced both the philosophy of Maimonides and the mystical teachings of the Zohar, which we shall consider shortly. First, let us look at the general conditions of medieval Jews.

Jewish Life in the Medieval Period

For the most part, Jews lived under the rule of Muslims (in Africa, Spain, and the Near East) and Christians (in most of Europe). Under Muslim rule, Jews were generally free to practice their own religion and to conduct their own courts of law, and they were assured security of life and property. There were occasional exceptions to these principles, and Jews were required to pay certain taxes to the Muslim rulers. But overall, the Jewish people fared quite well and established a large middle class.

Conditions under Christian rulers tended to vary considerably over the centuries. In the early centuries of the medieval period, European Jews emerged as successful moneylenders. (Church laws strongly discouraged Christians from participating in this profession.)

Left: The reign of King Philip II of France, from 1179 to 1223, was marked by persecutions and massacres of Jews, as depicted in this print.
Below: Jewish and Muslim women rally for peace in Israel in 1993.

This helped Europe's changing economy, and some Christians respected and appreciated the Jews with whom they had dealings. But the economic success of the Jews led to resentment among many Christians. Christians also felt a religious form of resentment toward the Jews, for Christians tended to regard them as "sons of the crucifiers" who intentionally rejected Christ.

Resentment led to open and violent persecution. Beginning in the twelfth century, Jews were commonly the victims of blood libels, which were false accusations that they had ritually murdered Christian children. Large-scale expulsions of Jews occurred in France, England, and Spain (which had come under Christian rule by the fifteenth century). Jews were also blamed for causing the Black Death, the devastating bubonic plague that killed about one-third of Europe's population in the mid-fourteenth century. For this, entire Jewish populations were massacred, mostly by wandering bands of Christian penitents. Meanwhile the Spanish Inquisition also targeted Jews, putting many to death.

To escape persecution, many Jews migrated eastward, especially to Poland, which welcomed them. By the mid-seventeenth century, Poland had the largest population of Jews (about 150,000) of any country in the Diaspora. Here Jews enjoyed a large degree of governmental autonomy, and the people lived in relative safety and prosperity. Polish rabbis made remarkable intellectual achievements. But even here the threat of persecution loomed. In 1648 a Cossack rebellion against Poland resulted in the brutal massacre of about one-fourth of its Jewish population.

The medieval period was clearly a time of great tribulation for many Jews. But we must not lose sight of the havens of relative peace and prosperity in which some Jews lived. Muslim Spain, home of the Jewish philosopher Maimonides and of the origins of Jewish mysticism, was one such haven.

Jewish Philosophy: Maimonides

Moses Maimonides (1135 to 1204) is representative of a great number of Jewish philosophers, teachers, and scriptural masters who contributed to the ongoing process of interpreting Torah. The tree trunk, with its concentric rings of interpretation, kept growing outward.

Maimonides applied the philosophy of Plato and Aristotle to the biblical tradition, fashioning a new and much debated Jewish theology. His most famous book, *The Guide for the Perplexed,* has stood through the ages as one of Judaism's most influential and challenging philosophical works.

In addition, Maimonides also contributed Judaism's most famous statement of beliefs, thirteen principles that set forth the backbone of Jewish theology:

Left: Jewish philosopher Maimonides

1. The belief in God's existence
2. The belief in His unity
3. The belief in His incorporeality
4. The belief in His timelessness
5. The belief that He is approachable through prayer
6. The belief in prophecy
7. The belief in the superiority of Moses to all other prophets
8. The belief in the revelation of the Law, and that the Law as contained in the Pentateuch is that revealed by Moses
9. The belief in the immutability of the Law
10. The belief in Divine providence
11. The belief in Divine justice
12. The belief in the coming of the Messiah
13. The belief in the resurrection and human immortality

(*The Ways of Religion,* pages 261–262)

The Kabbalah: Jewish Mysticism

While Jewish philosophy emphasizes reason, Jewish mysticism, or **Kabbalah,** teaches that God can best be known with the heart, through love. The mystics acknowledge the ultimate transcendence of God, but stress the immanence of God: God can be found by looking inward.

The most famous text of Jewish mysticism is the Zohar, probably written in thirteenth-century Spain by Moses de Leon. The Zohar incorporates rich symbolism based on numbers and esoteric language, and teaches that Torah can be interpreted on different levels, each revealing hidden meanings that bring one closer to God. Thus, though God is regarded as the "Infinite," transcending the fallen world of humanity, the mystic can come to know God through love and understanding of the hidden truth.

Though in many ways it is an alternative to traditional Judaism, the Kabbalah does not abandon the basic forms of Jewish practice. Kabbalists observe the commandments, and are renowned for their highly ethical behavior.

Judaism in the Modern Period

Great changes in European civilization began to occur in the eighteenth century. The period known as the Enlightenment, or Age of Reason, gave rise to new social theories asserting the equality of all. Monarchies began to be replaced by governments that were based on rule by the people.

These changes greatly affected religions, too, including Judaism. This section covers a wide variety of reactions to the new challenges of this period, which gave rise to different forms of modern Judaism.

Hasidism

Hasidism (from *hasid,* meaning "pious") arose in the eighteenth century in Eastern Europe. It draws from some of the mystical teachings of the Kabbalist tradition, holding that God is immanent and known first and foremost with the heart. Hasidism emphasizes personal relationships with God and the community, rather than study of the Torah and strict observance of the commandments.

The center of each Hasidic community is the leadership of the *zaddik,* a holy man who is believed to have an especially close relationship with God. Through the teachings

Right: A Hasidic teenager in New York City

5

Might the philosophy of Maimonides and the mysticism of the Kabbalah be used as two complementary approaches to God? Describe how you think the two approaches could work together.

and mere presence of the *zaddik,* Hasidic Jews are able to move closer to God. Large Hasidic communities still exist today in North America and elsewhere.

Zionism

Zionism originally referred to a movement arising in the late nineteenth century that was committed to the re-establishment of a Jewish homeland (Zion is a biblical name for Jerusalem). Now that the modern nation of Israel, established in 1948, does exist, Zionism refers generally to the support of Israel.

As we have seen, throughout the centuries Jews faced persecution, a phenomenon known as **anti-Semitism.** Despite the new ideals of social equality that arose with the Enlightenment, some Jews were convinced that the only way to ensure their safety was to have their own nation. Events of anti-Semitism in the twentieth century, most tragically the Holocaust, have confirmed the Zionist conviction regarding the need for a Jewish state.

The Holocaust

Of all the tribulations suffered by the Chosen People through the centuries, the Holocaust is surely the most horrific. Sometimes called Shoah (Hebrew for "mass destruction"), the **Holocaust** refers to the persecution of Jews by German Nazis from 1938 to 1945. Culminating in the use of highly efficient extermination camps, the Holocaust resulted in the murder of nearly six million Jews.

Along with the tragic consequences of such an immense loss of life, the Holocaust has confronted Judaism with religious challenges. Until this event, Jews could generally make sense of their difficult history. There had been tribulations, of course. But some reasoned that perhaps they were the result of the Jews' own failure to live up to the Covenant. Or perhaps God would right the wrongs by sending the Messiah to bring justice to the Jews. But in the face of the Holocaust, in which one-third of the Jewish people were senselessly murdered, such an-

Images from the Holocaust
Below: Children, location unknown
Bottom: Prisoners at the Dachau concentration camp celebrate the defeat of the Nazis.
Right: Jewish survivors at the Buchenwald camp included Elie Wiesel (second bunk from the bottom, seventh man from the left), whose book *Night* details his years as a prisoner.

The Precious Prayer

The true character of Hasidism is perhaps best exposed through its many stories. This one, called "The Precious Prayer," expresses the Hasidic emphasis on knowing God with the heart, through which God, in turn, knows human beings.

One Yom Kippur long ago, a rabbi was praying in the synagogue. An angel whispered in his ear about a man whose prayers had reached the highest heavens. The angel told the rabbi the man's name and hometown, and the rabbi went to find him.

When the rabbi reached that town, he asked for the man whose name the angel had given him. The only man by that name was a poor farmer. The rabbi found the farm, and the man invited him to enter the little hut in which he lived. Getting right down to business, the rabbi asked the farmer how he prayed. "But sir," replied the farmer, "I am afraid I cannot pray. For I cannot read. All I know are the first nine letters of the alphabet."

The rabbi was stunned. Could the angel have been wrong? So he asked, "What did you do on Yom Kippur?" The farmer said: "I went to the synagogue. I saw how intently everyone was praying, and my heart broke. So I began to recite the letters I know of the alphabet. And I said in my heart: 'Dear God, take these letters and form them into prayers for me, that will rise up like the scent of honeysuckle. For that is the most beautiful scent I know.' And I said that with all my strength, over and over."

When the rabbi heard this, he knew that God had sent him here to learn this: While humans see what is before their eyes, God looks into the heart. And that is why the prayers of the simple farmer were so precious. (Adapted from Schwartz, *Gabriel's Palace*, pages 86–87)

---

swers no longer make sense to many Jews. How could God have allowed such a horrible thing to happen?

Jews have responded to these challenges in a variety of ways. Some maintain that they deserved even this as punishment for their sins—most specifically, the sin of abandoning the ways of traditional Judaism. Others contend that the Holocaust can only mean that God has broken the Covenant. Another response, and a very prominent one, is Zionism, the ongoing support of the state of Israel.

The State of Israel

With the rise of the Zionist movement at the end of the nineteenth century, increasing numbers of Jews immigrated to Palestine. The Hebrew language was restored; the land was nurtured into fields fit for productive agriculture; and farming communities and cities were built. In 1948, in the wake of the Holocaust and with the sympathetic support of most of the world, Israel was granted statehood. Its political and cultural achievements since that time continue to be a source of pride for Jews. For the first time in over two millennia, the Jews have a national homeland.

Today the state of Israel provides a great deal of unity for Judaism. Most Jews, whether Israelis or not (less than half of the world's Jews live in Israel), and whether religiously observant or not, regard Israel as their earthly center and common cause. Vast financial and political support have been provided to the state, especially by North American Jews.

Along with this unity over the state of Israel, divisive problems persist. For one thing, the Palestinians also call this land their home. How is it to be shared? Deep divisions also exist between secular and religious Israeli

6

In "The Precious Prayer," the rabbi learns that "while humans see what is before their eyes, God looks into the heart." Compare this insight about prayer with that offered by Jesus in Matthew 6:5–6.

7

Review the opening section of this chapter, beginning with the passage from Abraham Joshua Heschel. What challenges do you think the Holocaust presents to this understanding of Judaism?

8

For some two thousand years prior to 1948, Jews endured without a national homeland. Imagine what your life would be like if your nation did not exist and you were living in exile in some foreign land. What important things would be missing? How would this situation affect your religious outlook? In general, how would it affect your priorities?

Jews. The task of reconciling such secular ideals as Western democracy with the ways of traditional Judaism poses a great challenge to Israel.

Modern Institutional Divisions

The same challenges of the modern period that prompted the development of branches of Judaism, such as Hasidism and Zionism, have also led to divisions within traditional Judaism. These divisions are most relevant in North America, where the three most prominent forms of Judaism are Reform, Orthodox, and Conservative.

Reform Judaism holds that being Jewish and being completely involved in modern society are compatible. As society changes, so must Judaism adapt to it. Reform Judaism is therefore relatively relaxed regarding the observance of the details of Jewish traditional practice. The worship liturgy is spoken in English, and the rabbi functions much like a

Christian preacher, rather than a traditional scholar and teacher of Torah. About one-third of Jews in the United States adhere to Reform Judaism.

Orthodox Judaism maintains that Torah is the standard of truth, and that life within society must always conform to it. Despite changes in society, Jewish life should change very little, for Torah is unchanging. This does not mean that Orthodox Judaism rejects all aspects of modernity; secular education, for example, is affirmed. But compared to Reform Judaism, Orthodox Judaism is deeply traditional. In the United States, the Orthodox often live in separate communities to help maintain their traditional ways. About 10 percent of Jews in the United States adhere to Orthodox Judaism.

Conservative Judaism occupies a middle position between Reform and Orthodox. While somewhat open to change and to modern ways, Conservative Judaism is quite strict regarding observance of traditional Jewish practices. The worship liturgy is in Hebrew, for example, and laws regulating diet and behavior on the Sabbath are strictly observed. Almost half of the Jews in the United States adhere to Conservative Judaism.

Each of these varieties of Judaism, even the Orthodox, continues to change. For example, women are becoming increasingly involved in both leadership and participation. Women often now serve as rabbis in both Reform and Conservative Judaism.

The Torah scroll is the focal point at this morning service in a synagogue.

The Sanctification of Life: The Way of Torah

We have learned that Judaism can be summarized as the sanctification of life. Life is sanctified through the moment-to-moment practice of observing Torah. Judaism is far more concerned with correct practice than with correct belief (and thus differs considerably from Christianity in this respect). Judaism places little emphasis on theology or statements of belief. Rather than focusing on what God is, Judaism focuses on how to worship God. Traditionally, therefore, a Jew is not a "believer" so much as an "observer of the commandments." In this section we will focus on just what this involves. As noted, different types of Jews are more or less observant; we will be mainly concerned with more traditional ways of being Jewish.

Daily Life

Traditionally, all aspects of Jewish life are guided by regulations derived from Torah, which categorizes acts as permitted or forbidden, obliged or free, and holy or profane. Torah thus defines both worship and ethical conduct.

Ethics

Observing Torah requires not only worshiping God but also leading an ethical life. In the Mishnah an esteemed rabbi puts it this way: "By three things is the world sustained: by the Law, by the [Temple-] service, and by deeds of loving-kindness" (page 446). We have already noted the importance of the study and interpretation of the Law, or Torah. Soon we will consider some details of service, or worship. As for deeds of loving kindness, we need only note the prominence of the Ten Commandments in God's revelation on Mount Sinai to realize the central significance of ethics. In addition to these famous ethical requirements (not to kill, steal, and so on), Judaism teaches many more. For example, Jews are obligated to give help to the needy, to give food and shelter to guests, and

to visit the sick. The traditional emphasis on ethics is reflected in the charitable and philanthropic work done by the Jewish community today.

Daily Worship Through Prayer

The predominant form of daily worship is prayer, which is mandatory only for males age thirteen and older. Women are traditionally excused because of their household responsibilities (which are themselves done in accordance with Torah, and so are an integral part of the sanctification of life). However, in recent times more women have been participating in prayer. In any event, males alone are required to wear certain ritual accessories. One is the *yarmulke,* or skullcap. Another is a set of small boxes containing biblical passages. These are secured to the forehead and to the left arm so as to be near the mind and the heart, the two primary means of serving God. A third accessory is the prayer shawl, which can be drawn over the head for privacy.

Prayers are said at least three times daily: in the morning, the afternoon, and the evening. They include a variety of traditional passages from the Bible and other authoritative sources. Prayers are usually recited at home, but are also frequently said in public

In Marc Chagall's painting *The Praying Jew,* the small boxes containing biblical passages can be seen on the man's forehead and left arm, and he is draped with his prayer shawl.

9

We often tend to think of religion as primarily a matter of believing in certain doctrines. Drawing from your own experiences, list several examples of religious practices. In your opinion are these practices meaningful if they are independent of beliefs?

A Jewish girl conducts a Sabbath blessing.

at the synagogue. Home and synagogue are the two centers of Jewish worship.

The Home and the Synagogue

The home is the most common place for Jewish worship, and it is the center of Jewish social life, which more than anything else focuses on the family. Rules based in Torah govern family relationships, so that children honor their parents, and parents care diligently for their children.

Jewish homes are often easy to identify. On the outside, just to the right of the door, many Jews attach the *mezuzah,* a small container with a scroll on which is written the Shema, "Hear, O Israel! The LORD is our God, the LORD alone" (Deuteronomy 6:4).

The social and religious center of the home is the dinner table. Along with festive meals in celebration of holy days and the Sabbath, ordinary meals, too, are important occasions. Traditionally, all the food must be kosher ("proper" according to Torah), meaning that certain dietary regulations apply. Pork, for example, is prohibited, as is the mixing of meat and dairy products.

In addition to the home, Jewish worship is commonly carried out in the synagogue (which Reform Judaism calls the temple). Since the Babylonian Exile (in the sixth century B.C.E.), synagogues have been centers for prayer, study, and communal fellowship. While the building designs vary, all synagogues contain a scroll of the five books of the Torah, which are encased in a box called an ark.

10

Read Deuteronomy 6:4–9. Identify parts of this passage that relate to the Jewish worship practices you have read about in this section of your textbook. Describe how you think the Shema (Deuteronomy 6:4) relates to the rest of the passage.

Rabbis are the leaders of the synagogues. The precise role of the rabbi varies among the different forms of Judaism. In general, "rabbi" simply refers to one who has mastered the sacred writings of Judaism, mainly the Bible and the Talmud. In other words the role of the rabbi differs from that of the Christian priest or minister because it does not imply such a formal distinction in status.

Sabbath

One of the Ten Commandments states, "Remember the sabbath day and keep it holy" (Exodus 20:8, Tanakh). This the Jews have done through the centuries with both reverence and festive joy. The **Sabbath** (also commonly known by its Hebrew name, *Shabbat*) begins at sunset on Friday and lasts until sunset on Saturday. (Some Reform Jews celebrate the Sabbath on Sunday.) It is both the religious and the social high point of the week.

The Sabbath is patterned after the seventh day of creation, on which God rested from labor and beheld the glory of the created world. Along with avoiding labor, Jews are required to refrain from many sorts of usual activities, such as driving, answering the phone, and (for the very observant) turning on an electric light, which would violate the biblical law prohibiting lighting a fire on the Sabbath.

Along with being a day of rest, though, the Sabbath is also a day of worship and celebration. Jews devote part of the time to Torah study and Sabbath services, both at home and at the synagogue. They enjoy festive meals of special foods that have been prepared before the onset of the Sabbath. It is a time of fellowship with family and other Jews of the community, and is joyful and celebratory.

The Annual Calendar of Holy Days

The calendar of holy days is a fundamental basis of Jewish life. These annual observances serve to ensure both the unity of the Jews and the continuity of their religious tradition. The Jewish calendar includes some sixteen important holy days. The first day of each month, marked by the new moon, is also observed. We will briefly consider the most important holy days: Rosh Hashanah, Yom Kippur, and Passover.

Rosh Hashanah

Rosh Hashanah, the festival of the new year, occurs in early fall and is observed for two days. Unlike the strictly secular celebration of the New Year, Rosh Hashanah is a religious event involving both celebration and serious contemplation. God's creation of the world is celebrated, but this is accompanied by individual reflection on the deeds of the past year and the need for redemption. The ram's horn, or *shofar,* is blown on Rosh Hashanah as a means of reminding the Jews of these spiritual needs. Rosh Hashanah marks the beginning of the "Days of Awe," a ten-day period of reflection.

Rosh Hashanah is also a time to reinforce social relationships. Festive meals are held for family and friends. Visits to the graves of family members reinforce bonds with the deceased, as well.

Yom Kippur

The Days of Awe conclude on the tenth day of the new year with **Yom Kippur,** the "Day of Atonement," Judaism's most important holy day.

Deeply personal and solemn, Yom Kippur emphasizes repentance through confession of sin. The day is observed through prayer and through abstaining from food, drink, and work. Services are held in the synagogue, during which prayers like the following are recited:

O my God, before I was formed, I was nothing. Now that I have been formed, it is as though I had not been formed, for I am dust in my life, more so after death. Behold I am before You like a vessel filled with shame and confusion. May it be Your will . . . that I may no more sin, and forgive the sins I have already committed in Your abundant compassion. (Neusner, "Judaism," in *Our Religions,* page 345)

Passover

The festival of **Passover** occurs early in the spring and lasts for eight days. It commemorates the Exodus of the Jews from bondage in Egypt, and is a time of great mirth and celebration.

The high point of the festival is the Seder feast, which features a recitation, called the Haggadah, of the events of the Exodus as well as a meal of traditional foods that symbolize these events. Throughout the eight days of Passover, only unleavened bread (*matzo*) is to be eaten. The *matzo* is symbolic of Abraham, Isaac, and Jacob, the forefathers of the Jewish people.

The Passover clearly illustrates a characteristic common to most of Judaism's holy days: the events of Jewish history are commemorated as having religious significance.

11
The Jewish Sabbath celebrates the creation of the world through avoiding labor in order to rest and to worship. Do you reserve time in your life for this kind of celebration? If so, describe what it is like. If not, reflect on what some of the benefits of doing so might be.

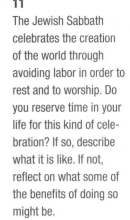

Jews in Israel celebrate the Passover Seder.

Growing Up Jewish in a Christian Town

Throughout history Jews have commonly lived in situations in which they were the minority. This is still the case for many Jews today. Stuart Miller tells of his experiences growing up Jewish in a small, predominantly Christian, city in Minnesota.

My parents were born overseas and immigrated to this country, my mother from Poland and my father from White Russia. Through different circumstances, they ended up in Winona, Minnesota (population twenty-five thousand), a town with only about ten Jewish families. I grew up with an older brother and a younger brother. My younger brother, Morrie, died in 1989 of cancer. My father, William, was an Orthodox Jew in the traditional sense. He observed the holidays, obeyed dietary laws, and prayed three times a day. My mother was not as religious. After my father's death, she shifted away from strict observance of Jewish Law, although she never lost her Jewish identity and remained totally devoted to Judaism.

When I was in grade school, a Jewish Sunday school teacher was brought to Winona from Minneapolis (about two hours away). There were about a dozen of us kids, of various ages. We studied Jewish history, Torah, and the Hebrew language—as much as the teacher could cram into those weekly sessions. My bar mitzvah was held in Winona, after I had received instruction from a medical student who came from Minneapolis. We celebrated the Jewish holidays in Minneapolis with my parents until my father got ill. Then we started going to synagogue in La Crosse, Wisconsin (a half hour from Winona). Through the years I received most of my learning of Hebrew, Torah, and Jewish history in La Crosse.

As a Jewish kid in a Christian community, the differences were most clear during the Christmas season. We celebrated Hanukkah, and the rest of the kids celebrated Christmas. It felt different. I was discouraged from singing Christmas songs, but I did anyway, with a compromise—I skipped certain words. The high holy days, Rosh Hashanah and Yom Kippur, also revealed differences. I missed school on those days in order to attend Jewish services. My younger brother, Morrie, was an excellent athlete. I remember a conflict when a high school football game was scheduled on Yom Kippur. Morrie missed the game that Friday. The coach was a little put off and was not able to understand my brother's decision. I was not a very good football player, so my absence never bothered my coach!

When I was in high school, a diplomat from Israel once came and spoke at an assembly. Due to my upbringing, I understood what he said about Israel, and it meant a lot to me. It was obvious that my classmates did not have the same emotional involvement that I did. Most neither understood nor cared about what he said.

Not once during my high school or college years did I experience firsthand any open anti-Semitism. However, in high school I knew of two brothers who were constantly teased and harassed for being Jewish. These same harassers never did that to me or my brothers, which made me wonder, why them and not me? I recall a specific incident concerning a gas station owner with whom my family did business. A customer of ours from out of town stopped at his station to ask directions to our business. The owner told him where "the Jews'"

business was—
not "the Millers'" business, but
"the Jews'." This astonished me. I thought
I knew that station owner better than that.

Now I am older and have a family of my
own. My eighteen-year-old daughter, Jessica,
attends college at Penn State. My older son,
Asher, is fifteen and is in high school. My
younger son, Joshua, is in grade school. My
wife, Sheryl, is also in school, working on a
degree in dental hygiene. Sheryl and I have
tried to instill in our children a love of Judaism.
Jessica celebrated bat mitzvah at age thirteen.
The synagogue had just changed from Orthodox to Conservative, and so she was the first
woman called to publicly read the Torah. Asher
celebrated bar mitzvah at age thirteen, and
Joshua will as well. We usually celebrate the
Jewish holidays as a family, the most important
being Rosh Hashanah, Yom Kippur, Hanukkah,
and Passover. I think we would agree that our
favorite is Passover. The special food, the Seder

night, the retelling of the
Exodus from Egypt—all combine to give
parents, children, and invited guests an appreciation of who they are and why their past is
so important. We try to go to synagogue as
much as we can, but kids (being kids) don't
want to go all the time. I was much the same in
my youth. I only hope that my children will have
a basis of Jewish faith, and that over time they
will expand upon this base on their own. Their
faith can help make them aware of bad things
and enable them to combat these bad things.

Growing up Jewish in a Christian town has
been an experience. One lucky thing for me
is that I was able to find a wonderful Jewish
woman to marry. It was difficult, but as I say,
I got lucky. There is anti-Semitism, but for the
most part it has been covered up by a thin
veneer of civility. I hope the veneer gets thicker
as time goes by so that my kids can be openly
proud of who and what they are, and appreci-
ate how they differ from other kids.

Rites of Passage

Like most other religions, Judaism prescribes rites of passage, or ritual events marking life's major changes. Rites of passage serve two primary purposes. First, they reflect the inevitable changes of life, while at the same time providing a sense of permanence through their unchanging rituals and the deeply rooted values they set forth. Second, rites of passage help to define the responsibilities of each stage of life, and to teach the means for advancing through them with appropriate maturity.

Birth and Naming

The rite of passage marking the birth of a child involves the giving of a name and, for boys, circumcision (removal of the foreskin of the penis).

The ceremony of circumcision takes place on the eighth day of life, usually at the home of the parents. In the Book of Genesis, circumcision is the sign established by God when entering into the Covenant with Abraham. This ritual therefore signifies entrance into the Jewish community of descendants of Abraham. Naming of the child also takes place during the ceremony of circumcision.

Girls are usually named at the synagogue during a Sabbath service. Reform Judaism, however, has developed a distinct ceremony for girls that is patterned after the ceremony of circumcision.

Coming of Age

The primary ritual marking the coming of age, that point at which a Jewish child takes on the religious responsibilities of an adult, is called **bar mitzvah** (son of the commandment) for boys, and **bat mitzvah** (daughter of the commandment) for girls. At this point the young person becomes responsible for observing the detailed practices of daily Jewish life.

Bar mitzvah takes place on a boy's thirteenth birthday. During the special service, the boy is a participant for the first time. He performs such tasks as reading from the Torah. Most Jewish girls celebrate bat mitzvah in a manner similar to a bar mitzvah. Bat mitzvah, however, is not observed in Orthodox Judaism.

Recently confirmation has become common among non-Orthodox Jews as a second means of observing the coming of age. Both girls and boys are confirmed, usually at age sixteen or seventeen.

Marriage

For Judaism, marriage is the ideal human relationship. Patterned after the relationship between Adam and Eve, marriage celebrates

12
Rites of passage are carefully observed in Judaism, as can be seen in the details involved in mourning the dead. How does this compare with the way a death is observed in secular society?

A girl celebrates bat mitzvah in New York.

God's creation by symbolically recreating the Garden of Eden. Marriage is a most joyous and festive occasion, and is almost always celebrated in a traditional manner, even by Jews who are otherwise not traditional.

Several symbols and events highlight the marriage ceremony. The bride and groom stand beneath the *huppah,* or bridal canopy, which creates a special, sacred space. Seven blessings, including the following, are read over a cup of wine:

Grant perfect joy to these loving companions, as You did to the first man and woman in the Garden of Eden. Praised are You, O Lord, who grants the joy of bride and groom. (Neusner, "Judaism," in *Our Religions,* page 350)

The ceremony concludes when the groom breaks a wine glass beneath his foot. This ancient custom may have originated as a symbol of the destruction of the two temples in Jerusalem. Today it serves to remind those present that marriage, like every aspect of life, will involve some difficulties and pain along with joy.

Death and Mourning

Death, the ultimate transition, poses unique challenges to the family of the deceased and to the community. Judaism deals with these challenges by carefully regulating the rituals and mourning activities that follow a death.

Several distinct stages of mourning are prescribed. The first stage lasts from death to burial, which preferably occurs on the day of death (though today this is usually not practical). When family members first learn of the death, they rip their clothes, and recite verses that acknowledge God as the "true judge." The mourners are restricted from certain activities, such as shaving and wearing leather. They are also relieved of many of the normal religious requirements, including the regular schedule of daily prayer. This allows them to attend to their grief and to special responsibilities, such as making sure the body is ritually washed and clothed in a shroud. It is buried in a plain wooden coffin.

A second stage of mourning begins after burial with the recital of the *kaddish,* a prayer

of mourning. This stage lasts for seven days. During this time community members visit the family. They discuss the merits of the deceased, and recite special prayers and psalms.

A third stage lasts until thirty days after burial. Most normal activities are resumed, but social gatherings and celebrations are avoided. If the deceased is one's parent, a fourth stage of mourning follows, this one lasting until the first anniversary of the death. During this stage the mourners avoid their usual seats at the synagogue, and they recite the *kaddish* during services. On the anniversary of the death, the mourners again recite the *kaddish.*

A woman reads a prayer book near the Western Wall in Jerusalem.

A rabbi blows the *shofar* for Rosh Hashanah at the Western Wall.

As we close this section on Judaism as the sanctification of life, it is timely to take careful note of how thoroughly Judaism deals with a rite of passage, in this case, death. This same thoroughness applies to all aspects of Jewish life. It is truly a religion of correct practice, from moment to moment, day in and day out.

The Tradition of the Chosen People

We began this chapter by noting three ways to summarize Judaism: First, it is the Covenant between God and the Chosen People; second, it is the interpretation of the history of the Jewish people; and third, it is the sanctification of life. Now that we have explored Judaism in some detail, it is possible to make sense of yet another summary statement, one that pulls all the others together: Judaism is tradition, the tradition of the Chosen People. To recall the words of Abraham Joshua Heschel cited at the beginning of this chapter, Judaism is "primarily living in the spiritual order of the Jewish people, the living *in* the Jews of the past and *with* the Jews of the present."

With only about thirteen million adherents worldwide, Judaism is among the smallest of the world's major religions. Many Jews today are gravely concerned that their numbers are decreasing, that the tradition is weakening, and that the Jewish people are losing their sense of identity.

Time will tell what is to become of Judaism. But given that it has endured against all odds for over two millennia, time seems to be on Judaism's side.

Glossary

anti-Semitism. Hostility toward Jews and Judaism, ranges from attitudes of disfavor to active persecution.

bar mitzvah, bat mitzvah (bahr meets-vah', baht meets-vah'; Hebrew: "son, daughter of the commandment"). The ritual celebration marking the coming of age of a Jewish child, at which time the person takes on the religious responsibilities of an adult.

Covenant. An agreement established between God and the ancient Israelites, first through Abraham and later through Moses, which designates the Jews as God's Chosen People with special rights and responsibilities.

Diaspora (di-as'puh-ruh; Greek: "dispersion"). The situation of Jews living away from their ancestral homeland, true of the majority of Jews ever since the classical period.

Hasidism. A form of Judaism arising in eastern Europe in the eighteenth century that emphasizes mysticism, a personal relationship with God, a close-knit community, and the leadership of the *zaddik,* a charismatic holy man.

Holocaust. The persecution of Jews by German Nazis from 1933 to 1945, resulting in the murder of some six million; commonly referred to by Jews as Shoah (Hebrew for "mass destruction").

Kabbalah (kab'uh-luh). Jewish mysticism, which teaches that God can best be known through the heart; developed mainly in the medieval period with such texts as the Zohar.

Mishnah (meesh-nah'). Written down in about 200 C.E., but contains collected teachings of the rabbis of the preceding four centuries; along with the Talmud, it is the most important text of the oral Torah.

Passover. The eight-day festival celebrated in early spring that commemorates the Exodus of the Jews from Egypt.

rabbis (ra'b/s; Hebrew: "my teacher"). Teachers of Torah and leaders of Jewish worship.

Rosh Hashanah (rohsh hah-shah-nah'; Hebrew: "the beginning of the year"). The festival occurring in early fall in commemoration of the new year.

Sabbath (in Hebrew, *Shabbat*). The day from sunset on Friday until sunset on Saturday (observed on Sunday by some Reform Jews) that is set aside for rest and religious celebration, as decreed by one of the Ten Commandments (Exodus 20:8).

Shema (shuh-mah'; Hebrew: "hear"). From Deuteronomy 6:4, Judaism's basic statement of monotheism: "Hear, O Israel! The LORD is our God, the LORD alone."

Talmud (tahl-mood'; Hebrew: "study," "knowledge"). The vast depository of the oral Torah, based on the Mishnah with extensive rabbinic commentary on each chapter; there are two versions, the Palestinian (completed about 450 C.E.) and the Babylonian (completed about 600 C.E.).

Tanakh (tah-nahk). A common way of referring to the Hebrew Bible, derived from the first letters of the Hebrew names of its three sections: Torah *(T),* Prophets *(N),* and Writings *(K).*

Torah (toh'rah; Hebrew: "instruction"). Generally, the revelation of God's will to the people; more specifically, the divine Law, especially as contained in the first five books of the Bible, which together are often called the Torah.

Yom Kippur (yohm' kee-poor'; Hebrew: "day of atonement"). Judaism's most important holy day, occurring in the fall on the tenth day of the new year and spent primarily at synagogue services in prayer for forgiveness of sins.

Zionism. Originally, the movement arising in the late nineteenth century that sought to re-establish a Jewish homeland; since 1948, the general support of the State of Israel.

Palestine at the Time of Jesus

Mediterranean Sea

GALILEE

Capernaum

Sea of Galilee

Nazareth

SAMARIA

River Jordan

JUDEA

Jerusalem

Bethlehem

Dead Sea

Damascus

13 Christianity

Who Is a Christian?

Nearly one-third of the world's population is Christian, making Christianity the world's largest religion. Christianity is the dominant tradition in the Americas, Europe, and Australia, and has significant followings in Asia and Africa as well.

What do the world's Christians, some one and a half billion people, have in common? To put it simply, Christians share three things: Christ, creed, and church.

To be a Christian is to acknowledge Jesus Christ as savior. The basis for knowing Christ is the New Testament, which describes the earthly life and ministry of Jesus, his Crucifixion and Resurrection, and the significance of these events for the early church and for humanity in general.

Christian creed, based on the New Testament, consists of the essential doctrines, or beliefs, of Christianity. In the centuries following the life of Jesus, church leaders and theologians strove to express their beliefs with ever greater precision. Classic

215

statements such as the Nicene Creed, formulated in the fourth century, present Christianity's core doctrines. The first core doctrine is the **Incarnation,** which asserts that Christ is both fully divine and fully human. The second core doctrine is the **Trinity,** which holds that God consists of three Persons—God the Father, Jesus Christ the Son, and the Holy Spirit—who are at the same time one God. To be a Christian is to believe in such doctrines as the Incarnation and the Trinity, central elements of the Christian creed.

Finally, to be a Christian is to belong to the church, the community of believers through which the creed is disseminated and Christ is celebrated. The New Testament decrees in various ways the essential role of the church, founded by Christ and his disciples, and guided and nurtured by the Holy Spirit.

Christ: Son of God, Savior

Early Christians, like some of their modern counterparts, used a concise and convenient symbol to express their understanding of who Christ was and what he meant for them. They drew a fish on their doors and elsewhere, indicating that they were Christians. In Greek the word for fish is *ixthus,* each letter of which begins a word (in Greek, that is) of the phrase, *Jesus Christ, Son of God, Savior.*

The New Testament itself is basically an elaboration of this summary depiction of Christ, recounting the earthly life of Jesus of Nazareth; explaining his identity as the Son of God; and describing his role as Christ the Savior, the Messiah who came to Earth for the salvation of all.

Drawing from the New Testament, we will investigate the life of Jesus, and the significance of his life and teachings for the New Testament authors and for Christians.

The Life of Jesus

The New Testament Gospels (Matthew, Mark, Luke, and John) are the primary sources of information about the life of Jesus. They focus almost entirely on the last few years of his life, from his baptism at around age thirty to his Crucifixion and Resurrection. Thus very little is known about Jesus' early life. One reason for this lack of information about Jesus' life is that the Gospel authors strove mainly to present Christ's teachings and to express the meaning of the events of his life, rather than to assemble a factual record. As a result we are not clear on all the details. The attempt by contemporary scholars to know the "historical Jesus" strives to overcome this shortage of readily available facts, but meets with only limited success.

With these circumstances in mind, let us sketch the life of Jesus as best we can.

Judaism at the Time of Jesus

Jesus was born a Jew, and he remained a practicing Jew his entire life. The twelve Apostles and other associates of Jesus were all Jews. Paul, the apostle to the Gentiles non-Jews, was also a Jew. It is therefore essential that we begin by noting a few facts about Judaism in Jesus' time.

The area of Palestine, the ancient homeland of the Jews, was conquered by the Romans in 63 B.C.E. When Jesus was a youth, most of Palestine, including Jerusalem, came under the direct rule of a procurator, a regional governor who reported directly to the Roman emperor. Pontius Pilate occupied this office from 26 to 36 C.E. The northern region of Galilee, where Jesus grew up and carried out most of his ministry, was ruled by Herod Antipas, a puppet king who himself was also ultimately under the rule of the Roman emperor. Being subject to the Romans placed the Jews in an extremely difficult situation. Tensions ran high, sometimes leading to conflicts and executions.

Jews responded to these difficulties in various ways. As noted in chapter 12, the Sadducees, Zealots, Essenes, and Pharisees all practiced different varieties of Judaism. The Sadducees, wealthy aristocrats who controlled the Jerusalem Temple, responded to Roman rule conservatively, generally remaining on friendly terms with the rulers. The Zealots believed that the only way to achieve Jewish independence was through armed rebellion. The Essenes chose to flee from the difficulties, leading lives of discipline and purity in desert communities. The Pharisees responded with moderation, obeying the traditional commandments of Judaism and developing the oral Torah.

Jesus fit none of these categories. He was not a conservative, like the Sadducees; he was a peaceful rebel who did not share the violent methods of the Zealots. And unlike the Essenes, he chose to remain within society. Jesus had much in common with the Pharisees, but they did not approve of his outreach to the lower strata of the Jewish community, or of his nontraditional ways of observing Torah.

1
Apocalypticism continues to this day to be an important perspective for many people. Based on the description given here, in what ways have you observed apocalypticism being manifested today?

2
The lower strata of Jewish society in Jesus' day included prostitutes, tax collectors, and others whom the Bible refers to as "sinners" and "outcasts." Who makes up the lower strata of society today?

Despite these differences, Jesus seems to have shared with many Jews some aspects of a basic religious perspective of that time: **apocalypticism.** According to this perspective, the world had come under the control of evil forces that caused Jews to live in an unjust situation. God, however, was still ultimately in control. The world's woes would become greater and greater until God would send the Messiah to conquer the forces of evil. This event, the end time, would divide "this age" and "the age to come." The dead would be resurrected, and all would be judged, leading to salvation for the righteous and damnation for the rest. Before sending the Messiah, God would reveal the plan to the elect through a revelation, or apocalypse, contained in certain writings. The last book of the New Testament, the Revelation (or Apocalypse) to John, is a primary example of apocalyptic writing. As we will see, apocalypticism seems to have informed the religious outlook of Jesus, and was central to Paul and to early Christianity in general.

Jesus' Early Life and Ministry

Jesus was born sometime between 6 and 4 B.C.E. (our system of dating based on Christ's birth was developed in the sixth century C.E.

and is off by several years). The Gospels of Matthew and Luke report that Jesus was born in Bethlehem, near Jerusalem, but he probably grew up in the town of Nazareth, in Galilee. Jesus likely became a carpenter, like his father. Jesus also seems to have become well versed in the Hebrew Scriptures, the sacred texts of the Jews of that time.

Jesus' ministry lasted about two years, and was carried out mainly in Galilee. It began shortly after Jesus was baptized by his cousin John the Baptist, whom Jesus apparently had followed as a disciple. John, clothed in animal skins and living off the land, preached the imminent coming of the judgment of God. The precise nature of Jesus' and John's relationship remains unclear, but it is evident that Jesus was baptized by John.

Upon beginning his ministry, Jesus attracted disciples, and eventually large crowds gathered around him. These facts alone are evidence of his charisma and of the relevance and effectiveness of his acts and teachings. The Gospels all portray Jesus as an exorcist (one who casts out demons) and a healer. He often taught in **parables,** ingenious stories cast in language and settings familiar to his listeners, but proclaiming radical lessons intended to disrupt conventional ways of thinking. Parables such as the good Samaritan and the prodigal son are among the best-known Gospel passages.

Jesus limited the scope of his ministry to fellow Jews, but unlike the Pharisees and other religious figures of his day, he constantly reached out to the lower strata of Jewish society: prostitutes, tax collectors, lepers, and other "sinners" and "outcasts."

Jesus' Message

Jesus said many insightful and compelling things. His astounding wisdom fills the Gospels, and his teachings have enriched Christians and non-Christians alike, for centuries. To summarize Jesus' message, we can note that he focused on two interrelated themes: the imminent coming of the Kingdom, or Reign, of God, and the urgent need for ethical transformation.

The first theme is summarized in Mark 1:15, in which Jesus proclaims: "'The time is fulfilled, and the kingdom of God has come near; repent, and believe in the good news.'" When Jesus spoke of the Kingdom of God, he seems to have been referring to God's intervention in history to right the wrongs of the world. The present age of injustice was rapidly coming to an end, and a new age was beginning, one in which God's Reign would prevail. Jesus' actions and teachings were directly linked to the coming of God's Reign. In Luke 11:20, for example, Jesus remarks on the significance of his role as exorcist: "'But if it is by the finger of God that I cast out the demons, then the kingdom of God has come to you.'"

The second theme of Jesus' ministry, ethical transformation, is also linked with the coming of God's Reign, for God's Reign was intended only for the righteous. Jesus taught that the need for ethical transformation was urgent. The heart of Jesus' ethical teachings can be found in his radical commandment on love:

"You have heard that it was said, 'You shall love your neighbor and hate your enemy.' But I say to you, Love your enemies and pray for those who persecute you, so that you may be children of your Father in heaven." (Matthew 5:43–45)

The notion of loving one's enemies must have struck Jesus' listeners as radical, but this is characteristic of his ethical teachings in general. Though Jesus did not reject the traditional commandments of Torah, he urged his listeners to go beyond the mere letter of the Law. The Reign of God demands more than a mere legal obedience to Torah; it demands a spiritual obedience as well. Love requires more than just following the rules; it depends on the transformation of the individual.

Along with teaching ethical transformation through his words, Jesus also taught by way of his actions, focusing his ministry on the lower classes of society. Jesus consistently practiced what he preached.

Jesus' Crucifixion and Resurrection

Jesus was crucified by order of the Roman procurator Pontius Pilate, probably in 30 C.E. It is tragic that a person as charismatic and innovative as Jesus should have met with such an early and painful death. Ironically it was precisely the radical nature of his teachings and ministry, and the agitated crowd of followers he attracted, that got Jesus in trouble with the authorities. Some of these authorities were Jewish, though the Gospels seem to overemphasize the involvement of Jews in Jesus' arrest and trial. In any event, only the Roman procurator had the authority to pronounce a death sentence. Jesus died the slow

Left: The Good Samaritan, by French painter Caruelle d'Aligny (1798 to 1871) *Above: Christ on the Cross,* by Dutch painter Rembrandt van Rijn (1606 to 1669)

3
How could you apply Jesus' commandment to love your enemies to your daily life?

4
Read the Sermon on the Mount (Matthew, chapters 5 through 7). Find three teachings (besides those mentioned) that you think clearly illustrate Jesus' ethical message.

and painful death of crucifixion, the manner of execution reserved for those condemned as political threats to the Roman Empire.

Of course this was not the end of the story. Indeed the religion of Christianity really began after the Resurrection, when Jesus' followers first experienced him as the Risen Lord. Though each of the Gospels gives a slightly different account of the discovery of the empty tomb, they all point to an event of profound significance and meaning. The conviction that Jesus had been raised from the dead by God moved Jesus' followers to spread the Good News far and wide. Some, such as Peter, were willing to die rather than deny their faith in this event.

The Gospel of Christ

The Christian message is often called the **Gospel,** which means "good news," and refers specifically to the Good News regarding Jesus Christ.

The New Testament authors have each provided a version of the Gospel that emphasizes certain aspects of the life and teachings of Jesus, and of his Crucifixion and Resurrection. By considering a sampling of the versions of the Gospel, the nature of Christ and his role as savior begin to come fully into focus.

The Gospel of Matthew: Revealing the New Torah

This chapter's earlier section on Jesus' message noted how he radicalized traditional ethical standards, urging a spiritual obedience to Torah. This is the main focus of the Gospel of Matthew, which presents Christ as the reveal-

er of God's new Torah. But this in no way implies that God's original revelation to the Israelites is to be disregarded: "'Do not think that I have come to abolish the law or the prophets; I have come not to abolish but to fulfill'" (Matthew 5:17). However, a new, radical obedience to Torah is now required, as we saw earlier regarding the commandment to love one's enemies: "'For I tell you, unless your righteousness exceeds that of the scribes and Pharisees, you will never enter the kingdom of heaven'" (Matthew 5:20).

The centerpiece of Matthew's presentation of Christ as revealer of the new Torah is the Sermon on the Mount (chapters 5 through 7), from which these passages are drawn. The Sermon on the Mount also contains the Beatitudes, the commandment to love one's enemies, and many other specific examples of radical obedience to traditional ethical laws. It is noteworthy that in Matthew's Gospel, Jesus reveals these teachings on a mountain (in the Gospel of Luke, similar teachings are presented on a plain). Matthew seems to intend for his readers to recall the original revelation of Torah to Moses on Mount Sinai.

The Gospel of Luke: Leading a Perfect Life

All the Gospels portray Jesus as one whom every Christian should strive to imitate. The Gospel of Luke emphasizes this point, portraying Jesus as a role model of the perfect way to live. Jesus reaches out to help people in all segments of society. Women receive more attention here than in the other Gospels, and many of the famous parables in Luke portray outcasts in a favorable light.

None does this more effectively than the parable of the good Samaritan (see Luke 10:29–37). Samaritans were historically on bad terms with the Jews, and thus were not expected to be kind toward them. But in the parable, a Samaritan aids an injured Jew who had been ignored by a priest and a Levite, members of what was supposed to be the most upstanding level of Jewish society.

The Gospel of John: The Incarnation of God

The doctrine of the Incarnation—that God's Son became fully human in Jesus Christ while remaining fully divine—is central to Christianity. This is the focal point of the Gospel of John, in which Christ is presented as the Word, who from the beginning was with God and was God (John 1:1). Christ was active in the creation of the world, and now, through the Incarnation, is the means for salvation. In the person of Jesus, "the Word became flesh and lived among us" (John 1:14). Salvation comes through knowing Christ and believing in who he is. This emphasis on the saving power of knowledge and belief is evident in the following passage, in which Jesus instructs his fellow Jews: "'Very truly, I tell you, anyone who hears my word and believes him who sent me has eternal life, and does not come under judgment, but has passed from death to life'" (John 5:24).

The Epistles of Paul: Christ Crucified and Risen

Paul's epistles, or letters, to the churches of Corinth, Rome, Galatia, and elsewhere are of paramount importance to Christian belief and theology. They are also quite challenging. It is therefore worthwhile to examine his main points in some detail.

Paul refers specifically to the Gospel, or "good news," in his First Epistle to the Corinthians:

Now I would remind you, brothers and sisters, of the good news that I proclaimed to you, which you in turn received, in which also you stand, through which also you are being saved, if you hold firmly to the message that I proclaimed to you—unless you have come to believe in vain.

For I handed on to you as of first importance what I in turn had received: that Christ died for our sins in accordance with the scriptures, and that he was buried, and that he was raised on the third day in accordance with the scriptures. (15:1–4)

Paul saw the power of Christ's Crucifixion and Resurrection as the source of salvation. Christ, in his death on the cross, carried away the consequences of humanity's sinfulness. With his Resurrection, Christ overcame death. Christians, having been forgiven of their sins through Christ's sacrificial death, will share in his Resurrection and experience eternal life. Thus, for Paul, salvation is the overcoming of sin and death.

The details of Paul's perspective on resurrection and eternal life remain predominant Christian beliefs. In spite of human sinfulness, God has offered salvation through the sacrificial death and Resurrection of Christ. In keeping with his apocalyptic view of the world,

5
Read the parable of the good Samaritan (Luke 10:29–37). While keeping its basic message intact, how would you retell the parable to make it more relevant for modern society?

Saint Paul preaches at Ephesus in this painting by French artist Eustache Le Sueur (1616 to 1655).

6

For Paul, God's giving of Christ marks the end of the era of Torah, but this in no way means that humans are released from ethical responsibility. Now, however, good behavior is to be rooted in faith and the spiritual transformation it brings, rather than in obedience to the letter of the Law. Think about ethical decisions you have faced. How might goodness rooted in the right spiritual perspective differ from goodness produced by following rules of correct behavior?

Paul understood Christ's death and Resurrection as one of the climactic moments of God's plan for salvation. Finally, when Christ returns to the world at the **Second Coming,** the dead will be raised, and all people—living and dead—will be judged. The good will be saved, and the evil condemned.

As we have observed, salvation is the overcoming of death, brought about at the time of the Second Coming of Christ. But salvation is also for the living, and it frees people from the bonds of sin and inspires a newfound peace and joy. God's goodness and grace overcome the power of sin so that those freed might enjoy the "fruit of the Spirit": "love, joy, peace, patience, kindness, generosity, faithfulness, gentleness, and self-control" (Galatians 5:22–23).

Paul emphasizes that this salvation comes only through the grace of God. Humans are not able to overcome sin on their own, but only through **grace**—God's presence freely given.

For Paul, God's giving of Christ marks the fulfillment of the divine plan for humanity, ending the era of Torah, in which Jews strove to be saved through observing the Law. Now

all people, Jews and Gentiles alike, can be saved through faith in Jesus Christ. Of course Paul did not teach the abandonment of ethical behavior. But this behavior now depends on faith in Christ, which transforms the believer, rather than on observance of the Law, which God had given to the Jews to serve as a "disciplinarian until Christ came" (Galatians 3:24).

Despite his conviction that Christ signifies the end of the Law, Paul insists that the Jews are still included in God's plan for salvation: "I want you to understand this mystery: a hardening has come upon part of Israel, until the full number of the Gentiles has come in. And so all Israel will be saved" (Romans 11:25–26). This remains an important passage in regard to the relationship of Christians and Jews.

Creed: What Christians Believe

The term *creed* comes from the Latin *credo,* "I believe," which begins the Latin version of the **Apostles' Creed.** The Apostles' Creed is one of Christianity's most important statements of belief:

I believe in God,
　　the Father almighty,
　　creator of heaven and earth.
I believe in Jesus Christ,
　　his only Son, our Lord.
He was conceived
　　by the power of the Holy Spirit
　　and born of the Virgin Mary.
He suffered under Pontius Pilate,
　　was crucified, died, and was buried.
　　He descended into hell.
On the third day he rose again.
He ascended into heaven
　　and is seated at the right hand
　　of the Father.
　　He will come again to judge
　　the living and the dead.
I believe in the Holy Spirit,
　　the holy catholic Church,
　　the communion of saints,
　　the forgiveness of sins,
　　the resurrection of the body,
　　and the life everlasting.
　　Amen.

Already in use by the end of the second century, the Apostles' Creed sets forth the foundations for two of Christianity's central doctrines: the Incarnation and the Trinity. Affirming both the divinity and the humanity of Christ, God incarnate, the Creed also refers to each of the three Persons of the Trinity: God the Father, Jesus Christ the Son, and the Holy Spirit. As we will see, today both doctrines are defined with greater precision, thanks to the work of theologians and church councils through the centuries.

The Incarnation: "The Word Became Flesh"

While clearly asserting the divinity of Jesus, the Apostles' Creed is notably insistent on his *human* nature, stating that he was "*born* of the Virgin Mary" and "*suffered* under Pontius Pilate, was *crucified, died,* and was *buried.*" The same is true of the Gospel of John, which emphasizes more than the other Gospels Jesus' humanness, making references to such things as his hunger and thirst, and pointing out that he wept on occasion. This focus on Jesus' humanity is in keeping with John's focus on the Incarnation, which we discussed earlier. Jesus is *fully* human, and, at the same time, fully divine. The first chapter

Far left: Easter Mass in Beijing, China
Left: Sunday Mass
Above: A Franscis-can monk lights candles at Saint Catherine's Franciscan Church.

of John establishes the foundation for the later formulations of the doctrine of the Incarnation. It identifies Christ as the Word (*Logos* in Greek), who from the beginning was with God and was God (John 1:1), active in the creation of the world. In the person of Jesus, "the Word became flesh and lived among us" (John 1:14), and because of this the salvation of humanity is possible.

For centuries the church strove to elaborate on the words of the Gospel of John and the Apostles' Creed, in order to state precisely the doctrine of the Incarnation. It was crucial that it be made clear that the Word actually *became* flesh, rather than merely appearing so, and that this union of the divine and human natures in Jesus was permanent, affecting humanity for all time.

The **Nicene Creed,** formulated by church leaders at the Council of Nicaea in 325, states that Jesus Christ is "the only Son of God, eternally begotten of the Father . . . true God from true God, begotten, not made, one in Being with the Father." This is obviously a much more elaborate, precise statement of the doctrine of the Incarnation than we see in the Apostles' Creed. Historically speaking, the most crucial point established at the Council of Nicaea is that Jesus the Son and God the Father are "one in Being" (*homoousios* in Greek). God became flesh in the person of Jesus, but in no way is Jesus a lesser being. Indeed he is the *same* being. This leads us directly into a consideration of the doctrine of the Trinity.

The Trinity

The doctrine of the Trinity is the centerpiece of Christian belief and theology. By definition the Christian God is a triune God, three Persons—God the Father, Christ the Son, and the Holy Spirit—in one Godhead. To think about God is therefore to think about the Trinity. Saint Thomas Aquinas, the great medieval theologian, expresses the centrality of the Trinity this way:

It is impossible to believe explicitly in the mystery of Christ without faith in the Trinity, since the mystery of Christ includes that the Son of God took flesh, that He renewed the world through the grace of the Holy [Spirit], and again, that He was conceived by the Holy [Spirit]. (*Summa Theologiae,* volume 2, part 2, question 2, article 8)

The doctrine of the Trinity states that the three Persons of God are distinct from one another, and yet of the same essence or substance. The Nicene Creed describes each Person of the triune God:

We believe in one God,
　the Father, the Almighty,
　maker of heaven and earth,
　of all that is, seen and unseen.

We believe in one Lord, Jesus Christ,
　the only Son of God

· · · · · · · ·

We believe in the Holy Spirit,
　the Lord, the giver of life,
　who proceeds from the
　Father and the Son.

In the Nicene Creed and later formulations, the distinctive features of the three Persons of

The Holy Spirit, symbolized as a dove, descends upon Jesus in this mosaic.

gence of new life in Christ. In addition, baptism, like the shared meal of the Eucharist, symbolized the unity and equality of Christians, who represented a cross section of Roman society. Some were rich, many were poor, and some were even slaves, but all were brothers and sisters in Christ.

The early church also developed a structure of leadership. By early in the second century, three distinct offices were in place: **bishops, presbyters,** and **deacons.** Bishops were seen as successors to Jesus' Apostles, and therefore were highly esteemed. Each bishop was the overseer of his church, and performed the central task of administering the Eucharist. From early times, Rome was generally regarded as the central location of the church, and the bishop of Rome was given a special degree of authority. Eventually the bishop of Rome came to have the title of **pope.** Because the Apostle Peter is traditionally thought to have been the bishop of Rome, the pope is his direct successor.

The presbyters (Greek for "elders") assisted the bishop, administering the Eucharist in the bishop's absence and taking charge of financial and disciplinary matters. Also assisting the bishop were deacons (Greek for "servants"), some of whom may have been women. While helping with a variety of tasks, the deacons also served as a link between the congregation and its bishop.

Christian scripture originally consisted of the Scriptures of the Jews. Paul's epistles, too, were eventually read. By the beginning of the second century, his epistles were widely circulated and regarded as scripture. Soon other writings, Gospels about the life of Jesus and various accounts of the Apostles, became known throughout the Christian communities.

In the fourth century, the church settled on a **canon** (which means "rule" or "standard") of twenty-seven writings. This collection is known as the **New Testament,** or New Covenant. As we have observed in the theology of Paul, Christians believed that the Gospel of Christ had fulfilled the Covenant with Israel in God's plan for the salvation of humanity.

Pope John Paul II arrives in Zaire in 1980.

Christ and Caesar: Christians in the Roman World

From the origins of Christianity through its first centuries of growth, Christians lived within the political, economic, and social structures of the Roman Empire. To a large extent, Christians carried on their spiritual lives independently of Roman constraints. However, some degree of conflict between Rome and Christianity was inevitable.

The Writings of the New Testament

The Gospels and Acts
Matthew • Mark • Luke • John
Acts of the Apostles (the second volume of Luke's two-volume work)

Paul's Epistles
Romans • 1 Corinthians • 2 Corinthians • Galatians • Philippians
1 Thessalonians • Philemon

"Deutero-Pauline" Epistles
(attributed to Paul, but were likely written by followers of Paul)
Ephesians • Colossians • 2 Thessalonians

Pastoral Epistles
1 Timothy • 2 Timothy • Titus

Letter to the Hebrews
Hebrews

Catholic Epistles
James • 1 Peter • 2 Peter • 1 John • 2 John • 3 John • Jude

Book of Revelation
Revelation

Chapter 11 mentioned that Roman worship of the emperor's genius, or guardian spirit, was primarily a display of loyalty toward the Roman state. Because Christians were monotheistic, they refused to worship the emperor, which made them seem to the Romans to be unpatriotic. This is one of the causes of persecution against Christians, who often died painfully as **martyrs** (witnesses), rather than violate their Christian convictions. Chief among other causes of persecution was a generally negative attitude of the Roman populace toward Christians.

Roman attitudes and policies toward Christians changed radically during the fourth century. As the century began, Christians were in the midst of the Great Persecution begun by the emperor Diocletian. At that time, only about 10 percent of the Empire was Christian. But by the end of the fourth century, Christianity was the Empire's only legitimate religion, and the vast majority of Roman citizens had converted. The key figure in this dramatic reversal of fortune was the emperor Constantine.

In 312 Constantine won a crucial victory that enabled him to become the uncontested emperor. He credited the victory to the intervention of Christ, and eventually he was baptized a Christian.

Constantine took significant steps leading to the prominence of Christianity in the Empire. In 313 he issued the Edict of Milan, declaring Christianity a legitimate religion and ending persecution of Christians. In 325 he convened the Council of Nicaea, at which the Nicene Creed was formulated to help unify the church. The theological arguments at the council were mainly taken up by the bishops, but Constantine's presence significantly strengthened the distinction between orthodox Christianity and heresies.

The Fall of Rome and *The City of God*

Among the many events leading to the fall of the Roman Empire, the sack of the city of Rome in 410 by the Visigoths was the most dramatic and alarming. Some Romans put the blame on Christianity, asserting that the gods were now punishing Rome for abandoning traditional pagan religion.

In response to this accusation, Augustine, bishop of Hippo in North Africa, wrote one of the great masterpieces of Christian theology: *The City of God*. Augustine argues in this work that all governments and nations are corrupt and have fallen to sin. Therefore, the fall of the earthly city is of little consequence. Only the heavenly city, the Kingdom of God, truly matters.

The significance of Augustine and his theology cannot be overstated. He set the stage for the great Catholic theologians of the Middle Ages, and was an inspiration for Martin Luther, leader of the Protestant Reformation.

Medieval Christianity and the Protestant Reformation

Christianity emerged in the fourth century as the premier religion of the Roman Empire. At this time the tradition of the orthodox, or **Catholic** (Greek for "universal"), church was well established. Theological debates still raged, and occasionally those whose views varied too greatly from the orthodox position were denounced as heretics. For the most part, though, the church was a united institution.

During the next seven centuries, however, Christian unity encountered many challenges, and a gradual divide took place in the church. By 1054 Eastern Orthodoxy, one of the three great limbs of modern Christianity, had officially become independent from the Roman church.

The Schism Between East and West

As early as the reign of Emperor Constantine, the foundation for a schism, or split, between the church in the east and the church in the west was already in place. Constantine established an eastern capital, Constantinople (modern-day Istanbul, Turkey), which quickly became a second center of the church, along with Rome. A number of problems arose. The distance between Constantinople and Rome caused communication problems, which were compounded by a language barrier: the eastern church used Greek, whereas the church in Rome used Latin. Further strife resulted from a gradual loss of political unity when the western part of the Roman Empire fell, and the eastern part survived (in the form of the Byzantine Empire).

Along with these divisive elements was the eastern Christians' refusal, starting in the late fourth century, to accept the authority of the pope in Rome. The final break occurred in 1054, when Pope Leo IX excommunicated the leader of the Greek church, the patriarch of Constantinople, who in turn excommunicated the pope. Attempts were made to reconcile the churches, but they failed. Eastern Orthodoxy and Roman Catholicism have been independent of each other ever since.

Catholicism in the Middle Ages

Through the Roman Catholic church, Christianity was established as the dominant culture of medieval Europe. For the most part, it was a period of triumph for Catholicism, though not without some serious shortcomings. Occasionally the pope and other members of the church hierarchy engaged in corrupt practices. The Crusades, which occurred from 1096 to 1270, were intended to take control of the Holy Land from the Muslims. Jerusalem was held for a time by Christians, but it soon fell back into Muslim hands. The Crusades, which were often senselessly violent, sometimes even involved Christians

7
Before Emperor Constantine legitimized Christianity in the fourth century, many Christians died as martyrs for their faith. Do you think Christian martyrdom is still possible in today's society? If so, can you think of any examples of modern Christian martyrs?

Cöment li roys loys liquarde la lignee huon chapet amisu

nomnes ma ognune oft onter per fur les samtzins

Above: Crusaders are depicted in this miniature painting from the medieval period.
Right: Notre Dame Cathedral, Paris

8

Saint Francis of Assisi lived a Christian existence that has been admired through the ages. Imagine a modern-day Saint Francis. What sort of lifestyle, goals, and virtues would such a person have?

fighting Christians; ultimately they accomplished very little.

But medieval Catholicism also accomplished much that has had lasting significance. The church continued to fortify itself as an organized institution with spiritual authority beyond that of any monarchs or other rulers. Great cathedrals were constructed, sometimes over the course of centuries. Monasticism, a lifestyle emphasizing community, simplicity, celibacy, and prayer, reached a new height of influence. Established communities of monks and nuns were reformed, and new ones, such as the Dominicans and Franciscans, were founded.

Saint Francis of Assisi (1182 to 1226), founder of the Franciscan order, remains one of the most revered Christians of all time. As one who loved nature and cared for poor people, Francis for the most part shunned the organizational constraints that were so much a part of the church. He and his loose-knit band of followers traveled the countryside in their simple, coarse garments, preaching the Gospel in the streets and marketplaces. Having put aside material possessions, they worked for food, and begged when work was not avail-

able. Their rewards were being close to nature and to God, and caring for the less fortunate. For many people Saint Francis is the perfect example of living in imitation of Christ.

Medieval theology culminated in the work of the great Dominican thinker, Saint Thomas Aquinas (1225 to 1274). Drawing from the philosophy of Aristotle, Aquinas explained the relationship between reason and faith, arguing that the two complement and need each other. For example, Aquinas taught that reason can prove the existence of God, but faith remains essential for full understanding of the truth, as it is revealed in the Bible and the teachings of the church. Aquinas's final and greatest work, the *Summa Theologiae*, was controversial at first, but became the standard work of Catholic theology. It remains very important to the present day.

The Protestant Reformation

The **Protestant Reformation** was a widespread phenomenon. It swept across much of sixteenth-century Europe, most notably in Germany, Switzerland, and England. Many Christians were frustrated with the church and were ready for change. Just then in Germany an individual stepped forth, almost by

accident, to lead a movement that would radically change Christianity as well as European society.

Martin Luther (1483 to 1546) was born to a peasant family. He originally set out to study law, but in response to his deep religious feelings, he became a monk of the Augustinian order. He was a highly devoted monk, but was unable to find freedom from his overwhelming sense of sinfulness. On a trip to Rome, Luther personally observed corruption within the hierarchy of the church.

Gradually Luther's feelings and experiences culminated in the birth of the Reformation. In Paul's epistles Luther discovered the foundation of his Christian faith: that humans are justified through faith in Christ, and not through external practices, or "works." One such external practice was the buying and selling of **indulgences,** pardons or reductions in the punishment due for sins committed. By giving money to the church, people believed they could reduce the time they would spend in the period of final purification after death, known as purgatory. Luther felt that this practice completely missed the point of Christianity.

In protest against the selling of indulgences, Luther wrote his famous Ninety-five Theses. According to the traditional account, he nailed them to the door of the church he served, which was considered a polite way of inviting discourse. He did not intentionally incite a major controversy, but, in fact, the Theses drew an enthusiastic—and highly controversial—response.

Luther defended his views with the Bible. According to him, much of what the church was doing did not conform to biblical Christianity. (To make the Bible more accessible to all Christians, including the common people, Luther later translated it into German. Because the printing press had been recently invented, Luther's German Bible was widely distributed.)

All the controversy Luther stirred up got him into trouble with the church. He was eventually excommunicated, but managed to evade punishment. Meanwhile local princes were given the choice between Protestantism (which the new movement was called, because it began as a "protest") or Catholicism. Most rulers in central and northern Germany and in the Scandinavian countries chose Protestantism. Former priests, monks, and nuns could now marry. Luther himself married a former nun, and they had five children.

Elsewhere in Europe other reform movements were taking place. In England a new English translation of the Bible appeared in 1526. This was such a radical step that its translator was condemned for heresy and burned at the stake. King Henry VIII (reigned 1509 to 1547) broke with papal authority due to his desire to remarry after divorcing his wife. King Henry declared himself head of the Church of England. Thomas More, the highest-ranking government official in England other than the king, refused to renounce the pope and was beheaded. The momentum of the Reformation in England was unstoppable.

In Geneva, Switzerland, a man named John Calvin (1509 to 1564) played a role in the Reformation second in importance only to Luther's. Calvin emphasized humanity's **original sin,** inherited from Adam and Eve.

9
Luther translated the Bible into German at about the same time as the invention of the printing press. Together these events greatly energized the Protestant Reformation by making the Bible widely available in the language of the common people. List other technological innovations that have caused a rapid spread of knowledge.

Some would be saved from sin, but only if God had already chosen them for salvation. The rest would be damned, regardless of how they lived their life. This doctrine of **predestination** was coupled with the idea that one's status among the saved is shown through good works and piety. For the Calvinist, therefore, a religious life is essential, even though the issue of salvation has already been determined by predestination.

The Protestant Reformation, begun almost accidentally by Martin Luther, had various effects besides the origin of Protestantism. For one thing, it sparked the beginning of the **Catholic Reformation** in 1545, which clarified church doctrine on a number of fundamental issues and cleaned up many of the corrupt practices Luther had protested against. Another effect, and a tragic one, was the Thirty Years' War (1618 to 1648) between Catholics and Protestants. Over half of Germany's population was killed, but the war settled nothing of real consequence. Within Protestantism, the motivating spirit of the Reformation itself—to protest any authority perceived to impede the Christian's relationship with God—continued to divide Protestants into new denominations.

Christian Divisions, Christian Unity

Today Christianity remains divided primarily into Roman Catholicism, Eastern Orthodoxy, and Protestantism. In this section we will consider the distinguishing characteristics of each. But even as we explore differences, it is crucial that we keep in mind the many beliefs and practices that unite Christians and form the basis of the movement known as ecumenism, which attempts to foster Christian unity.

Roman Catholicism

Most prevalent in central and southern Europe, Ireland, and Central and South America, and growing rapidly in Africa and Asia, Roman Catholicism today accounts for more than half of the world's Christians. Its most distinctive characteristic is its dependence on both the Bible and **Tradition** as the means of God's revelation of Christ. Tradition began with the Apostles, who handed it down to

their successors, the bishops and the popes. The bishops and the popes, in turn, are responsible for carrying on and clarifying anew in every age the Tradition passed on to them. The pope, as Peter's successor, is the highest authority in the church.

The Catholic church therefore has a special significance. As the earthly vessel through which divine truth is mediated, it is in some ways comparable to the Incarnation of God in the person of Jesus Christ. The fullness of the church, embodying all Christians, is understood as subsisting in the Catholic church. Other forms of Christianity are thought to exist in varying degrees of communion with the Catholic church. Eastern Orthodoxy, for example, is doctrinally closer to Catholicism than are most forms of Protestantism.

Catholicism recognizes seven sacraments, as does Eastern Orthodoxy (most forms of Protestantism recognize only two). Each of the sacraments is an outward, physical sign of an inward, spiritual reality. The seven sacraments are baptism, confirmation, the Eucharist (or Holy Communion), marriage, ordination (of deacons, priests, and bishops), reconciliation (or penance), and the anointing of the sick. Through the sacraments—especially baptism and the Eucharist—grace, the transforming presence of God freely given, flows forth into the person. The celebration of the Eucharist (or the Mass) is the summit of Catholic worship, and Catholics are expected to participate in the celebration each Sunday or Saturday evening.

Modern Catholicism has been strongly affected by the teaching of the **Second Vatican Council,** also called Vatican II. This worldwide council of bishops was convened by Pope John XXIII, and occurred from 1962 through 1965. The general aims of Vatican II were to update church teaching to respond to the needs of the modern world and to promote Christian unity. Many landmark documents were produced out of this council, including one acknowledging the holiness and truth that exists in non-Christian religions, and encouraging dialog with members of other religions. Other documents brought about changes in church liturgy and encouraged

Catholics to become engaged in life-giving, humanitarian struggles all over the world.

Amid the changes brought about by Vatican II, the Catholic church continues to take a stand on various issues, some of them quite controversial. But controversy is not new to the ancient tradition of Catholicism. Indeed the church's strength to stand up to controversy has always been a source of revitalization, as it has worked to be a beacon of light in the world.

Eastern Orthodoxy

Numbering nearly 250 million adherents altogether, the various churches of Eastern Orthodoxy are located mainly in eastern Europe, Russia, and the eastern coast of the Mediterranean Sea. Each of these churches (the Greek Orthodox church, the Russian Orthodox church, and so on) has its own leader, but all acknowledge the patriarch of Constantinople as the head of Eastern Orthodoxy. Unlike Catholicism's pope, however, the patriarch has no special doctrinal authority. This authority is held instead by the entire church body. Also in contrast with Catholicism, which regards Tradition as the process of clarifying the revelation of Christ through the ages, Eastern Orthodoxy limits its set of doctrines to those reached by seven ecumenical councils held prior to the year 787.

Eastern Orthodoxy observes the same seven sacraments as Catholicism. Its distinctive practices include a great emphasis on icons, which are artistic representations of the New Testament and early Christian saints. Theologically, Eastern Orthodoxy tends to focus on the Incarnation, encouraging a kind of mystical union with God through faith in Christ. This is the emphasis of the Gospel of John, which is especially popular in the Eastern church.

Presently Eastern Orthodoxy is challenged by great changes that have been taking place in the world and within the church itself. The breakup of the former Soviet Union has had pronounced effects, threatening the stability of the entire church. In North America, traditional ethnic identities of the various Orthodox churches are changing and eroding, and new membership among other ethnic groups is on the rise. This could prove to revitalize Eastern Orthodoxy, even as its deeply traditional ways are challenged.

Protestantism

As its name suggests, Protestantism originated as protest. This refers specifically to protest against any form of authority that it perceives as false—anything that stands in the way of the Christian's relationship with God through Christ. In general, Protestants focus on the Bible as the primary means of knowing

A Greek Orthodox church

10
Most of the sacraments of Catholicism and Eastern Orthodoxy function in part as rites of passage, marking divisions between one stage of life and the next. Given the nature of each sacrament, identify as many such divisions as you can. How might the sacraments function to celebrate the passage from one life stage to the next?

Christ, though different denominations vary considerably as to how they regard the Bible. For some Christians, called **fundamentalists,** the Bible is the direct word of God, and it must be read literally. For most Protestants, however, the Bible is a human product that conveys God's truth, as long as it is interpreted properly.

A second basic principle of Protestantism is justification by faith, as understood by Martin Luther. Faith is primary; as long as one has faith, good works will naturally follow. Sacraments are important, too, but only as accompaniments of faith. Most Protestant churches celebrate two sacraments: baptism and the Eucharist.

Protestantism is the predominant form of Christianity in northern Europe, England, Scotland, Australia, the United States, and Canada. It has four main branches, stemming from the days of the Reformation: Lutheran, Calvinist, Baptist, and Anglican (from which Methodism emerged). Today hundreds of separate Protestant denominations exist, many of them derived from one of these four branches.

The shape of Protestantism continues to change. New denominations are forming, and some that were divided at one time have now reunified. The main branches of North American Lutheranism, for example, recently merged to form the Evangelical Lutheran Church in America. Changes are also occurring within the denominations. For example, the number of women in the clergy is clearly on the rise. In some denominations the majority of ministers will soon be women.

Seeking Unity amid Diversity

The majority of Christians belong to one of the three main divisions we have just described. But there are also many smaller divisions, some of which challenge the very definition of what it is to be Christian. In fact, groups identifying themselves as Christian are not always regarded as such by other Christians. The Church of Jesus Christ of Latter Day Saints (the Mormons) and the Jehovah's Witnesses are two prevalent examples of such groups.

Amid this diversity are ongoing calls for unity. Many of the mainline Christian denominations advocate **ecumenism**—the promotion of worldwide Christian unity. One of the documents produced by Catholicism's Vatican II, for example, is devoted to a call for ecumenism. It begins as follows:

The restoration of unity among all Christians is one of the principal concerns of the Second Vatican Council. Christ the Lord founded one Church and one Church only. However, many Christian communions present themselves to [people] as the true inheritors of Jesus Christ; all indeed profess to be followers of the Lord but they differ in mind and go their different ways, as if Christ himself were divided. (*Decree on Ecumenism,* number 1)

United in Christ

The movement toward Christian unity is generally a cause for celebration, and it seems to be gaining momentum. Reflecting on the contents of this chapter, we can understand the logical appeal of the ideal of unity, even as we have noted the diversity among the many forms of Christianity. All these forms look to Christ and to the Christian creed as their common cornerstones. It stands to reason that there should be one church.

The Gospel of John sets forth Jesus' own prayer for Christian unity:

"I ask not only on behalf of [the Apostles], but also on behalf of those who will believe in me through their word, that they may all be one. As you, Father, are in me and I am in you, may they also be in us, so that the world may believe that you have sent me." (John 17:20–21)

Glossary

apocalypticism (From Greek *apokalypsis:* "revelation"). A common Jewish religious perspective of Jesus' time, which held that the world had come under the control of evil forces, and was heading toward a climactic end time, at which point God would intervene to usher in a reign of perfect justice and goodness. Early Christianity was generally in keeping with apocalypticism.

Apostle (From Greek *apostolos:* "messenger"). An early follower of Jesus recognized as one with authority to preach the Gospel; the Apostles included the twelve original disciples (with Matthias replacing Judas after the latter's death; see Acts of the Apostles 1:15–26) and Paul.

Apostles' Creed. A short statement of Christian belief that sets forth the foundations of the central doctrines of the Incarnation and the Trinity; traditionally thought to have been composed by the Apostles.

bishops. Officials within the early church who were regarded as successors to the Apostles. Bishops were responsible for overseeing the church and administering the Eucharist.

canon (From Greek *kanon:* "rule" or "standard"). An authoritative set of sacred writings, such as Christianity's New Testament.

Catholic (From Greek *katholikos:* "universal"). The largest of the three major divisions of Christianity. When it is not capitalized, catholic is used generally to denote the universal nature of the Christian church.

Catholic Reformation. A process begun in 1545, due partly to the Protestant Reformation, that clarified church doctrines and cleaned up corrupt practices.

church (From Greek *ekklesia* [ek-klay-see'ah]: "assembly"). The community of all Christian believers.

deacons. Officials within the early church who, like the presbyters, assisted the bishops, but were on closer terms with the congregation at large.

ecumenism. The promotion of worldwide Christian unity.

Eucharist. The Last Supper, or Communion meal, a central sacrament and ritual of Christianity patterned after the Last Supper shared by Jesus and his disciples.

fundamentalists. Those for whom a sacred text—for Christian fundamentalists, the Bible—must be read literally as the direct word of God.

Gospel (From Old English *godspel:* "good news"). General term referring to the Good News of the saving power of the life, Crucifixion, and Resurrection of Jesus Christ.

grace. God's presence freely given; a key doctrine for Paul and for Christianity in general.

heresies. Sects whose theological opinions were denounced as erroneous by orthodox Christians.

Incarnation. A core doctrine of Christianity stating that in Jesus Christ, God became fully human while remaining fully divine.

indulgences. Reductions or pardons in the punishment due for sins committed. The buying and selling of indulgences was a common practice in medieval Catholicism.

martyrs (From Greek *martyros:* "witness"). Those who choose to die rather than violate their religious convictions.

New Testament. A collection of twenty-seven writings which, by the late fourth century C.E., had been adopted by orthodox Christians as their primary sacred text.

Nicene Creed. Christianity's most important creedal statement, formulated by church leaders at the Council of Nicaea in 325 and setting forth in precise language the doctrines of the Incarnation and the Trinity.

original sin. Humanity's state of moral and spiritual corruption, inherited from Adam and Eve.

orthodox (From Greek *orthodoxos:* "right doctrine"). With respect to Christianity in general, the emerging version of Christianity that was deemed true by those with authority, and therefore accepted by the majority. When the word *orthodox* is capitalized, it refers to the major division of Christianity dominant in the eastern regions of Europe and the area surrounding the Mediterranean Sea.

parables. Stories that Jesus used to cast important moral lessons within the language and circumstances familiar to the common people.

pope. The title conferred on the bishop of Rome, the leader of Catholicism, who is considered by Catholics to be the direct successor of the Apostle Peter.

predestination. The doctrine, especially prevalent in Calvin's form of Protestantism, stating that God has already chosen those who will be saved from sin.

presbyters (From Greek *presbyteros:* "elder"). Officials within the early church who assisted the bishops.

Protestant Reformation. A widespread phenomenon in sixteenth-century Europe that resulted in the emergence of Protestantism from Catholicism.

Second Coming (In Greek, *parousia* [pahr-oo-see'ah]: "presence"). The anticipated return of Christ to the world, at which time the dead will be resurrected and all people will be judged.

Second Vatican Council. Also called Vatican II, a worldwide council of Catholic bishops convened by Pope John XXIII, occurring from 1962 through 1965. The council aimed to update church teaching to respond to the needs of the modern world and to promote Christian unity.

Tradition. A primary means of God's revelation of Christ, beginning with the Apostles and continuing in the present day through the church.

Trinity. A core Christian doctrine stating that God consists of three Persons—God the Father, Jesus Christ the Son, and the Holy Spirit—who are at the same time one God.

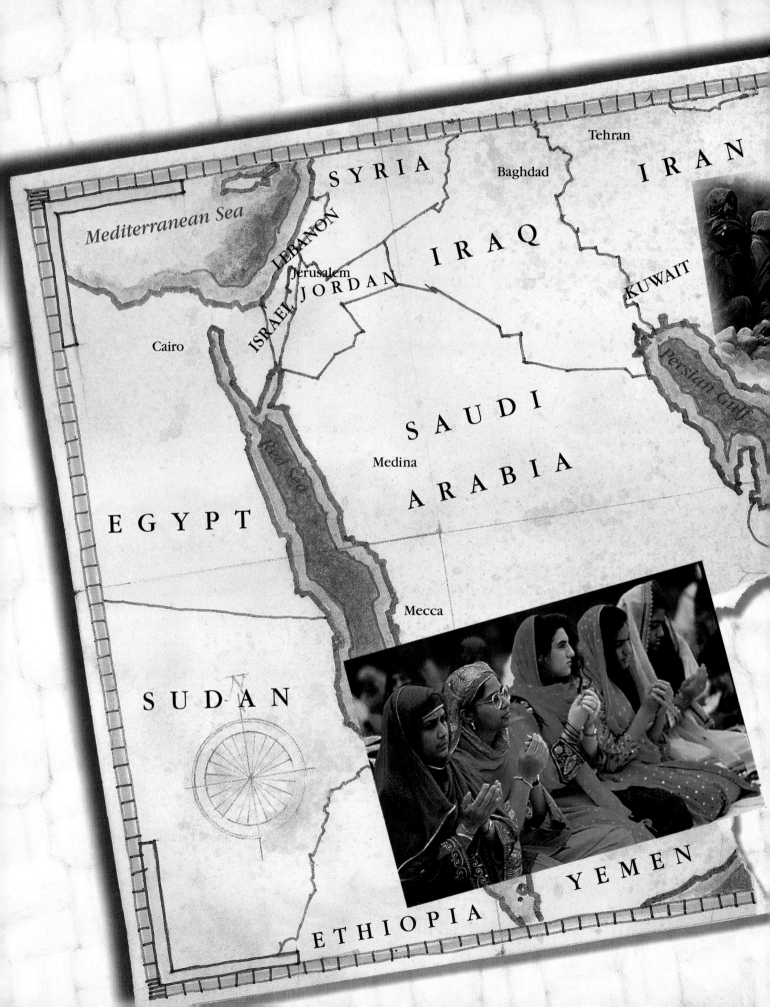

Mediterranean Sea

SYRIA

LEBANON

Baghdad

Tehran

IRAN

Jerusalem

ISRAEL JORDAN

IRAQ

KUWAIT

Cairo

Persian Gulf

SAUDI

Medina

ARABIA

EGYPT

Red Sea

Mecca

SUDAN

N

YEMEN

ETHIOPIA

14 Islam

Submission to the One God

The name Islam is derived from a root word meaning "surrender" or "submission."
In one simple phrase, this is the religion of Islam: submission to the one God, or Allah. The requirement of submission applies to every moment in the life of a Muslim
(which means "one who submits").

With nearly one billion adherents, Islam is the world's second-largest religion. It
is also the fastest growing. But for many Westerners, it remains something exotic, frequently mentioned in the news but rarely understood. Many are surprised to learn
that Islam is deeply rooted in the biblical tradition, and that it reveres Jesus Christ and
the great prophets of Judaism. Islam has also played a crucial role in the shaping of
Western culture, especially during the Middle Ages. But because most Muslims today
live in Asia and Africa, Islam no longer tends to be regarded as a Western religion.

Given its major role in world affairs, it is now more important than ever to understand Islam. Besides, it is a fascinating religion, with an astounding history and a
tradition of artistic and architectural splendor.

The Foundations of Islam

Something of the general nature of Islam can be understood simply by noting the degree of importance of each of its basic elements. First comes the **Qur'an** (also called the Koran), the primary sacred text and Islam's earthly center. Next comes the prophet Muhammad, who received the contents of the Qur'an from Allah and whose life provides Muslims with an example of human perfection. The central teachings of Islam, a third basic element, are derived from the Qur'an and from the life of Muhammad. Finally, the Muslim community, or Umma, bases its laws and lifestyle upon these teachings.

The Qur'an: Islam's Sacred Presence

The Qur'an is the earthly center of Islam. Its role can be compared to that of Jesus Christ for Christianity. Both are considered to be the sacred presence in the world. Just as Christ is the source of the foundational teachings of Christianity, so too is the Qur'an for Islam.

The Qur'an is about four-fifths the size of the New Testament, and is divided into 114 *surahs,* or chapters. It was originally written in Arabic, and there is only one Arabic version. This is logical, for the Qur'an is believed to contain the direct words of Allah, revealed to the prophet Muhammad and written down in its present form by his earliest followers.

The term *qur'an* literally means "reading" or "recitation," and oral recitation of the text has always been favored. The Qur'an is commonly regarded as the most beautiful work ever composed in the Arabic language. It is not possible to translate its full meaning into another language, owing to both its poetic quality and the subtle meaning that is conveyed visually through the Arabic script. The art of calligraphy was first used in the West by Muslims to celebrate the visual splendor of the Qur'an.

The Qur'an is revered as a miracle of God, especially because Muhammad is thought to have been illiterate. Today it is the world's most read and memorized book. It begins with a famous prayer called the Opening:

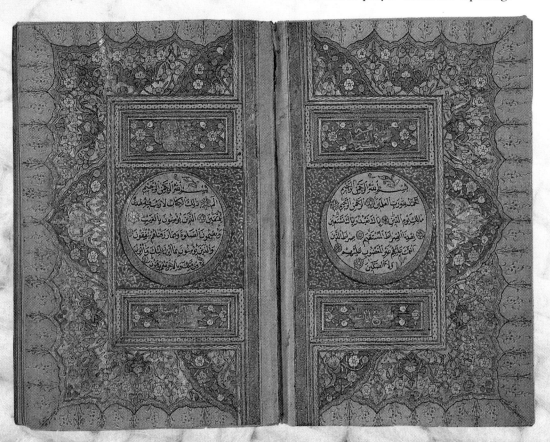

IN THE NAME OF GOD
THE COMPASSIONATE
THE MERCIFUL
Praise be to God, Lord of the Universe,
The Compassionate, the Merciful,
Sovereign of the Day of Judgement!
You alone we worship, and to You alone
   we turn for help.
Guide us to the straight path,
The path of those whom You have favoured,
Not of those who have incurred Your wrath,
Nor of those who have gone astray.

                  (Qur'an 1:1–9)

The Prophet Muhammad

Islam is purely monotheistic, and therefore carefully avoids regarding Muhammad as anything more than human. Even so, Islam celebrates Muhammad as the most perfect of all human beings, referring to him as a jewel among stones. The Prophet's combination of worldly success and religious genius make him a fascinating person, to say the least.

Muhammad's Life and Career

Muhammad was born about 570 C.E. into the leading tribe of Mecca, a city on the Arabian peninsula that was an important center of commerce and trade. Orphaned at an early age, Muhammad grew up with his uncle. He was an honest and dependable boy who worked hard as a shepherd and later in the trading business. He went to work as a caravan manager for a wealthy widow by the name of Khadija, whom he eventually married. Muhammad was twenty-five at the time, and Khadija was about forty. They had at least six children and enjoyed a long and happy marriage.

Along with being involved with his family and business pursuits, Muhammad spent much time in religious contemplation. He liked to retreat to a cave on nearby Mount Hira, where he could meditate on God in solitude. According to tradition, during one of Muhammad's visits to the cave, the archangel Gabriel appeared to him in a dream and commanded him, "Recite!" Muhammad

© Reuters NewMedia Inc./CORBIS.

protested that he was not capable. Twice more Gabriel issued his command, pressing hard on Muhammad's body. In desperation Muhammad asked him, "What shall I recite?" Gabriel answered:

Recite in the name of your Lord who created—created man from clots of blood.

   Recite! Your Lord is the Most Bountiful One, who by the pen taught man what he did not know. (Qur'an 96:1–4)

This event occurred in the year 610 C.E. and is celebrated as the Night of Power and Excellence. It marked the beginning of Muhammad's career as a prophet. This specific passage is the earliest "recitation" contained in the Qur'an. Muhammad would receive many more over the next twenty-two years, until his death in 632.

Left: Two pages from a seventeenth-century manuscript of the Qur'an
Above: A tribesman in Pakistan conveys goods using camel caravan, much as Muhammad did.

1

Consider the following characteristics of the Prophet Muhammad. For each one, discuss briefly how it might have affected his role as the founder of Islam:

- He was illiterate.
- He was married.
- He was an able businessman and a brilliant administrator.

Muhammad told Khadija about his experience, and she became the first convert to Islam. But in the early years, Muhammad found few who were willing to follow him. After ten years, several hundred families had converted. For the most part, though, Muhammad's fellow Meccans reacted to his message with hostility. This is not surprising, for Muhammad's teachings flew in the face of their accustomed ways. He taught that there was only one God, Allah. But Arabia was mostly polytheist, and in Mecca there were 360 shrines to various gods. Pilgrimages to these shrines earned much money for the city.

In addition, Muhammad's teachings on social and economic justice challenged his fellow Meccans, who were not ready to give up their established, and largely corrupt, standards of behavior.

In the face of this hostility, Muhammad and his followers migrated northward, to the city of Yathrib, in 622 C.E. City leaders there knew of Muhammad's reputation as an able businessman, and they invited him to become administrator of their city. The migration to Yathrib, of utmost significance to the history of Islam, is known as the **Hijra,** or "emigration." Muslims base their system of dating years on this event, using the abbreviation A.H. (after Hijra). The year 1622 C.E., for example, is 1000 A.H. by Islamic reckoning.

Muhammad proved to be a brilliant administrator, merciful and yet firm in his justice. The city of Yathrib soon came to be known as Medina, a shortened form of an Arabic phrase meaning "city of the prophet." Eight years later, after several battles with his Meccan opponents, Muhammad returned in triumph to his home city of Mecca. By the time of his death two years later, most of Arabia had converted to Islam.

Seal of the Prophets

Muhammad's unique significance for Islam rests in the belief that he is the final prophet, revealing the will of Allah fully and precisely, and for all time. Muslims believe that the prophets who came before Muhammad, such as Abraham, Moses, and Jesus, also revealed

Explorer, Paris/SuperStock.

God's will, but only partially. Muhammad, however, is the "Seal of the Prophets." There is no need for Allah to choose another.

We have noted that the Qur'an and Jesus Christ are both the sacred presence in the world for their respective religions of Islam and Christianity. Muhammad and Christ, however, have vastly different roles within these religions. Whereas Christ *is* the sacred presence, Muhammad *delivered* the Qur'an, which is the sacred presence. Muslims regard Muhammad as nothing more than human, with no supernatural qualities. Muslims regard Christ, on the other hand, as one of only two humans (Adam is the other) to have been conceived by God.

Muhammad is merely human, but he is revered as the best of all humans. His actions and his own teachings (which he carefully distinguished from the divine teachings of the Qur'an) together comprise the **Sunnah,** or "custom," of the Prophet. The Sunnah of Muhammad is the second most important authority for Islam.

Muslims admire and attempt to imitate Muhammad's earthly experience, but they also value the significance of a certain heavenly experience known as the Ascension to Heaven. Muslims believe that one night Muhammad was miraculously transported from Mecca to Jerusalem. From there he ascended with the archangel Gabriel through the seven heavens. He saw Moses, Abraham, and Jesus, and then was in the very presence of Allah. The Ascension to Heaven is one of two miracles involving Muhammad (the other is the production of the Qur'an). It is a central moment in Muslim piety.

Islam's Central Teachings

The teachings of Islam are ultimately based in the Qur'an and, secondly, in the Sunnah of the Prophet Muhammad. Nevertheless, great theological achievements have come through Islam, especially during its first two centuries. The fact that Muslim theologians through the ages have not always agreed helps to explain

why Islam tends to be somewhat diverse. This diversity is especially dependent on location. Islam as practiced in Saudi Arabia, for example, tends to be more conservative than Islam as practiced in Egypt. The following central teachings, however, are agreed upon by virtually all Muslims.

Allah: The One God

The Arabic name Allah literally means "the God." Allah was worshiped in Arabia before Islam. Muhammad's tribe, the Quraysh, regarded Allah as its special deity. But before Muhammad's call to be a prophet, Allah was considered to be one among many gods. Islam changed this decisively, for monotheism is one of the most emphasized teachings of the Qur'an.

Muslims understand Allah to be transcendent and suprapersonal, while at the same time immanent and personal. The suprapersonal transcendence is emphasized, however. Allah is thought to be genderless, for example, because being either male or female would suggest human qualities and thus limit God's nature. Muslims avoid artistic representations of Allah that in any way evoke human characteristics. As for the personal and immanent nature, Allah can be known in this manner, but only by the sage who has first experienced Allah's transcendence. The Muslim sage, or Sufi, will be examined more fully later in this chapter.

The transcendent, suprapersonal nature of Allah is made more accessible by the many names of God. Traditionally there are ninety-nine, including the Compassionate and the Real. These names provide Muslims with a variety of descriptive expressions for Allah, while maintaining their strict monotheism.

The Prophets: Messengers of Allah

Prophets provide the central link between Allah and human history; through them the divine will is revealed. Beginning with Adam and ending with Muhammad, many thousands of prophets have walked the Earth. An elite few are so important that they have changed the nature of humankind's relationship with Allah.

These few include Abraham, whom Muslims regard as the father of the Arab people, just as he is father of the Israelites. According to Islam, Abraham's son Ishmael moved to Mecca and became the ancestor of the Arabs. Abraham's prophecy centered on his pronouncement that there is only one God. Moses, Judaism's greatest prophet, is also revered by Islam. He pronounced Allah's ethical laws, the Ten Commandments. And then came Jesus Christ, who pronounced the Golden Rule ("Do unto others as you would have them do unto you"). Finally, Muhammad, the Seal of the Prophets, pronounced the Qur'an, and the revelation of Allah's will to humanity was complete.

Human Nature and Destiny

Islam teaches that human nature is essentially good, but people are all too capable of forgetting this. Forgetfulness is a key element in the Muslim interpretation of the Fall from perfection in the Garden of Eden. When Adam and Eve ate the forbidden fruit, they caused a state of forgetfulness to come upon them. When people momentarily forget their basic goodness, the passions can lead them to sin. Herein lies the need for the Qur'an and the other revelations of the will of Allah. Human beings need their directives for correct behavior so that goodness might prevail.

Human destiny is entirely dependent on the outcome of this struggle for goodness. The reward for the righteous is Paradise, and for the evildoers, Hell. The Qur'an vividly describes each realm, so that all Muslims are fully aware of the great consequences of their ethical decisions. Even more emphasis is placed on the Day of Judgment, at which time all humans will stand before Allah, and the destiny of each will be made known.

The Day of Judgment will be preceded by the coming of the Mahdi, a savior figure similar to Judaism's Messiah. The Mahdi will restore Islam and bring order on Earth. After this, Jesus Christ will return to Jerusalem and usher in the Day of Judgment.

The following passage from the Qur'an, an entire *surah* entitled "The Cataclysm," gives a typical description of the Day of Judgment:

When the sky is rent asunder; when the stars scatter and the oceans roll together; when the graves are hurled about; each soul shall know what it has done and what it has failed to do.

O man! What evil has enticed you from your gracious Lord who created you, gave you an upright form, and proportioned you? In whatever shape He willed He could have moulded you.

Yet you deny the Last Judgement. Surely there are guardians watching over you, noble recorders who know of all your actions.

The righteous will surely dwell in bliss. But the wicked shall burn in Hell upon the Judgement-day: nor shall they ever escape from it.

Would that you knew what the Day of Judgement is! Oh, would that you knew what the Day of Judgement is! It is the day when every soul will stand alone and God will reign supreme. (Qur'an 82)

The Nature of the World

Muslims believe that the natural world, being the creation of Allah, is good and worthy of reverence. Indeed the world is another form of revelation of God's will, and thus it is sometimes referred to as the cosmic Qur'an. Islamic civilization's great scientific advances are undoubtedly a result of this profound reverence of the natural world. Far from regarding science as somehow in conflict with their faith, Muslims celebrate science as a means of knowing more about Allah's perfect creation.

2
Now that you have read about Muhammad and some of Islam's other prophets, describe in your own words the function of prophecy in Islam.

3
"The Cataclysm" specifically describes the Day of Judgment. What can you infer from this passage about the Muslim perspective on Allah, human nature, and the role of Islam?

4
Muslims have always embraced science because it fits perfectly with their religious perspective about the natural world. From your perspective, how well do science and religion go together?

Muslim men in Houston, Texas, pray at a ceremony ending the month of Ramadan (see page 247).

Umma: The Community of Muslims

Islam emphasizes the community of all Muslims. Known as the **Umma,** this community transcends the boundaries of race, ethnicity, language, or other cultural factors. The Umma is a brotherhood and sisterhood based solely in religion.

Practically speaking the Umma is an ideal that is not always realized, for sometimes contention exists between certain groups of Muslims. Still, the ideal of community is a deeply held conviction and a basic element of Islam. And indeed, for most Muslims, the experience of belonging to the Umma is an everyday reality.

What is it about the religion of Islam that unites Muslims in this communal manner? It is the **Shari'ah,** or divine law. Drawn from the Qur'an and the Sunnah, the Shari'ah divides actions into five categories: obligatory, recommended, indifferent, disapproved, and forbidden. It is all-encompassing, setting forth in detail how to actually practice Islam—submission before Allah. To ignore the Shari'ah is to stop being a Muslim.

In the Islamic civilizations of the past, the Shari'ah was the law of the land, both religiously and politically. This is how the Shari'ah was intended to be applied. In modern times the Shari'ah is the basis of government in several countries with Muslim majorities, including Saudi Arabia, Iran, and Pakistan.

We now turn to some aspects of the life of the Muslim community at large, as it is shaped by the divine law.

5

Many Muslims live in countries governed by the Shari'ah, or divine law, of Islam. Imagine what it would be like if your own country came to be ruled by a religion. What would be the most notable changes?

Basic Practices and Social Teachings

One of Islam's great strengths is its practical approach to religious life. It describes the requirements and the rewards of righteous living with order and clarity, and it spells out in detail how to act in order to meet the requirements and reap the rewards. The Shari'ah, then, is a very practical form of divine law, conceived by God but fashioned for human beings' day-to-day life.

The Five Pillars

The order and clarity of the directives for living righteously is nowhere more apparent than in the **Five Pillars** of Islam. Each pillar calls for specific actions, and together the Five Pillars provide a basic framework for life.

Confession of Faith

The first pillar of Islam is its central creedal statement, the confession of faith known as the **Shahada:** *"La ilaha illa'Llah. Muhammadun rasulu'Llah."* This statement of faith is translated: "There is no god except God. Muhammad is the messenger of God." Stating this confession freely and with conviction officially makes a person a Muslim.

The contents of the confession refer to two of the basic teachings of Islam: monotheism and the uniqueness of Muhammad as a prophet. Though these beliefs are essential, most of Islam's teachings, like those of Judaism, involve correct practices. The rest of the Five Pillars demonstrate Islam's emphasis on correct practice.

Prayer

The second pillar of Islam is prayer. All Muslims, women and men, are required to pray five times each day: early morning, noon, midafternoon, sunset, and evening. Muslim prayer requires ritual washing of the hands and face, prostration in the direction of Mecca, and other ritual movements. Usually the prayers are performed on a rug specifically designed for this purpose.

On Fridays, public prayers are conducted in the **mosque,** a structure that traditionally includes a prayer hall and an enclosed courtyard, with towers called minarets at each corner. Public prayers may also be conducted in an open field or in the desert if there is no mosque nearby. Friday prayers are led by an **imam,** a "leader" who has been designated to conduct worship (though in Shi'i Islam, as we will see, Imam has a special meaning). The *imam* also delivers a sermon.

Three images of
Muslims at prayer

Fasting

The third pillar calls for fasting. Fasting takes place during the month of **Ramadan.** From dawn until sunset, Muslims are to avoid eating, drinking, smoking, and engaging in sex. Some are exempt from this requirement, for example, those who are sick, those who are making difficult journeys, and women who are breastfeeding.

Islam uses a lunar calendar, so Ramadan occurs during different seasons throughout the years. When it occurs during the summer, the requirements of fasting are particularly challenging, especially in the many desert and tropical regions of Muslim lands. (When it occurs in winter, it poses difficulties for the growing number of Muslim players in the National Basketball Association.)

Fasting is believed to be beneficial in many ways. Deprived temporarily of the material goods and sensual pleasures that are often taken for granted, Muslims gain insight into the situations of people who are less fortunate. Fasting also nurtures an awareness of mortality, and helps focus attention on moral and religious concerns, which fosters spiritual fortitude.

Wealth Sharing

Islam's fourth pillar, wealth sharing, helps assure the economic welfare of the entire Muslim community. It requires that Muslims contribute $2\frac{1}{2}$ percent of the value of their possessions to a public treasury. Poor people are exempt from this requirement. In fact, they are among the recipients of the shared wealth. It can also be spent on public concerns, such as educational or cultural institutions.

Wealth sharing is considered a form of worship, and thus provides benefits beyond the economic advantages it offers the community. Along with the specific requirement of wealth sharing, Islam teaches that acts of charity should be performed regularly.

Pilgrimage

Once in their lifetime, if they can afford it and are physically able, all Muslims are to journey to Mecca. The pilgrimage, or ***hajj***, is the fifth pillar of Islam. The *hajj* has great religious significance, for Allah forgives the sins of those who make the journey with reverence. Any pilgrim who dies on the journey to or from Mecca is a martyr, and enters Paradise.

The pilgrimage vividly captures the communal ideal of the Umma, because Muslims from around the world gather together in Mecca to celebrate their common religion, regardless of their worldly differences. Male

6

Islam places great emphasis on its primary pilgrimage, the *hajj*. It involves several symbolic features, all of which have great religious significance for Muslims. Try to identify at least three of these symbolic features. Does anything in your own life have symbolic meaning similar to that of the *hajj*?

pilgrims wear plain white clothing that signifies their basic equality, and is also symbolic of ritual purity. Female pilgrims, on the other hand, wear simple but colorful clothing that is typical of their own homeland. Together the white cloth of the men and the colorful dress of the women symbolize Islam as a global religion that brings its diverse adherents together in the unity of the Umma.

The pilgrimage takes place during a specific month of the year and lasts for at least fifteen days. It involves several ritual acts, including the circling of the **Ka'ba,** a stone cubical structure in the courtyard of the Great Mosque of Mecca. It is believed that Abraham built the Ka'ba, and it has been a site of religious significance since pre-Islamic times. Muslims regard the Ka'ba as the "navel" of the Earth, and as their sacred center, geographically.

The Personal and Social Life of Islam

7

The Five Pillars of Islam provide a basic framework for life. Now that you have read about each of the pillars, state in your own words how they provide this framework.

The Shari'ah, or divine law, spells out details of Muslim life that go far beyond the requirements of the Five Pillars. Let us consider just some of the standards of personal and social behavior that contribute to Islam's clear and ordered directives for living righteously.

Care of the Body

Islam holds that the body ultimately belongs not to the individual but to God. This basic principle leads to specific teachings on the care of the body. These teachings celebrate physical joys while controlling desires.

The body is to be kept clean; recall that washing is part of the Muslim prayer ritual. Clothing should be neither overly seductive nor overly luxurious, but there is nothing wrong with choosing clothes that are fashionable and attractive. Perfumes are especially popular. Muhammad himself once mentioned three particular joys: the company of women, prayer, and perfume. Good aromas tend to remind Muslims of Paradise.

Like Judaism, Islam regulates the diet. The Shari'ah distinguishes between permitted and forbidden foods. The eating of pork and the drinking of alcohol, for example, are forbidden. Several passages in the Qur'an condemn wine and other intoxicants.

Sexuality is celebrated as one of Allah's greatest gifts, but one that is to be enjoyed only within marriage. Premarital and extramarital sex, and even having lustful thoughts for another, are forbidden, as are homosexuality and prostitution. Muslims are urged to marry as early in life as possible. Marriages are traditionally arranged by the parents; dating is generally not practiced. This of course contrasts sharply with the Western perspective on marriage, for which romantic love is the foundation. In Islam, marriage is first and foremost a legal contract; love is expected to grow once the couple has begun their married life.

Women in Islam

The status of women in Islam is a controversial issue. Western critics tend to accuse Islam of being chauvinistic and of denying basic rights to women. Muslims, in turn, tend to be frustrated and irritated by these accusations, dismissing them as meddlesome and unfair.

On the whole, the Qur'an itself, and the ideals of Islam, regard men and women as equals, but with different roles. Often these ideals are realized in daily life. For example, while men usually have predominant roles in economic and public life, women generally have greater influence within the family, Islam's central social institution.

Three specific points of contention are commonly cited by Western critics: divorce, polygamy, and the wearing of the veil.

According to the Shari'ah, either the husband or the wife may initiate a divorce, although traditionally it has been easier for the man. In the practice known as repudiation, a man can divorce his wife simply by stating, "I divorce you" three times. Usually a waiting period is required between the utterances, however, to allow opportunities for reconciliation. In some Muslim countries, repudiation is no longer legal, and men and women are generally on equal footing when it comes to initiating a divorce. In any event, Muhammad denounced divorce as being detested by Allah, even though it is categorized as a "permitted" act.

As for polygamy, the Qur'an technically allows it, but sets limits:

You may marry other women who seem good to you: two, three, or four of them. But if you fear that you cannot maintain equality among them, marry one only. . . . (Qur'an 4:3)

This passage is open to interpretation. Some Muslims contend that it actually recommends monogamy, because to be perfectly equitable toward two or more wives would be nearly impossible. In most regions polygamy is very rare. In some situations, however, Muslims condone the practice as the right thing to do. If there are many more women than men (in periods following warfare, for example), or if an older woman is widowed, it is better that men have multiple wives than that women remain alone. Muhammad himself had many wives late in life, though for twenty-five years he had been married to Khadija only, until her death. His practice of polygamy, moreover, was mainly for the sake of political unification, and not for sensual pursuits.

Like polygamy, the wearing of the veil is referred to in a passage in the Qur'an that has been interpreted in different ways:

If you ask [the Prophet's] wives for anything, speak to them from behind a curtain. This is more chaste for your hearts and their hearts. (Qur'an 33:53)

8
Compare Islamic teachings on the care of the body with those you have been taught.

Left: The Ka'ba is surrounded by pilgrims during the *hajj.*
Above: A veiled Muslim woman

9
Very few Muslims practice polygamy, though it is technically allowed by the Qur'an. How do you interpret this Muslim teaching, as set forth in the passage quoted from the Qur'an?

Some Muslims require that women cover every part of their body, and hide their face behind a veil. Others define veiling simply as covering the hair while in public. Veiling was a pre-Islamic practice in Arabia, and it is no longer universal among Muslim women. In the last few decades, educated women in relatively modernized countries like Egypt have intentionally returned to wearing the veil. For them it is perceived as a means of embracing their own traditional heritage, not as a form of male domination.

Jihad: "Struggle"

Jihad, which means "exertion" or "struggle," is a principle that applies to all aspects of Islamic life, personal and social. It is sometimes counted as the sixth pillar of Islam.

On a personal level, *jihad* refers to the individual's spiritual struggle against anything that detracts from revering Allah and from acting in accordance with the divine will. Socially, *jihad* refers to the preservation of the order that Allah has willed for the world. To some extent the expansion of Islam is considered part of this order.

The term *jihad* is also used in a more controversial way. In a narrow context, it refers to armed struggle, and is sometimes thought of as meaning "holy war." The Qur'an, however, supports armed struggle for the sake of Islam only if it is done in self-defense.

Expansion and Varieties of Islam

Like most religious traditions, Islam has taken various forms over the centuries. But there are only two major historical divisions: Sunnism and Shi'ism. Sufism, the mystical form of Islam, draws its adherents from both of these historical divisions, and therefore is not a separate division. Before taking a closer look at the forms of Islam, we will review Islam's noteworthy history of rapid expansion.

The Expansion of Islamic Civilization

Following the death of Muhammad in 632 C.E., Muslims were led by **caliphs** (successors) chosen by the community. The first caliph was Muhammad's father-in-law, Abu Bakr. These caliphs oversaw a remarkable phenomenon. First, all of Arabia, which had never managed to unite over anything in the past, embraced Islam. Soon the peoples of vast stretches of territory converted to the new religion, most often by their own free will and not because of armed force.

Within one century of Muhammad's death, Islam was the religion of the entire Middle East, Persia, North Africa, and almost all of Spain. If Muslim forces had not been defeated in the Battle of Tours in southern France in 732, they may well have conquered France and the rest of Europe.

The religion of Islam, by its very nature, is also a system of government and the foundation for a literary and artistic culture. In other words, Islam is also Islamic civilization. And so it was that in these vast regions, great centers of Islamic civilization developed. Muslims, Jews, and Christians lived side by side in Muslim Spain, and civilization flourished even as the rest of Europe endured the Dark Ages. A mathematical system, called *al-jabar* in Arabic, was invented; in English we know this system as algebra. The library of Cordoba, the main city of Muslim Spain, housed four hundred thousand titles. It is through these Arabic translations that some of the classics of ancient Greece and Rome have survived to this day.

Other Muslim empires arose, and in widely diverse regions. The Mogul Empire ruled India from 1526 to 1858. The Ottoman Empire, centered in modern-day Turkey, endured from 1326 all the way into the twentieth century.

For the most part, the flourishing of Islamic civilization came to an end during the era of European colonization. Many lands with a majority Muslim population came under the rule of European nations, and the normal functioning of Islam as a system of government within a religion was crippled. Today Islam seems to be in the midst of a rapid recovery from the effects of colonization.

Where Muslims Live

Presently the nations with the greatest concentration of Muslims are located in the northern half of Africa, all of the Middle East and southwestern Asia (including Turkey, Iraq, Iran, and Afghanistan), South Asia, and the islands of Malaysia and Indonesia.

Arabia and the Muslim World

Islam crosses many boundaries of language, ethnicity, and culture. It cannot simply be equated with Arabia or the Arabs, who comprise only about 20 percent of the entire Muslim population. By way of comparison, 35 percent of the world's Muslims live in the South Asian nations of Pakistan, Bangladesh, and India. Still, the Arabian region enjoys a special status in Islam for several reasons: Arabic involvement in Islam goes back to the earliest history of Islam; Arabia is the location of Muslim sacred sites; and Arabic is the language of Islam.

Islam in the United States

Between four and six million Muslims live in the United States, where Islam is the fastest-growing religion. About 40 percent of the U.S. Muslim population is made up of African Americans, some of whom can claim a Muslim heritage. It is estimated that nearly 20 percent of Africans brought to North America as slaves were Muslim.

Far left and center: Views of Muslim Spain
Left: The Islamic Center in Cedar Rapids, Iowa, is the oldest mosque in the United States.

Partly due to this heritage, some African Americans have argued that Islam is better suited for their community than Christianity, which they regard as the religion of their white oppressors. This is a central principle of the Nation of Islam, a twentieth-century movement that has been led by such notable men as Elijah Muhammad, Malcolm X, and Louis Farrakhan. The Nation of Islam upholds only some of the practices of traditional Islam, and most Muslims do not regard it as an authentic part of their religion. These differences were highlighted in the 1960s when Malcolm X, after making a pilgrimage to Mecca, rejected the Nation of Islam and formed a more traditional Muslim movement. For one thing, whereas the Nation of Islam teaches racial separatism, Malcolm X embraced the interracial unity he observed firsthand in Mecca.

The majority of Muslims in the United States, however, are immigrants from Muslim countries and their descendants. Some arrived by the end of the nineteenth century, from the Middle East and eastern Europe. Large-scale immigration first occurred in the 1960s, caused by troubles in Muslim homelands. These immigrants tended to maintain their own ethnic ways within small communities of fellow Muslims. Their children, however, have been more affected by Western influences. Today many of them are as typically American as they are Muslim. Islam is rapidly settling in as a common feature of the religious landscape of the United States.

Historical Divisions Within Islam

Though we are about to consider the divisions within Islam, let us first note the more prominent theme of unity that holds together the brotherhood and sisterhood of Muslims, whether Sunni or Shi'i. Various specific reasons underlie this theme of unity. Only one Arabic version of the Qur'an exists, regarded by all Muslims as the direct word of Allah. The Sunnah of the Prophet allows all Muslims to share in the inspiration of Muhammad's life and teachings. Ritual practices, such as those required by the Five Pillars, are common to all.

10
Have you observed any aspects of Islam in your own community or nation? What have you been able to learn from these observations about Muslims and their religion?

Bearing in mind these unifying features, let us now consider the interesting characteristics that distinguish Shi'i from Sunni Islam.

Sunnism

Sunni is drawn from a longer phrase referring to the people who follow the established custom, or sunnah, meaning the Sunnah of the Prophet. It is simply the common name for the form of Islam practiced by the majority (about 87 percent) of Muslims. In this respect, then, it is Islam as described in the preceding pages of this chapter.

Shi'ism

Shi'i comes from *shi'at 'Ali,* which means "partisans of Ali." Ali was the cousin and son-in-law of Muhammad. Three times he was passed over before finally being named caliph, and eventually he was assassinated. These events led to the origins of the Shi'i movement by Muslims who favored Ali as the true successor of Muhammad. Shi'ism was consolidated into a distinct form of Islam when Ali's son, Husayn, was assassinated in 680 c.e. The martyrdom of Husayn continues to be observed within Shi'i Islam as a significant event, and Husayn himself is revered as a great hero.

The origins of Shi'i Islam, then, were due primarily to historical circumstances. Today Shi'ism can be distinguished in part by geography. The nations of Iraq and Iran have Shi'i majorities. Kuwait, Afghanistan, and Pakistan also have significant Shi'i populations.

In terms of its teachings, Shi'ism is most notably distinguished by the figure of the **Imam.** While not a prophet, the Imam is believed to have special spiritual insight, and is revered as the true earthly authority. Most Shi'is believe there have been twelve Imams, all of them descended from Muhammad through his daughter Fatima and her husband, Muhammad's cousin Ali. The twelfth Imam, Muhammad al-Mahdi, is thought to have been hidden away at a young age. At the end of time, he will return to restore Islam and bring on the Day of Judgment.

This belief in the return of Muhammad al-Mahdi, and the general emphasis on the Imam as an authority figure, has made Shi'ism more politically volatile than Sunnism. In the Iranian Revolution of 1978 to 1979 and its aftermath, for example, the late Ayatollah Khomeini was thought to have special authority, and sometimes was even regarded as the Imam.

Sufism: Islamic Mysticism

Islam, as practiced by the majority of Muslims, Sunni and Shi'i alike, emphasizes the transcendence and suprapersonal nature of Allah. Worship focuses on living in accordance with the divine will, through following the Shari'ah. An abyss lies between the religious understanding of the individual and the great magnificence of Allah.

Sufism strives to cross that abyss, to experience Allah as immanent, dwelling within the worshiper. A Sufi saying expresses this in the words of Allah: "'My Earth and My Heaven contain Me not, but the heart of my faithful servant containeth Me'" (quoted in Arberry, *Sufism,* page 28).

Sufism's Place Within Islam

The term *sufism* is derived from *suf,* the coarse wool garment that is traditionally worn by Sufis. Despite the simplicity of the name's origin, the place of Sufism within Islam is a complicated and controversial issue.

Recall the first verse of the confession of faith, the first pillar of Islam. It declares, "There is no god except God." Sufism extends this a step further, declaring that there is nothing *but* God. If this is the case, then the worshiper, too, must be one with God. This is the guiding principle of Sufism. The **Sufi** experiences oneness with Allah, and through this experience gains spiritual fortitude.

Sometimes this perspective has landed Sufis in trouble with orthodox Muslims. A great Sufi by the name of al-Hallaj, for example, was crucified by his fellow Muslims in 922 for having stated, "I am the Real." The Real is one of the ninety-nine names of God, so al-Hallaj was in fact claiming identity with Allah. To orthodox Muslims, this was blasphemous. For Sufism, it was a description of the pinnacle of religious experience.

Despite such events born of controversy, in the past Sufism generally fared well alongside orthodox Islam. In fact, it played an enormous role in attracting new adherents to Islam, especially in the East. Today, however, with the rise of more traditionalist forms of orthodox Islam, Sufism is commonly blamed for having caused Islam to stray from the true path, and is therefore frowned upon by many.

Sufi Methods

Similar to Christian monasticism, Sufism is made up of groups known as orders. Each is led by a **shaykh,** a master and teacher. He leads his disciples through a variety of spiritual disciplines to help them achieve union with God. These disciplines include recitation of sacred names and phrases, breathing exercises, and the chanting of odes. Perhaps the most famous Sufi discipline is a dance form best known in the West as the whirling dervish.

Sufis identify the aim of their disciplines as **al-fana,** or "extinction." This refers to the extinction of the person's sense of ego, of the notion of separate existence. Once this notion is annihilated, the separation between self and God disappears, triggering the experience of union with the divine. This aspect of Sufism is similar to some of the mystical teachings of Hinduism.

The late Ayatollah Khomeini, a Shi'ite Muslim, was an influential and controversial leader in the Iranian Revolution of 1978 to 1979.

11
Given what you now know about Islam, state in your own words why you think al-Hallaj was crucified, and why Sufism is commonly frowned upon by orthodox Muslims today.

Muslim Life

Nizar Najjar is a university student in the United States. He grew up in Tunisia, a predominantly Muslim country on the Mediterranean coast of North Africa. He was asked to remark on a few topics.

What is it like to be a Muslim here, compared to Tunisia?

There are big differences. In Tunisia, a Muslim country, we have the call to prayer, we go to the mosque, and in Ramadan everyone fasts and prays together. We can freely butcher the lamb needed for our feast at the end of Ramadan. Here, if you go to your home and butcher a lamb, you can get into trouble. Also, when I am fasting here during Ramadan, I see everyone else eating. That gives me an un-comfortable feeling. Back home, the whole community is supportive and synchronized. If a Muslim chooses not to fast, that is fine. But it is considered wrong to eat or to smoke outside, in front of others, because they are fasting, trying to resist the urge to eat or to smoke.

As for prayer, in the United States we do not have the call to prayer. We use our watches instead. Here there is no mosque. We must find an empty, clean room for prayer, and determine the direction to Mecca before praying. We students are trying to buy a place and transform it into a mosque, so that we can at least perform our prayers.

What is involved in the practice of prayer?

Preparation for prayer involves ablution, or ritual washing. But even before ablution, you have to have good intention, by purifying your heart. Ablution is not going to do you any good if you don't purify yourself spiritually before praying. Praying is not simply a duty that you can perform just to get rid of it. What you need to do is purify yourself. You also wash yourself—your hands, face, and other parts of your body, all in a certain order. Then, if your inside is pure and your outside is clean, you are ready spiritually to perform the prayer.

In prayer we are in the presence of Allah. He is metaphorically—though not physically—in front of us. So when you are praying, it's strictly forbidden for anyone to cross in front of you. It would interrupt your sacred time of worship. It would interrupt your concentration, which is vital to prayer.

Prayer must be done with good intention. Still, it is a duty. Allah deserves our prayer. It is the least thing we can do to obey Him and to satisfy Him and to appease Him.

How would you describe the Prophet Muhammad?

Muhammad is great. Muhammad is wonderful. Muhammad had lots of accomplishments. Muhammad was successful. Muhammad transformed the whole nation. Muhammad was a political leader, he was a war strategist, he was a good economist. He was all these things. But the bottom line is, he was just a human being. He doesn't have the presence that Jesus has in the heart of Christians. We have lots of respect for Muhammad, but he was just a human being, and we do not idolize and worship him. Allah and the Qur'an are first. When we need advice, we go first to the Qur'an. If we don't find anything in the Qur'an that will guide us, *then* we go to the sayings of the Prophet. This is the importance of the Prophet. Some aspects of daily life and social problems were addressed by the Prophet. So we are required to follow his teachings.

What do you most want readers to know about Islam?

Just know that Muslims do not hate Christians. Actually, Muslims are the closest religion, or the closest people, to Christians. Muslims are not enemies, as the media sometimes tend to present them. Islam is the only non-Christian religion that makes it an article of faith for its followers to believe in Jesus, to believe that Jesus was one of the mightiest messengers of God, or of Allah, as we call Him. We believe in Jesus' miracle birth. We believe that he healed the blind and the lepers, by God's permission. And we believe that he is coming back. So we have lots of similarities. The only difference we have is that we do not believe that Jesus was the Son of God. But this is a separate issue. Actually, Jesus appears in the Qur'an more frequently than does Muhammad. An entire chapter in the Qur'an is dedicated to Mary, just to honor the mother of Jesus.

We have some differences with Christians, but there is no way a Muslim could hate a Christian just because he's a Christian. That's absurd. Basically we love everybody, especially Christians and Jews, who follow the Scriptures, who do good deeds. There is no difference, except in the form of worship. We love everybody. We just want everybody to love us. That's it. We don't deny that we have shortcomings. We have people who are fanatics, who want to go bomb places. But a true Muslim disagrees with these people. We don't send people to kill innocent people—that is absurd. So don't judge us based on what some bad people, some bad Muslims, do. Just judge us as persons, and judge our religion.

Islam and the World

Islam is distinctive among the great religions of the world for the extent to which it embraces the totality of life. There is simply no recognition of a division between what is religious and what is secular. The very meaning of the term *religion* in Arabic implies the need to repay one's debt to God; every aspect of life is indebted, and every action should tend to this need.

The all-encompassing nature of this, the world's second-largest religion, makes Islam an especially relevant subject of study. How does Islam see its place within our pluralistic world? Can a religion that understands itself as embracing the totality of life truly be tolerant of other religions?

The answer to such questions is twofold. Muslims regard Islam as the final revelation to all religions, just as the Qur'an itself is believed to be the final revelation of the divine will. But Muslims also acknowledge that other religions include expressions of the divine will. Judaism and Christianity, especially, have a favored place in the eyes of Islam, which regards their followers as "People of the Book."

We often hear of conflicts involving Muslims: Palestinian Muslims fighting Israeli Jews, Hindus at war with Muslims in India, conflicts in eastern Europe; the list goes on. As we have seen at other points in this chapter, it is important to realize that as with every religion, the ideals of Islam are not always put into practice. It is appropriate that we close with a Muslim's statement on the ideal of unity. This is from the great Sufi poet Rumi:

I am neither eastern nor western, neither
    heavenly nor earthly,
I am neither of the natural elements nor of
    the rotating spheres.
I am neither from India nor China,
    from neither Bulgaria nor Tabriz,
From neither the country of Iraq nor the land
    of Khurasan.
My sign is without sign, my locus is without
    locus,
It is neither body nor soul for I am myself the
    Soul of souls.
Since I expelled all duality, I see the two
    worlds as one.
I see the One, I seek the One, I know the
    One, I call upon the One.
    (Nasr, "Islam," in *Our Religions,* page 522)

Glossary

al-fana (ahl-fuhn'ah; Arabic: "extinction"). The extinction of one's sense of separate existence before achieving union with Allah; the aim of Sufi mystics.

caliphs (Arabic: "successors"). The military and political leaders of the Muslim community who succeeded Muhammad after his death.

Five Pillars. Specific religious and ethical requirements for Muslims: the confession of faith (Shahada), prayer or worship, fasting during the month of Ramadan, wealth sharing, and the pilgrimage to Mecca *(hajj).*

hajj (haj). The fifth of the Five Pillars, the journey to Mecca that all Muslims are to make at least once in their lifetime, if they can afford it and are physically able.

Hijra (hij'ruh; Arabic: "emigration"). The emigration of Muhammad and his followers from Mecca to Yathrib (thereafter called Medina) in the year 622 c.e., the founding event of the Muslim community.

imam (i-mahm'; Arabic: "leader"). The leader of the Friday worship service who leads the prayers and delivers a sermon. For Shi'i Islam, when the word *Imam* is capitalized, it refers to an early successor to Muhammad and leader of Islam (most Shi'ites acknowledge twelve Imams), believed to have special spiritual insight.

jihad (ji-had'; Arabic: "exertion," "struggle"). Sometimes counted as the sixth pillar of Islam, the general spiritual struggle to be a devout Muslim. In a more narrow context, *jihad* refers to armed struggle ("holy war") for the sake of Islam, which the Qur'an supports only if it is done in self-defense.

Ka'ba (kah'bah). The stone cubical structure in the courtyard of the Great Mosque of Mecca, believed to have been built by Abraham and regarded by Muslims as the sacred center of the Earth.

mosque. The Muslim place or building of worship, traditionally including a prayer hall and courtyard, with towers called minarets at each corner.

Qur'an (kuh-ran'; Arabic: "recitation"). Islam's primary sacred text, regarded by Muslims as the direct words of Allah, revealed to Muhammad through the angel Gabriel.

Ramadan (ram'uh-dahn). The ninth month of the Islamic lunar calendar during which Muslims fast, in accordance with the third of the Five Pillars.

Shahada (shuh-hah'duh; Arabic: "witnessing"). The confession of faith, the first of the Five Pillars and central creedal statement of Islam: "There is no god except God. Muhammad is the messenger of God."

Shari'ah (sha-ree'ah). The divine law, derived from the Qur'an and the Sunnah, all-encompassing in scope and setting forth in detail how Muslims are to live.

shaykh (shayk). A teacher and master in Islam, such as the leader of an order in Sufism.

Shi'i (shee'ee). From *shi'at 'Ali,* "partisans of Ali," the division of Islam dominant in Iraq and Iran, originating as a result of an early dispute over leadership; distinguishable from Sunni Islam mainly by the figure of the Imam and strong messianic expectations.

Sufi (soo'fee). An adherent of Sufism, the form of Islam characterized by a mystical approach to Allah, who is experienced inwardly.

Sunnah (soon'nuh; Arabic: "custom" or "tradition"). The teachings and actions of Muhammad recorded in writings known as *hadith,* which provide the model for being Muslim; Islam's second most important authority (after the Qur'an).

Sunni (soon'nee). The division of Islam practiced by the majority of Muslims (about 87 percent), named after the Sunnah.

Umma (oom'muh; Arabic: "community"). The community of all Muslims.

Epilogue   Endings and Beginnings

In one respect we have reached the end of our journey. We have encountered and discovered many things about the world's religions. But such discoveries also mark new beginnings. Old questions answered lead to new questions. Knowledge gained sparks a yearning for more knowledge.

And so the journey continues, although in many ways we are better informed than when we first set forth. For one thing, we have considered the religions' various answers to some basic religious questions introduced at the start of this course: What is the human condition? What is salvation? What is our destiny? What is right, what is wrong? What is the nature of the world? What is ultimate reality, and how is it revealed?

As our study has shown, these questions are indeed basic for the world religions, but they are also quite complex, with widely divergent answers. Let us review just a few responses to the first question: What is the human condition? Hindus respond by referring to *samsara,* the wheel of rebirth on which we are trapped due to our ignorance. Only through *moksha,* liberation from *samsara,* can humans be freed from this predicament, and with *moksha* human individuality vanishes. Islam offers a very different answer, contending that each individual is created and loved by Allah, and that humans are by nature good. Christianity understands humans to be sinful, having fallen from the original state of innocence, and therefore in need of redemption.

The list of varying answers does not end there, of course, nor does the list of questions. But as we conclude our study, we can try to make some sense of this dizzying diversity of religious perspectives.

We can begin with the obvious: all of the world's religious traditions have valuable wisdom teachings to offer us. Examples of these teachings abound: Taoist reverence for nature, Christian love of neighbor, Buddhist emphasis on mental clarity and vigor, Jewish care for tradition, Confucian devotion to the family, Muslim transcendence of racism through the ideal of community—the list could go on almost without end. Such teachings are precious sources of wisdom. Only in recent times has extensive knowledge regarding the religious traditions of the world been made widely available. We are fortunate to live in this modern era of the global community, in which the world's great wisdom traditions are now more than ever gifts to be shared.

Living in this global community presents another important reality, one that the study of religions can help us deal with. In our diverse world, we increasingly encounter people who have grown up in different traditions and therefore see the world in ways that are sometimes quite foreign to us. Getting along well with such people requires that we know something about them and their traditions. To recall a term defined in the first chapter of this book, we need to practice *empathy,* to walk a mile in the moccasins of the other. Studying the world's religions is essential if we are to practice empathy effectively.

An event several years ago serves to highlight just how relevant the study of religions has become now that we are living in a global community. In 1993 the Parliament of the World's Religions convened in Chicago. It was in part a celebration of the one hundredth anniversary of the first such parliament held in 1893. The 1893 parliament was a milestone for the study of world religions because it introduced the great richness of the various traditions to a vast number of people.

At the 1993 parliament, hundreds of religious leaders from around the globe approved the "Declaration of a Global Ethic." Drawing on the wisdom of the world's religions, this document provides guidelines designed to nurture the value of all life on Earth. While acknowledging the diversity and uniqueness of the world's religions, the document highlights certain principles common to all the religions: preservation of life through nonviolence; respect for all living things; honest and fair dealings with one another; speaking and acting truthfully; respecting and loving one another.

The "Declaration of a Global Ethic" illustrates some important points related to our study of the world's religions. For one thing, it makes clear that although the world's religions are diverse, they all share some basic principles. Secondly, the need for this document affirms that we are living in a global community and that the religions of other people are relevant to all of us. Finally, the creation of such a document, along with any attempts to put it into practice, demonstrate that the study of world religions is relevant and powerful. People of different traditions can come to agreement and work in harmony only when they understand one another.

We can expect the world to become more and more a shared global community. Projects such as the one that produced the "Declaration of a Global Ethic" can help to make the world a better community for all in which to live. Whether or not you continue to study the world's religions, you can be sure that the journey we have undertaken will become more important as we encounter, with empathy, our diverse global community.

Glossary Pronunciation Key

Note: Accent marks in the glossaries come after the accented syllables.

Symbol	Sound
a	hat
ah	father
ahr	hard
air	hair
aw	law
ay	hay
b	box
ch	chill
d	dad
e, eh	set
ee	need
f	fine
g	gap
h	hit
hw	whether
i	sit
i	lie
ihr	ear
j	jump

Symbol	Sound
k	key
kh	ch as in German *buch*
ks	hex
kw	quit
l	lamb
m	most
n	nest
ng	bing
o	tot
oh	low
oi	toy
oo	foot
oo	hoot
oor	floor
or	more
ou	cow
p	pass
r	ring

Symbol	Sound
s	sew
sh	shell
t	toe
th	thick
tw	twine
uh	ago
uhr	sir
v	van
w	water
y	yak
z	zebra
zh	vision

Index

Italic numbers are references to photos or illustrations.

Acknowledgments *(continued)*

Studying and writing about the world's religions is a pleasurable task that has been enhanced by many people.

The staff at Saint Mary's Press, especially Steve, Barbara, and Michael, have blessed me with the opportunity to write this book, and with their steadfast assistance and good company. I shall miss the laughter and edification of our meetings!

Professors Birger Pearson, Richard Hecht, Gerald Larson, and other esteemed faculty in the department of religious studies at the University of California Santa Barbara have taught and inspired me in many ways. In particular, a word of gratitude to Professor Ninian Smart, whose ideas, especially his dimensional approach to religions, are echoed here. For elucidating introductions to the dimensional scheme, see his *Worldviews: Crosscultural Explorations of Human Beliefs* or the introductory chapters in *The World Religions* or *The Religious Experience.*

Many friends and family members (all of whom are also friends) have generously provided their assistance, support, and encouragement—so many that it would be impossible to mention them all. But to Kelly, a special thanks for "minding the store." And to my dear wife, Jill, who assisted in that way and in others, some ineffable but all of them wonderful.

The scriptural quotations in the introduction and in chapter 13 are from the New Revised Standard Version of the Bible. Copyright © 1989 by the Division of Christian Education of the National Council of the Churches of Christ in the United States of America. All rights reserved.

The extract on page 8 from *Declaration of the Relation of the Church to Non-Christian Religions,* number 2, and the extract on page 8 from the *Dogmatic Constitution on the Church,* number 16, are quoted from *Decrees of the Ecumenical Councils,* volume 2, edited by Norman P. Tanner, SJ (London: Sheed and Ward, and Washington, D.C.: Georgetown University Press, 1990), pages 969 and 861. English translation copyright © 1990 by Sheed and Ward Limited and Georgetown University Press.

The extracts from Pope John Paul II's 1986 Day of Prayer for Peace message quoted on page 9 are reprinted from "The Challenge and the Possibility of Peace," number 2, in *Origins,* 6 November 1986, page 370.

The excerpt on page 17 is from *C. G. Jung Speaking: Interviews and Encounters,* edited by William McGuire and R. F. Hull (Princeton, NJ: Princeton University Press, 1977), page 428. Copyright © 1977 by Princeton University Press.

The excerpt on pages 30–31 is from *Lame Deer, Seeker of Visions: The Life of a Sioux Medicine Man,* by John Fire/Lame Deer and Richard Erdoes (New York: Simon and Schuster, 1972), pages 11, 14–16. Copyright © 1972 by John Fire/Lame Deer and Richard Erdoes. Permission applied for.

The excerpt by Shri Ramakrishna on page 37 is quoted from *The Spiritual Heritage of India,* by Swami Prabhavananda (Hollywood, CA: Vedanta Press, 1963), page 353. Copyright © 1963 by the Vedanta Society of Southern California.

The quote from the Rig Veda on page 38 is quoted from *A Source Book in Indian Philosophy,* edited by Sarvepalli Radhakrishnan and Charles A. Moore (Princeton, NJ: Princeton University Press, 1957), page xxvii. Copyright © 1957 by Princeton University Press.

The excerpts by Mahatma Gandhi on pages 38 and 48 are from *The Moral and Political Writings of Mahatma Gandhi,* volume 1, *Civilization, Politics, and Religion,* edited by Raghavan Iyer (New York: Clarendon, Oxford University Press, 1986), pages 542–543 and 461. Copyright © 1986 by Navajivan Trust. Used by permission of Oxford University Press.

The excerpts on pages 39–41 and 50 are from *The Upanishads: Breath of the Eternal,* selected and translated from the original Sanskrit by Swami Prabhavananda and Frederick Manchester (Hollywood, CA: Vedanta Press, 1948), pages 70 and 17. Copyright © 1948, 1957 by the Vedanta Society of Southern California. Used by permission of Vedanta Press.

The excerpts from the Bhagavad-Gita on pages 42 42, 46 (first), 46 (second), 48 (first), 48 (second), 53–54, and 54 are from *The Bhagavad-Gita: Krishna's Counsel in Times of War,* a translation by Barbara Stoler Miller (New York: Bantam Books, 1986), 2:12,13,22; 2:31–33; 5:3; 3:27; 2:47; 4:6–8; and 9:27–29, respectively. Translation copyright © 1986 by Barbara Stoler Miller. Used by permission of Bantam Books, a division of Bantam Doubleday Dell Publishing Group.

The excerpt from Chandogya Upanishad on page 45 is from *The Thirteen Principal Upanishads,* second edition, translated from the Sanskrit by Robert Ernest Hume (New York: Oxford University Press, 1931), page 233.

The excerpt by Mahatma Gandhi in page 55 is from *Young India (1919–1922),* second edition (New York: B. W. Huebsch, 1924), page 804. Copyright © by S. Ganesan, Triplicane, Madras SE.

The excerpt from the Padmapurana on page 57 is quoted from *A History of the World's Relgions,* ninth edition, by David S. Noss and John B. Noss (New York: Macmillan College Publishing, 1994), page 118. Copyright © 1994 by Macmillan College Publishing Company.

The excerpt by Gautama on page 68 is quoted from *Buddhism in Translations,* translated from the original Pali into English by Henry Clarke Warren (New York: Atheneum, 1984), page 109. Originally published by Harvard University Press.

The excerpt on pages 73–74 is from *Old Path White Clouds: Walking in the Footsteps of the Buddha,* by Thich Nhat Hanh, translated by Mobi Ho (Berkeley, CA: Parallax Press, 1991), page 407. Copyright © 1991 by Thich Nhat Hanh. Used by permission of Parallax Press, Berkeley, California.

The excerpt by Wei Wu Wei on page 74 is from *Ask the Awakened: The Negative Way* (London: Routledge and Kegan Paul, 1963), page 1. Copyright © 1963 by Kegan Paul.

The story on pages 77–78 is from *The Hungry Tigress: Buddhist Legends and Jataka Tales,* by Rafe Martin (Berkeley, CA: Parallax Press, 1990), page 130. Copyright © 1990 by Rafe Martin.

The mantra on page 84 is from *The Buddhist Religion: A Historical Introduction,* third edition, by Richard H. Robinson and Willard L. Johnson (Belmont, CA: Wadsworth Publishing Company, 1982), page 94. Copyright © 1982 by Wadsworth Publishing Company.

The excerpt on page 87 is from the Acaranga Sutra, book 1, lecture 4, lesson 1.1–2, as quoted in *Sacred Books of the East,* volume 23, translated by various Oriental scholars and edited by F. Max Müller (New York: Oxford University Press, 1968), page 36. Copyright © by Motilal Banarsidass.

The excerpt on page 96 is from *Perspectives in Jaina Philosophy and Culture,* edited by Shri Satish Kumar Jain (New Delhi, India: Ahimsa International, 1985), pages 45–46. Copyright © 1985.

The excerpt from the Avashyaka Sutra on page 97 is quoted from *The Jains,* by Paul Dundas (New York: Routledge, 1992), page 148. Copyright © 1992 by Paul Dundas.

The excerpts on pages 104 (first and second) and 108 (second) are from *The Sikhs: Their Religious Beliefs and Practices,* by W. Owen Cole and Piara Singh Sambhi (London: Routledge and Kegan Paul, 1978), pages 9 and 10, and 69, respectively. Copyright © 1978 by W. Owen Cole and Piara Singh Sambhi. Used by permission of the publisher.

The excerpts on pages 104 (third), 106, and 108 (first) are from "Sikhism," by Khushwant Singh, in *The Encyclopedia of Religion,* volume 13, edited by Mircea Eliade (New York: Macmillan Publishing Company, 1987), pages 316, 319, and 319, respectively. Copyright © 1987 by Macmillan Publishing Company.

The excerpt on page 110 is from *Fighting for Faith and Nation: Dialogues with Sikh Militants,* by Cynthia Keppley Mahmood (Philadelphia: University of Pennsylvania Press, 1996), pages 144–145 and 150. Copyright © 1996 by Cynthia Keppley Mahmood. Used by permission of the University of Pennsylvania Press.

The excerpt by Tu Wei-ming on page 118 is from "Confucianism," the excerpts by Jacob Neusner on pages 207 and 211 are from "Judaism," and the excerpt by Seyyed Hossein Nasr on page 255 is from "Islam," in *Our Religions,* edited by Arvind Sharma (New York: HarperSanFrancisco, 1993), pages 149;

345 and 350; and 522, respectively. Copyright © 1993 by HarperCollins Publishers. Used by permission of HarperCollins Publishers

The excerpts on pages 120 (all five), 123 (first, second, and fourth), 124 (first and second), 125 (first, second, third, and fourth), 126, 127–128, 129 (second), 129–130, 130 (first five), and 131 (all seven) are from *Confucius: The Analects,* translated with an introduction by D. C. Lau (New York: Penguin Books, 1979), pages 90, 91, 88, 86, 63; 80, 86, 73; 61, 78; 72, 72, 121, 135; 101; 63; 74; 115–116; 66, 107, 89, 69, 129; and 65, 73, 128, 125, 136, 122, 74, respectively. Copyright © 1979 by D. C. Lau. Used by permission of Penguin Books.

The excerpts on page 122 are from *A Chinese Childhood,* by Chiang Yee (New York: W. W. Norton and Company, 1963), pages 79–80, 83, and 86. Copyright © 1952. Used by permission of W. W. Norton and Company and Methuen, a division of Random House.

The excerpts on page 123 (third), 125 (fifth), 127 (first), and 130 (sixth) are from the Analects, as quoted in *A Source Book in Chinese Philosophy,* translated and compiled by Wing-tsit Chan (Princeton, NJ: Princeton University Press, 1963), pages 23, 42, 22, and 22, respectively. Copyright © 1963 by Princeton University Press. Used by permission.

The excerpt from The Great Learning on page 128 and the excerpt from *Records of Rituals* on page 129 are quoted from *Chinese Religion: An Introduction,* fifth edition, by Laurence G. Thompson (Belmont, CA: Wadsworth Publishing Company, 1996), pages 12 and 11. Copyright © 1996 by Wadsworth Publishing Company.

The excerpt from the Book of Mencius on page 128 is quoted from *Mencius,* translated with an introduction by D. C. Lau (New York: Penguin Books, 1970), book 3, part A, number 4, page 102. Copyright © 1970 by D. C. Lau.

The poem on page 133 is from *The Way of Chuang Tzu,* by Thomas Merton (New York: New Directions, 1965), page 65. Copyright © 1965 by the Abbey of Gethsemani. Copyright © 1977 by the Trustees of the Merton Legacy Trust. Used by permission of New Directions Publishing, New York, and Gerald Pollinger, England.

The excerpt on page 134 from *Shih Chi,* by Ssuma Ch'ien, is quoted from *Lao Tzu and Taoism,* by Max Kaltenmark, translated from the French by Roger Greaves (Stanford, CA: Stanford University Press, 1965), page 8. Copyright © 1965 by Editions du Seiul, Paris.

The excerpts on pages 135 (first), 137 (both in main text), 137 (second in sidebar), 139 (first), 141 (first, second, third, fourth, sixth), 143 (first), 144 (third), and 145 are from *The Way of Lao Tzu (Tao-te ching),* translated by Wing-tsit Chan (New York: Bobbs-Merrill Company, 1963), pages 97; 144, 160; 97; 101; 224, 184, 212, 236, 139; 139; 130; and 174, respectively. Copyright © 1963 by the Liberal Arts

Press, a division of Bobbs-Merrill. Reprinted by permission of Prentice-Hall, Upper Saddle River, New Jersey.

The second *Tao Te Ching* excerpt on page 135 and the third excerpt in the sidebar on page 137 are quoted from *The Way and Its Power: A Study of the "Tao Te Ching" and Its Place in Chinese Thought,* by Arthur Waley (New York: Grove Press, 1958), pages 210 and 141.

The excerpts on pages 135 (third), 138, 141 (fifth), 143 (second), and 144 (first and second) are from the *Tao Te Ching,* by Lao Tsu, translated by Gia-fu Feng and Jane English (New York: Vintage, Random House, 1989), pages 21; 30; 72; 26; and 31, 70, respectively. Copyright © 1972 by Gia-fu Feng and Jane English. Used by permission of Random House and Gower Publishing, England.

The excerpts on pages 136 and 139 (second) are from the *Chuang Tzu,* as quoted in *Three Ways of Thought in Ancient China,* by Arthur Waley (New York: Barnes and Noble, 1939), pages 54 and 27.

The first excerpt in the sidebar on page 137 is from *Living Religions of the World,* by Frederic Spiegelberg (Englewood Cliffs, NJ: Prentice-Hall, 1956), page 300. Copyright © 1956 by Prentice-Hall.

The fourth excerpt in the sidebar on page 137 is from *The Way of Life: Lao Tzu,* translated by Raymond B. Blakney (New York: New American Library, 1955), page 53. Copyright © 1955 by Raymond B. Blakney. Copyright © renewed 1983 by Charles Philip Blakney.

The final excerpt in the sidebar on page 137 is from *Lao Tzu: Tao Te Ching,* translated with an introduction by D. C. Lau (New York: Penguin Books, 1963), page 57. Copyright © 1963 by D. C. Lau.

The excerpt on pages 139–140 is from *Chuang Tzu: Basic Writings,* translated by Burton Watson (New York: Columbia University Press, 1964), page 113. Copyright © 1964 by Columbia University Press. Used by permission of the publisher.

The excerpt on page 142 is from *The Monastery of Jade Mountain,* by Peter Goullart (London: John Murray, 1961), pages 30–31. Copyright © 1961 by Peter Goullart. Used by permission of John Murray.

The excerpts on pages 147, 149 (second), 150 (second), 151, 152 (first), and 153 (second and third) are from *Zen Flesh, Zen Bones: A Collection of Zen and Pre-Zen Writings,* compiled by Paul Reps (Garden City, NY: Anchor Books), pages 96; 39; 55; 5; 25; and 22–23, 19–20, respectively. Used by permission of Paul Reps.

The excerpts on page 149 (first) and 150 (third) is from *Essays in Zen Buddhism (First Series),* by Daisetz Teitaro Suzuki (New York: Grove Press, 1961), page 13.

The first excerpt on page 150 is from *The Three Pillars of Zen,* twenty-fifth anniversary edition, by Roshi Philip Kapleau (New York: Doubleday, 1989), page 195. Copyright © 1980 by the Zen Center. Copyright © 1965, 1989 by Roshi Philip Kapleau.

The second, third, and fourth excerpts on page 152 are from *Zen Comments on the Mumonkan,* by Zenkei Shibayama, translated by Sumiko Kudo (New York: Harper and Row, 1974), pages 74, 272, and 54, respectively. Copyright © 1974 by Zenkei Shibayama. Used by permission of HarperCollins Publishers.

The third excerpt on page 150 and the excerpt by C. G. Jung on page 153 are quoted from *An Introduction to Zen Buddhism,* by Daisetz Teitaro Suzuki (New York: Grove Press, 1964), pages 38 and 10.

The excerpts on page 154 are from *Pure Heart, Enlightened Mind,* by Maura O'Halloran (New York: Riverhead Books, 1994), pages 102–105, 233, and 301. Copyright © 1994 by the Estate of Maura O'Halloran. Used by permission of Charles E. Tuttle Company.

The poem on page 156 is from *A Zen Wave: Basho's Haiku and Zen,* by Robert Aitken (New York: Weatherhill, 1978), page 25. Copyright © 1978. Used by permission of the publisher.

The poem on page 157 is from *RIPRAP and Cold Mountain Poems,* by Gary Snyder (San Francisco: Grey Fox Press, 1958), page 44. Copyright © 1958, 1959, 1965 by Gary Snyder. Used by permission of the publisher. Foreign rights applied for.

The excerpt by Motoori Norinaga on page 160 is quoted from *Religion in the Japanese Experience: Sources and Interpretations,* by H. Byron Earhart (Encino and Belmont, CA: Dickenson Publishing Company, 1974), page 10. Copyright © 1974 by Dickenson Publishing Company.

The excerpts on pages 166–167 are from *A Year in the Life of a Shinto Shrine,* by John K. Nelson (Seattle: University of Washington Press, 1996), pages 125–129. Copyright © 1996 by University of Washington Press. Used by permission of the University of Washington Press.

The excerpts on pages 173 and 175 are from *Early Zoroastrianism,* by James Hope Moulton (London: Williams and Norgate, 1913), pages 367–368 and 374.

The excerpt from the Gathas on page 174 is from *Textual Sources for the Study of Zoroastrianism,* edited and translated by Mary Boyce (Manchester, England: Manchester University Press, 1984), page 35. Copyright © 1984 by Mary Boyce. Used by permission of Mary Boyce.

The excerpt from *Agamemnon* on page 178 is from *The Oresteian Trilogy,* translated by Philip Vellacott (London: Penguin Books, 1956), page 48. Copyright © 1956, 1959 by Philip Vellacott.

The excerpt from *The Odyssey* on page 181 is from *Homer: The Odyssey,* translated by E. V. Rieu, revised by D. C. H. Rieu (London: Penguin Books, 1991), page 173. Copyright © 1946 by E. V. Rieu. This revised translation copyright © 1991 by the Estate of the late E. V. Rieu, and D. C. H. Rieu.

The excerpts on page 185 are from *Aelius Aristides and the Sacred Tales,* by C. A. Behr (Amsterdam: Adolf M. Hakkert, 1968), pages 224 and 261–262. Copyright © 1968 by A. M. Hakkert, Amsterdam, Netherlands.

The excerpt from *The Metamorphoses* on page 188 is quoted from *The Ancient Mysteries: A Sourcebook,* edited by Marvin W. Mayer (San Francisco: Harper and Row, 1987), page 158. Copyright © 1987 by Marvin W. Mayer.

The excerpt from Pliny's letter to Emperor Trajan on pages 188–189 is quoted from *The New Testament in Context: Sources and Documents,* by Howard Clark Kee (Englewood Cliffs, NJ: Prentice-Hall, 1984), page 44. Copyright © 1984 by Prentice-Hall.

The excerpts from the Tanakh in chapter 12 are from *Tanakh: A New Translation of the Holy Scriptures According to the Traditional Hebrew Text* (Philadelphia: Jewish Publication Society, 1985). Copyright © 1985 by the Jewish Publication Society.

The excerpt by Abraham Joshua Heschel on page 191 is from *Man's Quest for God: Studies in Prayer and Symbolism* (New York: Charles Scribner's Sons, 1954), page 45. Copyright © 1954 by Abraham Joshua Heschel.

The excerpt from the Talmud on page 195 is quoted from *The Essential Talmud,* by Adin Steinsaltz, translated from the Hebrew by Chaya Galai (New York: Basic Books, 1976), page 3. Copyright © 1976 by Bantam Books.

Maimonides's dogmas on page 201 are quoted from *The Ways of Religion: An Introduction to the Major Traditions,* second edition, edited by Roger Eastman (New York: Oxford University Press, 1993), pages 261–262. Copyright © 1975, 1993 by Roger Eastman.

The excerpt on page 203 is adapted from *Gabriel's Palace: Jewish Mystical Tales,* selected and retold by Howard Schwartz (New York: Oxford University Press, 1993), pages 86–87. Copyright © 1993 by Howard Schwartz. Used by permission of Oxford University Press.

The excerpt on page 205 is quoted from *The Mishnah,* translated from the Hebrew by Herbert Danby, DD (Oxford, England: Oxford University Press, 1933), page 446.

The excerpt on page 224 from *Summa Theologiae,* volume 2, part 2, question 2, article 8 is translated by the Fathers of the English Dominican Province and is quoted from *Great Books of the Western World,* volume 20, edited by Robert Maynard Hutchins (Chicago: Encyclopedia Brittanica, 1952), page 398. Copyright © 1952.

The excerpt on page 236 from the *Decree on Ecumenism* is quoted from *Vatican Council II: The Conciliar and Post Conciliar Documents,* revised edition, edited by Austin Flannery, OP (Northport, NY: Costello Publishing Company, 1988), number 1, page 452. Copyright © 1975, 1984, and 1987 by Harry J. Costello and Rev. Austin Flannery.

The excerpts from the Koran on pages 241 (first and second), 244, and 249 (first and second) are quoted from *The Koran,* translated by N. J. Dawood (New York: Penguin Books, 1956), pages 9 and 60; 298; and 420 and 429, respectively. Copyright © 1956, 1959, 1966, 1968, 1974, 1990, and 1993 by N. J. Dawood. Used by permission of the publisher.

The excerpt on page 253 is from *Sufism: An Account of the Mystics of Islam,* by A. J. Arberry (New York: Harper Torchbooks, 1970), page 28. Copyright © 1950 by A. J. Arberry.

Photo Credits

Tsafrir Abayov, Impact Visuals: page 214

G. Abegg, Sygma: pages 40 (bottom left), 43

Alinari, Giraudon: page 205

Paul Almasy, © Corbis: pages 187, 232 (right)

Roberto Arakaki, International Stock Photo: page 63

Tony Arruza, Corbis: page 223 (left)

Arte Video Immagine Italia srl, Corbis: pages 182 (right), 186 (right), 228

Art Resource, New York: page 49

Asian Art and Archaeology, Inc., Corbis: pages 128, 140

Mark Avery, AP/Wide World Photos: pages 2 (top and middle), 210, back cover (top and middle)

Baldev, Sygma: pages 107 (left and right), 108

Dave Bartruff, Corbis: pages 147, 223 (right)

Annie Griffiths Belt, Corbis: pages 100 (bottom), 112 (left and right), 195 (left and right), 197 (right), 247 (left)

The Bettmann Archive: pages 177 (top left), 241

Daniel Blatt: pages 191, 196, 217

BO, Giraudon: pages 90, 91

Bonora, Giraudon: pages 64, 66, 80 (right)

Jeffrey Brodd: pages 52, 83, 178 (left and right), 254

Jon Brodd: pages 55, 239 (top)

Michael Busselle, Corbis: page 151

Sheldon Collins, Corbis: pages 94, 95

Kirk Condyles, Impact Visuals: pages 109 (right), 113

Alexander Contos, Impact Visuals: page 239 (bottom)

© Corbis: page 86 (bottom)

Corbis-Bettmann: pages 135 (top), 165 (bottom)

Gianni Dagli Orti, Corbis: pages 181, 183

Bennett Dean, Eye Ubiquitous/Corbis: page 100 (top)

Dinodia, Impact Visuals: page 50

C M Dixon: pages 40 (bottom right, middle, top left, and top right), 67, 77, 88, 172, 177 (middle), 188, 200, 220

J. L. Dugast, Sygma: pages 3 (middle), 76, front cover (middle)

Chad Ehlers, International Stock Photo: page 68

Johan Elbers, International Stock Photo: page 24

Ric Ergenbright, Corbis: page 86 (top)

Eye Ubiquitous, Corbis: pages 133, 247 (right)

Jack Fields, Corbis: pages 118 (right), 126

Owen Franken, Corbis: pages 150, 222

Craig Fuji, Impact Visuals: page 51

Arvind Garb, Impact Visuals: page 109 (middle)

Berto Gian Vanni, Corbis: page 87

Giraudon: pages 80 (left), 216, 218, 219, 232 (left), 233, 240, 242

Giraudon, Art Resource, New York: pages 14, 193

Frank Grant, International Stock Photo: pages 45 (left), 47, 60 (top)

L. Greenfield, Sygma: page 132 (bottom)

Tom and Michele Grimm, International Stock Photo: pages 12 (bottom), 45 (right)

Patrice Habans, Sygma: pages 104, 105

Abu Hander, International Stock Photo: page 248

Robert Holmes, Corbis: pages 93 (left and right), 98

Norma Holt, Impact Visuals: page 206

E. D. Hoppé, Corbis: page 20 (top)

Jeremy Horner, © Corbis: pages 89, 104 (bottom)

Anthony Howarth, International Stock Photo: page 60 (bottom)

Hulton-Deutsch Collection, Corbis: pages 202 (bottom left and left), 253

Miwako Ikeda, International Stock Photo: pages 56 (right), 163 (bottom left and middle), 171 (top)

Mimmo Jodice, Corbis: page 177 (top right), page 182 (left)

Wolfgang Kaehler, Corbis: page 249

William Karel, Sygma: page 149

Kelly-Mooney Photography, Corbis: page 143

Keystone, Sygma: page 56 (left)

Gabe Kirchheimer, Impact Visuals: page 58

Lauros, Giraudon: pages 13, 84 (bottom), 121

Charles and Josette Lenars, Corbis: page 173

Pascal Le Segretain, Sygma: front cover (bottom), page 3 (bottom)

Meryl Levin, Impact Visuals: pages 84 (top), 109 (left), 215

Library of Congress, Corbis: page 32

L'Illustration, Sygma: page 38

Philip Little, International Stock Photo: pages 75 (left and right), 79

Christopher Loviny, Corbis: page 146 (bottom)

Araldo de Luca, Corbis: pages 177 (bottom), 186 (left), 189

James Marshall, Corbis: page 197 (left)

Stephanie Maze, Corbis: page 124

Photograph on page 209 is courtesy of the Stuart Miller family.

Kevin Morris, Corbis: pages 116 (top), 119

The National Archives, Corbis: pages 161, 202 (bottom right)

The National Gallery, London, Corbis: page 221

Charlie Neibergall, AP/Newsfeatures Photo: page 251

Photograph on page 226 is courtesy of Chau Ngo.

Michael Nicholson, Corbis: page 179

Richard Nowitz, Corbis: pages 201, 204, 207, 211, 212

Illustration on page 154 was used with the kind permission of Ruth O'Halloran.

© Orion, International Stock Photo: pages 62 (top), 159

Christine Osborne, Corbis: pages 101, 102

Tim Page, Corbis: page 139

F. Paolini, Sygma: pages 21, 29

Sarah G. Partridge, Corbis: page 22

P. Perrin, Sygma: page 190

Ed Peters, Impact Visuals: page 37 (top)

PhotoDisc, Inc.: sand background in part 1

Phyllis Picardi, International Stock Photo: pages 36, 59

L. A. Raman, Impact Visuals: page 48

C. Rancinan, Sygma: page 46

Vittoriano Rastelli: page 229

Reuters/Corbis-Bettman: pages 165 (top), 199 (right)

Scala/Art Resource, New York: pages 15, 16, 171 (bottom)

Kevin Schafer, Corbis: page 235

Jane Schreibman: page 44

Seattle Art Museum, Corbis: pages 26, 27, 152

SEF, Art Resource, New York: pages 170, 174, 175

Leonard de Selva, Corbis: page 199 (left)

James Shaffer: page 224

Vernon Sigl: pages 70, 71

Peter Southwick, AP/Wide World Photos: page 236

Sean Sprague, Impact Visuals: pages 12 (top), 62 (bottom), 72, 81

Sharon Stewart, Impact Visuals: 238, 245

Johnny Stockshooter, International Stock Photo: pages 158 (bottom), 163 (bottom right and top left)

Keren Su, Corbis: pages 125, 135 (bottom)

Tung Yuan Sung, Corbis-Bettmann: page 136

Chuck Szymanski, International Stock Photo: page 250 (left and right)

Joe Tabacca, AP/Wide World Photos: page 192

Hardie Truesdale, International Stock Photo: page 138

Penny Tweedie, Corbis: page 25 (left and right)

UPI/Corbis-Bettman: page 158 (top)

USDA-Forest Service, Corbis: page 33

J. Van Hasselt, Sygma: page 23

Michael Ventura, International Stock Photo: page 116 (bottom)

Brian Viander, Corbis: page 117

Victoria and Albert Museum, London, Art Resource, New York: page 37 (bottom)

David Wells, Corbis: page 246

Werner Forman Archive, Art Resource, New York: page 20 (bottom), 142, 144

Jim Winkley, Ecoscene, Corbis: page 225

Janet Wishnetsky, Corbis: page 104 (top)

Alison Wright, Corbis: page 118 (left)

Michael Yamashita, Corbis: pages 132 (top), 146 (top)

Dost Yayinlari, Giraudon: page 243